Portrait of a Turkish Family

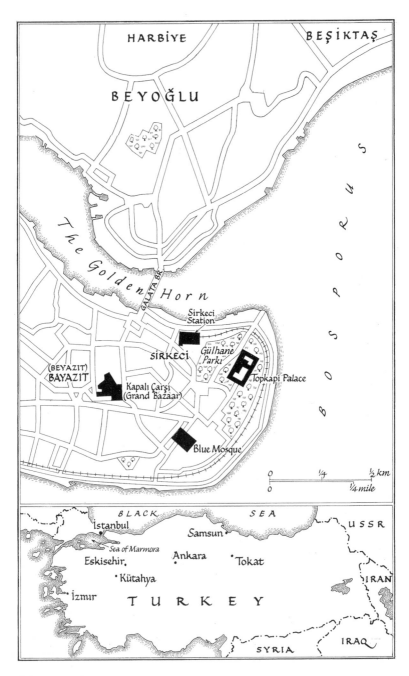

Turkey and Istanbul

Portrait of a
Turkish Family

IRFAN ORGA

London

First published by Victor Gollancz in 1950
First published by Eland in 1988

This edition first published by Eland Publishing Ltd
61 Exmouth Market, London ECIR 4QL
in association with Galeri Kayseri,
Divanyolu 58, Istanbul, in 2004

Text and afterword © Ateş D'Arcy-Orga 2006

ISBN 978 0 907871 82 8

Cover designed by Robert Dalrymple
Cover image: Dolmabahçe by Fausto Zonaro
© coll. of Mafalda Zonaro

Printed in Spain by GraphyCems, Navarra

CONTENTS

To
MARGARETE
My wife, with love

CHAPTER I

INTRODUCING THE FAMILY

I WAS BORN in Istanbul, on the 31st of October 1908. I was the eldest son of my parents, my mother being fifteen at the time of my birth and my father twenty. Our house was behind the Blue Mosque, looking over the Sea of Marmora. It stood at the corner of a small cul-de-sac with only a low stone wall between it and the sea. It was a quiet, green place and a very little Mosque stood near it, and amongst my earliest recollections is the soft, unceasing sound of the Marmora and the singing of the birds in the gardens. Our house was a big wooden house, painted white with green shutters and trellised balconies front and rear. It belonged to my grandfather and my grandmother and we lived there with them.

Looking back, it seems to me that the whole of early childhood is linked with the sound of the sea and with the voices of my parents and grandparents as they sat eating breakfast on the terrace overlooking the gardens. Still can I feel the content of childhood's awakening in the low, sunny room filled with the reflected white light from the sea; still hear faintly the domestic sounds from the kitchen and the high-pitched, smothered laughter of our black cook. I would creep out of bed, absurd in my old-fashioned nightshirt, and lean my head against the protective iron bars on the windows and call down to the family group below me. This calling was the signal for my father to toss aside his napkin and shout up to me that he was coming. I would hastily scuttle back to my bed, laughing a bit with anticipation for I had already learned that I was an important member of the household, and each day for me began with the throwing aside of my father's breakfast napkin, his running footsteps on the stairs then his repeated tossing of me into the air, to the accompaniment of my excited, terrified screams. But it was a terror I could not resist and my day would not have properly begun if my father had omitted this thrilling game. Attracted by my laughter Inci would appear, her black eyes rolling in her small dark face and her mouth screwed up with laughter. Inci was my nursemaid, coal black and only thirteen years old yet she had full charge of me.

She was the daughter of Feride, the upstairs maid, and had been born in Istanbul whilst her father was a servant in the palace of the Sultan. After the death of her father, my grandmother had taken her and her mother to our house and after my birth Inci had been given to me. I loved her very much and could not have imagined life without her. She was always good-humoured and used to make me shout with laughter when she rolled her eyes at me or pulled funny faces. Even when I was more than usually fractious, screaming at her or stamping my feet with temper, she would remain good-humoured, merely administering a good, sharp slap where it hurt most then leave me to kick out my tantrums alone.

With the arrival of Inci each morning my father would stand me on my feet, telling me to be a good boy, pat Inci's crinkly hair then leave us. Inci and I would stare at each other solemnly for a moment or two then she would start to make her funny faces and waggle her flat hips and the pair of us would burst into laughter and I would run to her, flinging my arms about her. She would begin to dress me, and washing was one long battle. Firmly would she grasp me under one arm and hold me over the shallow china basin, lathering my face and neck with soap—most of which used to get in my eyes. And all the while I kicked the air, struggling futilely to get free. The combing of my hair was the next torture to be endured. I had thick curls which were my mother's pride and joy, Inci's too when they were arranged, but the arranging of them was torn with my cries of temper and distress and Inci's commands to keep still and let her finish. My hair finally arranged to her satisfaction, we would glare at each other, my scalp still smarting from the tugging of the comb and my eyes still red-rimmed from soap. It was a daily battle and as much a part of existence as the sound of the sea or my father's kiss, and in five minutes it was all forgotten and I would go dancing down the stairs ahead of Inci to see my mother and my grandparents. My mother's kiss set the seal of perfection on the day. All the things which preceded it—my waking to a light-filled room, my father's tossing me into the air, my battle with Inci—were only the sweet high prelude to my mother's kiss. The kiss that was cool and light and held the perfume of roses in it.

She was very beautiful. Hair that was black and shining and coiled into smooth curls on top of her head. A face that was pale and oval with a small, uptilted, humorous mouth and great melancholy eyes that lightened like jewels when she smiled. She was always very slender and liked to dress in pastel colours, soft shimmering silks that smelt of lavender water or eau-de-Cologne, and she wore long gold necklaces, twisted two or three times around her throat. She was a gentle, silent person, her hands delicate and useless-looking and weighted down with the number of flashing rings that she invariably wore. She did the most lovely embroidery and petit-point and she would take each ring off very carefully before she started, dropping them with a little chink into a small satin-lined box kept solely for that reason. She was very elegant and might have been a noted beauty had she been born in Europe. But because she was a Turkish lady and had to wear a veil to cover her face whenever she went out, she was unknown save to the members of her family. She married my father at the age of thirteen, having been promised to him at the age of three. She rarely went out and never alone but spent most of her time on the terrace or sitting under a fig-tree in the garden, much as the women of her family had done for generations before her. She appeared perfectly happy, content to be solely an ornament in her husband's home. My grandparents were a devoted couple and spoiled me very much, perhaps because I was the eldest grandchild. They seemed very old to me, although looking back to the time of which I write, Spring of 1914, my grandmother must have been only in the early forties since she too had married very young. But to the eyes of a child a bit over five, she seemed incredibly old.

It is strange now to sit here and look back to the past and see them so clearly before me, the people who made me and moulded me and are, in part, responsible for whatever I am to-day. The people who are now dead and forgotten by all who knew them, forgotten by me too until I started to look backwards to my far-off childhood. I did not know I was capable of remembering so much, but now that I have started the subconscious yields its secrets and the memories come crowding thick from the buried years. I cannot describe my grandfather, yet I remember dimly the tall old man who used to give me sweetmeats and fruit fresh from the garden, with the

dew still on it. He used to take me for walks whilst Inci
attended to my small brother or helped Feride with the upstairs
work. It was the custom after breakfast for my grandfather to
go to a coffee-house and smoke the nargile, or hookah-pipe,
and after my fifth birthday I used to be taken with him. He
would sit in front of an open window in the coffee-house,
leaving me to play in the gardens, ever under his watchful eye.
But sometimes he would engage in earnest conversation with his
friends and his eye become not quite so observant, and then I
used to play with the dirt, making mud-castles for myself, a
lost rapt little boy, absorbed with the wet feel of the mud
running through my fingers. I would be oblivious to the stones
cutting into my knees but presently a sharp slap on the arm would
recall me to the present. I would let the remaining mud trickle
dreamily through my fingers then look up to find my grandfather staring down at me with eyes that pretended to be fierce.
All the way home he would make me walk a little behind him,
like a puppy with its tail between its legs, crestfallen and very
conscious of the old man's displeasure. Upon arrival at home I
would be delivered into the hands of Inci, who would take a
severe look at the dirt on my person and on my clothes then
whisk me off to be washed in time for luncheon.

One day I remember playing in the coffee-house gardens
and had wandered over to the large, ornamental pool in the
centre, intent upon playing 'boats'—a game that was as thrilling
to me then as it is to-day to my small son at the Round Pond in
Kensington Gardens. My game however was not played with
boats but with various piece of sticks. On this particular day,
in my absorption, I leaned too far over and in I fell with a
terrible splash—in up to the neck and icy cold. My clothes
held me down and I thought I was going to drown. My
piercing screams brought my grandfather and a couple of
waiters running at the double and I was unceremoniously
fished out, blue in the face and coughing up what seemed to
be gallons of water. And oh! the safety of my grandfather's
arms. I was taken into the coffee-house, stripped of all my
clothes and wrapped in a blanket, whilst a messenger was
despatched to my home for dry clothing. Hot milk was forced
through my chattering teeth and my grandfather, looking
white and shaken, scolded me without ceasing. I was finally
taken home in dry clothes, still trembling with fear and cold

and my grandfather refusing to speak to me. After that episode I was left to kick my heels at home for days on end. My grandfather's morning kiss became fraught with ice and he would pay no attention to me when I timidly enquired after his health. He would stalk off to the coffee-house, leaving me on the terrace with my mother and my grandmother. I used to play in the garden under an apple-tree. It was my apple-tree and my retreat when the burdens of the world became too much. When I grew tired of being alone I would wander back to the house in search of Inci. Hacer, the cook, would perhaps softly call me into the kitchen, giving me lokum to eat then 'shooing' me off quickly lest my grandmother discover me there. Hacer, like Inci, was my friend. She was enormously, grotesquely fat and when she laughed her whole body rippled and her eyes were lost in rolls of flesh. She had been with my grandmother for many years and was intensely jealous of Feride, whom she suspected of receiving more favours than herself. She used to make secretly for me little pastas with funny faces or give me cloves to eat, forbidden luxury, and sometimes when I knew my grandmother to be safely out of the way I would steal in to Hacer and she would give me cakes. If she were in an especially good humour she would dance for me and sing quaint old Turkish songs which made the heart shiver with melancholy. Her dancing was a joy for me. Her gigantic old stomach performed lewd posturings, her unconfined breasts shook merrily and her backside did a little dance all on its own. Attracted by my shouts of laughter, Inci would come in search of me to pull me sharply by the ear out of the kitchen or, worse still, my grandmother would hear me and come in like the silent wind, her face a stony threat, and poor Hacer's demented breasts would give a final, horrified leap into the air, her performance coming to an abrupt end.

My mother was most likely to be found in the salon, that is if she were not sitting out in the garden or paying calls with my grandmother. But my grandmother only occasionally liked to ride behind the cream-coloured horses in the phaeton, and as my mother was not permitted to go driving alone, she consequently rarely left home. If this arrangement bored her she gave no sign. She displayed no temper, being invariably tranquil. If I were to wander into the salon to find her sitting there, she would lay down her embroidery, pat the seat beside her and invite me to tell her what I had been doing with myself. More often than not I would refuse the invitation, feeling constrained in the face of such perfect tranquillity and preferring the more robust ordinariness of Inci. But Inci in the mornings was usually helping Feride, or doing something for Mehmet, my baby brother, and the upper regions of the house were also forbidden territory for me. Bored and lonely I would seek the garden again, climbing the little apple-tree to watch the passing boats on the Marmora. Many long childish hours I dreamed away in that tree, listening to the soft crying of the seagulls and only being recalled to the present by Inci's voice ordering me to come into the house.

One morning my father awakened me early and after tossing me two or three times into the air, told me that my grandfather wanted to see me in his room. I rushed to him, peering cautiously through the door and saw him sitting up in his bed, his eyes twinkling under the white nightcap pulled low over his forehead. He looked comical and called to me to come in. I leaped into his bed joyfully for I had smarted under his displeasure and was wildly happy to be here in this great, adventurous bed again. That bed which was so exciting to explore and held such possibilities of terror for a small boy who ventured too far beneath the clothes, delving deeper and deeper into the blackness whilst a grandfather pretended to be a fierce old lion, emitting the most awful roars. When my screams became too hysterical, he would pull back all the clothes and I would creep back to normality again, my heart still pounding with terror. He would instruct me to ring for Feride and when she appeared would ask for my breakfast to be served with his. The morning of which I write was no exception to the general rule. We played and romped and growled fearfully at each other, and when I was taken away to be dressed, my grandfather called after me that I could accompany him to the coffee-house later on. Then I really knew that we were friends again.

Yet we did not go to the coffee-house after all, for he suddenly changed his mind as we were setting out. And it is perhaps this one thing that makes that day, with all its events, still remarkably clear in the memory. For we walked that day by the Marmora, the first and last time I ever walked and talked with my grandfather, for never before had I been any farther with him than the local coffee-house. We walked that day like old comrades, that brilliant young day. Nowadays whenever I walk beside the Marmora on just such a soft young day, I am again a child of five skipping along beside the lost figure of the kindly old man. And that morning, for all his talk, he seemed to lean more heavily on his stick and presently he sat down on a rock, saying he was tired. He told me I could play with the sands, provided I did not go too near the sea. I started to hunt for shells, and whenever I found a particularly nice one I would shout to him, telling him of my find. But once when I shouted he did not reply and when I turned to look at him he was gesturing to me with his hands. I ran to him feeling, as children instinctively feel and with that little extra sense of perception that is in them, that something had gone wrong with the morning. Yet equally instinctively refusing to recognise the perception, so that even though I ran to him I was rebelliously shouting that I wanted to play, I wanted to play. . . .

He said: 'Grandfather is not well, my darling. Let us go home quickly.'

And I gathered my shells mutinously but with a very little icy thread of fear touching my heart.

It is odd how intuitive are children and animals. To-day if any danger threatened I doubt if I would have the clear warning I had as a child. Sophistry and the years have combined to stifle, to overlay that quick animal sense and I believe I could actually walk into danger without so much as a flicker of the heart. But that day I felt it surrounding my grandfather like an aura.

I held his hand tightly, my heart almost suffocating me with the premonition I had. Half-way home we met the Imam from the little Mosque and he came up to us, looking concerned, and spoke softly to my grandfather. I felt a great, overwhelming relief that some other human was here to share my fear. The Imam took my grandfather's arm and slowly, painfully slowly, we ascended the last long hill that led to home.

Once at the house I was delivered to Inci, who was in the garden with Mehmet. Mehmet was eighteen months old at that time, just starting to walk. He was supposed to be delicate and I resented him, for whenever I wanted to shout and run, I was inevitably hushed by Inci or my mother and warned that he was sleeping. It seemed to me that he never did anything else but sleep and I despaired of the day ever coming when he would be considered big enough for me to play with. But I also sometimes loved him and liked to stroke his soft cheek and feel the down on his head. Now and then he would call me to him, curling his fingers over my hand and chattering. The day we brought my grandfather home I was unable to respond to the laughter in his eyes for I was consumed with uneasiness and curiosity. Inci's dark eyes were big with question and she asked what it was that had happened on the walk.

We stayed out in the hot garden all through the morning, and when we went into the dining-room for luncheon, my mother looked odd and lonely seated alone at the great table. We children and Inci used to eat at a smaller table in a little recess, and all through that meal I was conscious of my mother as she toyed with her food and poured many glasses of water for herself from a crystal carafe. In the middle of luncheon Feride came hurriedly in, announcing that the doctor had arrived, and without any ceremony, and leaving her meal half touched, my mother left the room. Inci called to Feride and asked what was the matter, but Feride, with a quick, warning look at me, said she did not know.

During the afternoon my father was sent for and I remember his thin worried face as he passed me, without being aware of me, where I stood in the hall.

Inci took us to the playroom for it was too hot to play any more in the garden. I vaguely recall playing with bricks, with Mehmet crawling over a large mat on the floor and Inci sitting in a rocker by the window, a pile of mending by her side. We were all listless with the heat. After a little while my father came for me and, picking me up in his arms, said:

'Grandfather is very ill but he wants to see you. Will you be a good, brave man and come with me?'

I nodded dumbly and we left the room together, the tall young man and the solemn little boy who was once again overcome by the events of the morning.

In my grandfather's room it was twilight. The windows stood open but the cool green shutters had been fastened against the glare of the afternoon sun.

My mother was seated on one side of the bed, holding a silver pitcher which I knew to be filled with water from the grave of Mahomet. I knew also that this precious water was only to be used in times of extreme emergency. My grandfather had once made the pilgrimage to Mecca and had brought this water back with him and afterwards he was always known by the title of Haci, signifying he had been to Mecca. My grandmother stood by one of the windows, her eyes straining through the little spaces in the shutters. The fierce white glare from the gardens must have hurt her eyes yet she seemed oblivious to it. She stood perfectly still, like a statue, and the tears poured unchecked down her cheeks. It was a shock to see my usually composed grandmother crying so unrestrainedly and it tightened the feeling of fright that already half-paralysed my heart.

A doctor was washing his hands in a corner, quietly, quietly, making scarcely any sound.

As we came in my mother put down the silver jug on a side table and took me from my father. He went to the other side of the bed and took up the Koran, beginning to read aloud from it in his soft, musical Arabic. I stood looking at my grandfather, awed by the unaccustomed sight of so much solemnity surrounding him. He moved his fingers and my mother lifted me up to him, saying, ' Father, this is Irfan.'

He laid his heavy, old hand on my head as though giving me his blessing, then his fingers moved feebly through my curls and down, down, slowly down over my face. I kissed his hand and ached with unshed tears. He tried to say something and the doctor came quickly over, motioning to me with his head, and my mother took me out. She told me to go back to Inci then left me and returned to my grandfather's room, the door closing gently behind her. I started to cry suddenly, there on the quiet landing, and still I remember, as if it were yesterday, how a big fat wood-pigeon flew past the window, coo-cooing in his soft throaty voice.

It is still the best-remembered sound from that day.

CHAPTER II

AN AUTOCRAT AT THE HAMAM

Now and then, usuaily about once in a week, my grand-mother had a sociable turn of mind and when these moods came upon her she invariably went to the Hamam. Hamams, or the Turkish Baths, were hot-beds of gossip and scandal-mongering, snobbery in its most inverted form and the excuse for every woman in the district to have a day out. Nobody ever dreamed of taking a bath in anything under seven or eight hours. The young girls went to show off their pink-and-white bodies to the older women. Usually the mothers of eligible sons were in their minds for this purpose for these would, it was to be hoped, take the first opportunity of detailing to their sons the finer points of So-and-so's naked body. Marriages based on such hearsay quite frequently took place, but whether or no they were successful few of us had any means of knowing.

In the hot rooms of the Hamams little jealousies and rivalries were fanned into strong fires and very often fights took place between the mothers of attractive daughters vieing for the favours of the same young man.

As against the mothers of daughters the mothers of sons took pride of place. There was a sort of sharp dividing line drawn between them and it was quite easy for a stranger to tell which of the plump, matronly ladies had the best wares for sale. For whereas the mothers of daughters were inclined to laugh a lot, to draw attention to their family groups, the mothers of sons lay aloof on their divans—too conscious of their own superiority to contribute to the general noise and scandalising. They would lazily nibble fruit, eye the simpering, posturing young girls critically and sometimes accept the offer of having their backs washed by some ravishing young creature but with such condescension that immediately the wildest speculations were engendered in the other female breasts as to why such an obvious favour had been shown at all. The back-washing con-cluded, the ravishing young creature would be dismissed and one by one the mothers of the ignored daughters would sidle up to the devilish old autocrat who had just had her back washed and whisper the most damning things about the character of the recent, elated, now vanished back-washer. My grandmother had no eligible sons for sale but nevertheless this did not prevent her from making her presence felt. Sociability would develop in her over a period of days until one morning she would grandly announce to my mother that on such and such a day she would go to the Hamam. My mother, having no social interests, or the nature maliciously to enjoy intrigues or broken or pending romances, rarely accompanied her to the baths. Generally she sighed at the thought of all the extra work my grandmother's decision was going to make for the servants.

Quite frequently I was taken by my grandmother, although after my fifth birthday it was strongly doubted by the other members of the family as to the seemliness of taking such a grown-up young man to a place full of naked women. My grandmother, however, who would have been the first to object to this in other people, always set aside the idea that five was a great age and would insist on taking me with her.

She always engaged private rooms for herself at the Hamam, a room for disrobing and another for washing herself, feeling quite definitely that she could not be expected to mix entirely with the common herd. Sociability could only go so far.

I well remember the flutter she caused in the household when she announced one day that on the morrow she would go to take her bath. It practically paralysed the administration, so to speak, for it could not be lightly decided just like this that one was going to the Hamam less than twenty-four hours hence. Preparation was necessary. Special foods had to be bought and cooked and packed. The private rooms had to be booked. My mother vainly tried to persuade her to wait a day longer but this interference unfortunately only had the result of making my grandmother's determination all the stronger and more fervent.

Feride was sent to the Hamam to warn them of our arrival on the morrow—for it had already been decided that I should go too. Looking back, I have a suspicion that Feride rather liked this sort of mission for she had lived so long with my grandmother that she quite enjoyed creating sensations and bullying the servants of others by right of her exalted position as personal factotum to my grandmother, whose social position was undoubtedly the greatest in the neighbourhood.

The owners of the Hamam were of course well acquainted with the various foibles and idiosyncrasies of my grandmother and thought nothing of giving her private rooms whenever she wished—even on occasion dispossessing women who had previously engaged them. My grandmother was a great force and, because she knew this very well, shamelessly took advantage of it and altogether behaved like royalty.

The rooms having been reserved for her the next thing of importance was to have long and futile discussions with Hacer as to the sort of food she wished to have prepared for eating in the Hamam. Murat, the coachman, was despatched post haste to the market, just as my mother was wanting him for something else, with a basket almost as big as himself, for he was a small man, and he arrived back with enormous quantities of food—most of which would undoubtedly be wasted. But my grandmother, at her most gracious now that she had gained her own way and hospitality simply dripping from her, explained this extravagance away by saying she liked a large selection of food from which to choose and that in any case she liked to feel that the unfortunate ones left at home would enjoy the same delicacies as she herself would be enjoying at the Hamam. Food was good at all times in the house for she always ordered everything herself—certainly never allowing my tranquil mother to express any preference, completely disbelieving that anybody's ideas could be better or more original than her own. Furthermore she did not encourage originality of thought, cherishing the belief that this when related to food ruined the digestion, perished the lining of the stomach, tore the nervous system to little pieces and was the cause of every known disease.

All the memorable day Hacer was kept busy over the cooking-stove. Dolmas were made from vine-leaves, stuffed full of savoury rice and currants and nuts and olive oil. Every few minutes my grandmother would dart into the kitchen to interfere and offer her unwanted advice to the more experienced phlegmatic Hacer. My grandmother tasted everything. This was an awful business for Hacer and on these nerve-racking occasions I would wait for her to burst into wild tears of rage or swipe all the crockery off the tables and have a fine display of hysterics. Poor Hacer was always the luckless one. She would stare apprehensively as my grandmother critically poked and sniffed at her cooling dolmas, and nine times out of ten she was ordered to prepare and cook fresh ones as those already made were only fit for the Christians to eat. Feride was called in to superintend the making of kadin-ğöbeği, heavy, syrupy dough-nuts which when properly made are light as air and heaven to eat. I was very fond of kadin-ğöbeği and purposely delayed in the kitchen looking for a chance to steal one of them as they were cooling in the rich syrup. The advent of the supercilious Feride caused sulkiness to mount in the breast of Hacer and she muttered many unmentionable things beneath her breath.

Her beloved Feride safely installed in the kitchen and nothing likely to go wrong, or so she fondly hoped, my grandmother next went upstairs to her bedroom taking Inci with her, to my mother's annoyance, since this left Mehmet and me with no supervision. Inci was instructed to sort out the clean linen and bath-robes and innumerable towels that would be required at the Hamam. Bars of soap and a large bottle of eau-de-Cologne were brought from their hiding-places and all the other appurtenances needed for the correct toilette of a lady about to take her bath. Inci was told to pack all these things in little embroidered cloths, which were kept especially for this pur-pose, and I was several times called upstairs and warned of all the things I must not do at the Hamam. By the time my grand-mother had herself uselessly run up and down the stairs several more times, she suddenly came panting into the salon and threw herself without the least semblance of elegance into a large chair. She fanned herself vigorously then complained to my mother that she was very tired and that she could not understand why it was that whenever she wished to take a bath it was she who had to do all the work about the place. Hacer, she said, was more than ever useless and she did not know why she continued to keep her, excepting perhaps that it was because she felt pity for her, knowing that no other household in the world would keep her for more than a day. My mother, who had a soft spot for the maligned Hacer, here interrupted to tell my grandmother that—on the contrary—when she went to the Hamam she completely disorganised the entire house. Warming to her subject in the face of my grandmother's dis-believing attitude, she said that here was she—starving, with none to prepare a meal for her, her children were hungry too and that as Hacer had already been twice told to throw away all the dolmas she had spent the entire morning cooking, she felt that the rest of the day would go by in similar fashion until we would all die with the hunger.

This considerably enraged my grandmother, who thought the whole accusation very unjust indeed, and she then added chaos to chaos by impetuously ringing for Murat and ordering him to run immediately to the butcher to buy meat as everyone was hungry. Murat, who was hungry himself, went with great haste lest my grandmother changed her mind again. She, with great indignation at being so unjustly accused, went off in a temper to the kitchen to instruct Hacer to leave everything and prepare luncheon since my mother, worn out with all the embroidering she had done that morning, was starving.

She suddenly recollected that henna had to be applied to her hair and called Feride away from the kadin-göbeği, demanding to know why the henna had not been prepared before this time. Her obstreperousness affected us all, and me in particular so that I was continuously fractious, eventually reducing Inci to weak tears of rage.

'If I go to the Hamam,' she ground out at me through tightly clenched teeth, 'you will come home looking like a lobster. I shall hold your head under the boiling water until you die and pull your nose until it is as long as an elephant's nose!'

Sufficiently intimidated I fled to Hacer who gave me sugar to eat and sat me on a high chair so that I could watch what she was doing. But the hot smell of food overcame me and in any case I was far too excited to sit still for very long, so I demanded to be lifted from the high chair and went in search of my grandmother. I discovered her in her bedroom and as she was in a gracious mood she permitted me to enter just inside the door to watch what Feride was doing. I could not help laughing when I saw her because she looked so funny. She was sitting in a straight-backed chair in front of a long mirror, Feride beside her placing layer after layer of clean white paper over the revolting brown mess of henna which covered her hair. A silver cup with the remains of the brown mess adhering to its sides stood on a low plaited stool beside them and next to it was a Moorish table piled with snowy towels and a tray of small gold hairpins.

Because my grandmother had henna on her hair she was unable to go to the salon or the dining-room, so she stayed in her room and ate lokum (Turkish Delight) out of a large dish on her lap and drank rose sherbet. She then languidly refused the tray of luncheon brought to her by Inci, saying she was not hungry and that she needed very little to keep her going. I begged to be allowed to eat the tray of refused food and permission was indulgently granted but my mother was furious when she heard of it and sent Inci to fetch me to the dining-room. I regretted having to leave the close, scented atmosphere of my grandmother's room and bit Inci's finger on the way downstairs in revenge.

After luncheon was over Feride re-prepared all the bathrobes and lingerie Inci had so carefully packed during the morning. Feride put little bags of lavender between each fold, annoyed because Inci had forgotten to do this. The smell of lavender always lingered in our house for all the drawers and cupboards were full of it, tied into little muslin bags and placed between the linen.

Every year the wild, gaunt-looking gipsies used to gather it in the hills then come down to the city to sell laden baskets full of its sweet perfume. Lavender grew in a corner of the garden too but we always bought from the gipsies. I remember a merry-eyed gipsy girl who used to come to the house when I was small. She would stand in the street singing her lavender song and then she would be brought into the house by Feride, who would bargain astutely for the lavender. Hacer would make Turkish coffee for her to drink and I would steal into the kitchen to look at the dark, alien face of the gipsy girl as she sat on the table and swung her long, bare legs. Sometimes my grandmother would order Hacer to give the gipsy a good meal and afterwards she would be called to the salon to read the future for my mother and grandmother, who both had a child-like belief in such things. She would be given a cushion and would sit on this, just inside the door, fearful to advance too far into the elegant room, careful not to put her bare, dirt-grimed feet on the carpets. Having read the amazing things revealed in her shining crystal ball and thoroughly fevered my imagination, she would take out a handful of dried broad beans from a bag attached to the wide belt she wore, extricate a handkerchief remarkable for its cleanliness and some blue glass beads and begin the fortune-telling all over again. When this was finished my grandmother would toss her a gold coin which she would catch dexterously.

She had long slim fingers, I remember, the filbert-shaped nails always tinted with henna, and a brown little face with a wide mouth that always seemed to be laughing. She wore strange, exotic garments of every hue and her shining black hair had twisted through it many vividly hued glass beads. She would tell us about her life in the tents and of her husband, who made baskets to sell to the peasants or sometimes to the rich houses of Istanbul. She gave one the impression that she was sharp as a monkey and oddly alluring, and I used to imagine a fine, swashbuckling husband for her, with swarthy face and gleaming white teeth and gold earrings dangling, flashing in the sun as he moved his leonine head. A tall, muscular man he would be with magnetism to match the strange charm there was about her. I was very disappointed one day when he accompanied her to our house, wishful to sell one of his baskets to my grandmother for Murat's use. He was small and thin and ugly in a frightening way with a pock-marked face and a cruel mouth and eyes which looked as if they were perpetually narrowed by avarice. He exuded danger and dark deeds on a windy night and I was very afraid of him. He was jealous of the gipsy girl who was his wife and I noticed she was very subdued in his presence, the laughter dimmed in her eyes. He was very free with Feride, who became taut and haughty and almost incredibly like my grandmother in a rage. He slapped Hacer's rolling backsides several times, roaring with laughter each time she protested. I fled from the kitchen to the salon, my eyes for some reason or other blinded with tears. I felt a helpless, childish rage against him and his coarseness, and pity for the poor, merry gipsy girl he had married. I did not know that life and people are seldom what one expects them to be.

When my father arrived home that evening hampers of food which had been parcelled by Feride were stacked in the hall and the packages containing the clean linen and various other sundries stood beside them. My father began to laugh when he saw them, remarking to my mother that all the world knew when my grandmother was going to take a bath.

She came down the stairs as he was saying this, her hands

blazing with jewels and a large, brightly coloured silk scarf tied over her head. She looked extremely odd with her small, slender body and the swollen head. The drying henna and the innumerable towels still covered it but she had made a concession to polite society by winding her gay scarf over them all so that she could eat in the dining-room with the rest of the family.

'I am going to the Hamam to-morrow,' she said, and my father, with a very grave face and making a gesture in the direction of the parcels, said that this was not difficult to understand. He frowned however when he heard that I was going also and said that I was too big for this sort of thing now. My grandmother very soon over-rode his objections and with a pretty little display of femininity promised that this would be the last time she would take me.

When my father finally gave in to her cajolery I was so excited I could scarcely eat a thing for the thought of his almost certain refusal had been gnawing at me all day.

Murat arrived at the front gates with the polished phaeton and the restive, impatient, cream-coloured horses, their harness jingling musically each time they tossed their beautiful heads. Feride handed Murat the things needed for our day then importantly returned to the house to escort my perfectly capable grandmother into the carriage. I walked behind them feeling rather grand and Murat looked reproving when he saw me, making the expected remark that I was too big to be taken with the women. Secure in parental permission however I ignored him and took a tight, defiant hold of my grandmother's hand. When we arrived at the Hamam the attendants came out to meet us, bowing very deeply to my grandmother but looking a little startled and uncertain when they caught sight of me beside her. They did not make any remark however but led the way to the disrobing room which had been prepared for us.

I had difficulty in keeping up with my grandmother's quick, disdainful steps but nevertheless refused to leave hold of her hand. We passed through a vast marble hall with divans grouped against the walls and little, frosted glass doors which opened off to the private rooms. There were many women lying about on the divans, and in the centre of the hall was a pool and a fountain, the waters making a cool, tinkling sound as they rose and splashed into the stone basin. Many bottles of gazoz, a type of soda water, stood cooling in the pool, for this was a communal room and it was here that all the women would eat and gossip when they had completed their washing. We passed through without looking to right or to left, in fact I kept my eyes firmly on the ground as I had been warned to do. Feride had taken hold of my arm and, stealing a glance at her, I noticed the disdain on her black, finely featured face, the nostrils lifted as though there was a bad smell beneath them. Up a flight of stairs we went and were shown to a small room where we started to undress ourselves. I was the first ready and then Feride went to assist my grandmother. An attendant hovered outside the door waiting for orders, and when we were ready Feride called to her and handed our soaps, eau-de-Cologne and the large silver cup which was used for rinsing our bodies.

We wore takunyas on our feet, a sort of wooden sabot. Mine were painted gold, I remember, with richly coloured red roses outlined on the fronts. My grandmother wore black ones with jewel-studded heels and we made a terrible noise with them on the bare stone floor. She looked very elegant in her rose-coloured bath-robe, her hair caught back from her ears and temples with little gold-topped combs. Feride managed to convey all the dignity of the East in a plain, severe white robe wrapped closely about her lean figure. Solemnly we left the disrobing-room and followed the attendant to the room where we would wash ourselves and later eat all the food we had brought with us.

We had again to pass through the communal wash-room and some of the women were still washing themselves, whilst others lay about on the divans. There was a great deal of noise in this place. The high-pitched voices shouted across each other's heads the scandal and the bits of gossip they had all retained until this meeting in the room of the Hamam—for nowhere else would gossip be so spicy in the relating.

As graciousness and sociability were the keynotes of my grandmother's mood on Hamam days, she naturally halted our little procession whilst she enquired after the healths of the women who, a little overcome by this magnificent condescension, were practically reduced to silence.

My grandmother looked at the naked young girls with the

critical eye of a connoisseur and now and then, when a figure displeased her, she would clap her hands together in a very expressive gesture denoting disapproval—saying that So-and-so was too thin altogether, that her backside rattled and that she would never be able to find a husband until her figure improved. 'Give her plenty of baklava,' she advised the mother, and everybody would feel embarrassment for the blushing girl and the naturally affronted mother but my grandmother was always unaware that she embarrassed anybody.

She next singled out a ripe young beauty for approval and patted the plump thighs appreciatively. This drew the attention of all the mothers of sons, and my grandmother stated with great simplicity that if *she* had a marriageable son, this was the very girl she would select for him.

The small girls eyed her with dislike but as she did not notice this it did not matter. She only had eyes for the budding, well-made young maidens of thirteen years old or thereabouts and she would tell some delighted mother at great length that she would certainly be well advised to marry such a daughter as soon as possible to the strongest young man that could be found.

'He will know how to delight her,' she would boom loudly, 'but make sure he is as strong as a lion, otherwise with those fine legs of hers she will kill him.'

This caused a great silence and then the women suddenly caught sight of me lurking in the background and gasped with horror that a young man of the advanced age of five years had been brought amongst them, a witness to their nakedness. They curled into the most unnatural positions, trying to cover their bodies, and sniggered into their protective arms rude remarks about my male organs. My grandmother frowned at this levity however. She might be outspoken herself regarding other people's property but none might dare to make a remark about hers.

Sociability temporarily suspended she drew herself up haughtily and made a sign to the patiently waiting attendant that she was ready.

Our little procession moved on again, the clattering of our takunyas effectively drowning the remarks which were being made about me, and about my grandmother too for that matter.

Before we reached the room where we were to wash we had to cross a narrow channel where the dirty water was running to the drains. We could not cross this however until we had all solemnly spat three times into the dirty water and said, 'Destur bismillah' to appease the evil spirits which always lurk in dirty places. In old Turkey one had to be very civil to the evil spirits. If one did not say 'Destur bismillah', meaning 'Go away in the name of God', the evil spirits of the drains might very likely feel insulted by the lack of respect shown towards them and give one a push in the back guaranteed to land one face downwards in the channel of dirty water, or they might even cause one side of one's body to become temporarily afflicted with paralysis. Therefore we never took any chances with them. We were always most respectful.

Having on this occasion discharged our obligations, we were able to cross the dirty water freely and proceed without any further hindrance to the washing-room with light hearts. This room was very large, but because it was for private use there was only one kurna or large water-basin in it, instead of the twenty or so in the communal washroom. In one side of the marbled wall was a niche where Feride immediately placed our baskets of food. The attendant put the soap, the towels and the eau-de-Cologne on another shelf and left us, and Feride promptly pulled a curtain, made of rough towelling, into position over the arched doorway so that none might catch sight of us at our ablutions. She then proceeded to wash the kurna and the walls and the floor with soap which had been brought with us for that purpose. All the time she laboured my grandmother exhorted her to wash everything three times, otherwise they could not be said to be washed at all, and if everywhere was not perfectly clean evil spirits would cling to the dirt and perhaps do us some injury whilst we were washing. I sat on the cleaned part of the floor, apprehensive lest Feride should omit to wash anywhere thoroughly and visualising grinning, destructive demons lurking invisibly in the air waiting to pounce on me when I disrobed.

Perspiring freely by the time she had finished everywhere, Feride placed more towels about the floor for us to sit on and then she lay down herself and blew soap bubbles to amuse me, and succeeded in making me forget all about the evil spirits. Washing was the worst part of the visit to the Hamam for Feride, like Inci, had no mercy on me and lathered me from head to foot three times, making sure I could not escape from her by holding me securely between her strong legs. She put a sort of loofah glove on her right hand and scrubbed and kneaded my body with it until great, ugly lengths of black dirt were brought to the nearly bleeding surface and released. Despite my fierce cries she never relaxed and just when I thought the worst was over, she repeatedly filled the silver cup with what seemed to me practically boiling water and threw it over my head and body until I finally emerged smarting and tingling all over and looking like a lobster.

Whilst my grandmother was being subjected to similar treatment, with the wily Feride all the time admiring the delicate, unlined texture of the creamy skin, I was forced to lie down to rest, wretched and bored by this part of the day and longing for the excitement of food to be given me. Food always had twice its appeal if offered in the Hamam. I did manage once however to slip out of the room unnoticed and wandered into the communal room, without my bathrobe, thinking to cool myself with the sound of the cool fountain that played there.

The women watched me with a sort of hostile interest and sharply called the younger children to their sides, and I stood alone in the middle of the large room, awkward and shy yet reluctant to return to the steam and overpowering boredom of the private room. A fat Armenian woman called me over to her and offered me an apple but I had been taught never to accept anything from anyone outside my family so I could only thank her and decline the offer, even though my stomach turned over with the longing to bite at the cool, red apple in her hand.

She coaxed me over to her side and put a fat, kindly arm about me, and a young woman called impudently;

'Madame! It would have been better to have brought your husband here. Why, he's not as big as my little finger and I doubt if he would be of much use to you.'

The other women laughed coarsely at this and the fat Armenian woman grew red with anger and annoyance.

' You would be better not to let the grandmother hear you talking like that about him,' she said, and many more remarks were passed about me and some of the women stopped eating to see if there was going to be a fight between the fat Armenian and the young Turkish woman. I escaped and ran back to the private room to the more kindly influence of my grandmother and Feride and even my posterior seemed to be blushing with the dreadful sense of embarrassment which I felt.

When I got back my grandmother was resting and Feride in the act of setting out plates of food on a white tablecloth which was spread over a section of the floor. We all sat cross-legged in our bathrobes and ate with great appetite the lahana dolmasi (stuffed cabbages) which the despised Hacer had somehow managed to cook to perfection after all. We ate köftes (a savoury meat rissole), börek (a pastry stuffed with white cheese, eggs and parsley), turşu (a salad consisting of pickled vegetables, mostly cabbages), green peppers and fat golden cucumbers.

An attendant brought us iced gazoz to drink and then we ate Feride's speciality, kadin-göbeği, and afterwards were so overcome with sleepiness that my grandmother became quite querulous at my slowness in finishing. She brusquely ordered Feride to clear away the dirty remains of our feast and said that she wished to sleep. I curled myself up in a ball beside her, belching unashamedly to show my appreciation of all the good food I had eaten and then I went to sleep too.

When I awoke, the day at the Hamam was almost over. My grandmother was in the act of bathing herself for the last time and Feride, noticing my awakening, promptly seized the opportunity to wash me again. Renewed by her sleep she put as much energy into washing as though the dirt of centuries lay over me.

The day was dying. Crockery, dirty linen and the silver washing-cup were packed away by Feride, the empty eau-de-Cologne bottle lay forlornly in the centre of the floor. It would not be wanted again.

My grandmother put on her rose-coloured bath-robe and helped me into mine, and we went down the long, echoing corridor to the room where we had left our clothes this morning, which now seemed a lifetime away.

I averted my eyes as we passed the groups of remaining women. Many of them who were here this morning had already gone home but those who still remained called out respectfully to my grandmother, wishing her good health and continued prosperity, but she was in no mood for trivialities. She ignored them all. The time for sociability was over for another week.

CHAPTER III

A PURELY MASCULINE SUBJECT

THE LONG HOT summer sped by and my grandfather's death was eclipsed for me by the autumnal approach of my sixth birthday and—CIRCUMCISION!

Circumcision was only a word to me but as time went on it became the most exciting word in the world. It cropped up frequently in my parents' conversations. My father would start the ball rolling by perhaps remarking that Ali, the son of the local schoolmaster, had been circumcised a few days ago and that the whole neighbourhood was still talking of his bravery. This was the signal for my grandmother to look disbelieving, furiously clack her knitting-needles and remark, disparagingly, 'What! That unhealthy-looking child! Impossible for him to show any bravery, it isn't in his blood!' and she would go off at a tangent into some long story about his father and his grandfather and their lack of bravery, until I would begin to wriggle impatiently and she would check herself and end triumphantly, 'Wait until they all see *my* grandson.'

And because she meant me a hot thrill of pride would surge through my veins.

My mother would contribute in her cool voice: 'You are quite right, of course. My son will be as brave as a lion and we shall all be proud of him.'

Nobody ever explained what this terrible ordeal was which lay before me, requiring the courage of a lion, and I was too timid to ask though becoming more and more curious about it. One day I asked Inci to explain but she only laughed and told me to wait and see. So then I flew to Hacer for advice and she popped freshly made baklava into my mouth and grinned coarsely. She made a gesture somewhere in the lower regions of my anatomy but I did not understand and probably looked very puzzled, for she sobered her grinning and told me to run away and not to be bothering my head with such things. My mother was little more explicit but at least she tried to form some sort of picture in my mind. She told me that all little

Muslim boys had circumcision and that it would be the start of my 'manhood' and that lovely new clothes were to be prepared for me, for the act of circumcising was a great ceremony in Turkey. I thought about her words but, without knowing it, she had given me a new problem to wrestle with in my already overflowing mind. What had she meant by the word 'manhood'? Had it anything to do with my father—whom I had heard referred to as a 'man'? It was all very odd to a small boy's mind, but all these conversations had the desired effect of making me impatient and eager to experience circumcision.

Every evening I used to climb on my father's knee and ask when it would happen. He would pretend to look very grave and would ask my mother if I had been a good boy that day. The answer was always yes. Indeed, since the idea of circumcision had taken hold of me, I had walked in saintliness. So then my father would promise to arrange everything before my birthday and I would swell with pride and the days could not pass quickly enough.

It became my custom to wait each evening at the side of the house for my father to return from his business. When I saw him turning the corner, I would run to open the gate for him and examine his bulging pockets, usually filled with toys or sweets for Mehmet and me. One evening he was carrying a large cardboard box under his arm and when I demanded to know what was inside it, he told me it was my circumcision robe. I was almost delirious with excitement and begged to be allowed to carry it into the house. In the hall we met my mother and I pointed out the box to her, almost bursting with pride at the thought of what it contained. She restrained my high enthusiasm and I rushed off to find Mehmet and Inci to tell them the news.

Mehmet was now two and he began to cry because the robe was for me and not for him. He wanted a new dress too, he wailed. Inci popped sweets into his mouth, telling him to stop crying for he was lucky not to be having circumcision, since it would hurt him.

It was the first time anyone had mentioned anything about hurt and I felt the first chill of apprehension. I remember that Inci stared at me with round, appalled eyes because she had told me something she had obviously been warned to keep to herself. I rushed from the playroom, down the stairs and into the salon, in my panic forgetting to knock at the door and wait for permission to enter. As I burst in my father looked at me in astonishment.

'What is the meaning of this?' he demanded sternly.

And I burst out passionately: 'Baba! Inci says it will hurt me. Will it?'

My father looked swiftly at my mother, then back to me and replied:

'Nothing will hurt you. It's all very simple and quick, and now let us look at your robe and see if you like it.'

The subject was dismissed but I noticed that my mother gathered up her sewing and quickly left the room. I knew she was going in search of Inci and had a moment's swift regret for what she was about to say to her.

However my father's words had partially reassured me so it was with a light heart that I went out to the hall table, where lay the precious package, and brought it back to the salon. My mother returned in time to open it for us and I stole a glance at her face. She looked very composed but there was a slight tinge of colour in her cheeks.

The robe was the most beautiful thing I had ever seen. Blue it was, thick blue silk that slid against the face, embroidered lavishly with threads of gold and silver and rose. There was a blue cap in the same material, a sort of fez, and written across the front, in letters of brightest gold, was the word—'Maşallah.'

I was so overcome with emotion that I could not speak and my grandmother imperiously called for Feride and Hacer and Inci to come and see the pretty thing. Amidst their exclamations and cries of delight I strutted proudly as a peacock and was only shaken once when I saw Mehmet put out a tentative small hand to take the hat. Fortunately Inci coaxed him away from the shining wonder and my heart began to function again.

After this I became consumed with impatience. I wanted a definite day to be told me, to hold in my mind—and my shadowy fears began to grow bolder, threatening to swamp my mind. Inci had told Mehmet it would hurt. My father had assured me it would not. I trusted my father implicitly but I trusted Inci too. I could not remember a time in my life when I had not seen her black laughing face bent over me. She was as much a part of life and existence as were my fingers and toes. I began to have frightening dreams but had nobody to whom

I could run for consolation. Oh the dim, incomprehensible fears of childhood and the total inability to share or lessen those fears!

At times I would run to my mother, putting my head in her lap and bursting into floods of tears. She would take me on her knee and I would smell the comforting, familiar smell of her eau-de-Cologne as I nestled against her shoulder. She would ask me to tell her what was the matter but shame and pride forbade me discussing such a purely masculine thing as circumcision with her. But one unexpected day fear and doubt became things of the past—things to be looked back on with amusement and a certain lingering shame.

That morning dawned differently from the others. In the first place my father did not go to his office and all the house was caught up in the bustle of extra cleaning. Poor Hacer was almost beside herself in the kitchen, with my mother and grandmother constantly going to inspect what she was doing. Feride was ordered to finish her work upstairs quickly in order that she might assist the near-hysterical Hacer. Inci was taken from Mehmet and me and we were left in the garden with my father, who would have been almost certainly better in his office, since the uproarious house was no place for him.

In the middle of the afternoon I was whisked off to be bathed, an unheard-of thing—since my normal bath-time came prior to going to bed. Whilst Inci was drying me, she told me that I was going to be circumcised. Just then my mother arrived, in a flutter, with a bottle of her own especial eau-de-Cologne, and practically drenched me in its sickly, overpowering smell, damping and flattening down my curls with it and rubbing it across my body. Inci screwed up her little button of a nose and said I smelled like a woman, then quickly stuck her tongue between her teeth to make me laugh. When they finally let me go—having powdered and perfumed me to their hearts' content—the blue robe was lifted from its box and lowered over my head. The cap was placed over my flattened hair at a becoming angle, for Inci had a great sense as to how a fellow should wear his headgear.

I could hardly stand still with excitement and was several times sharply reprimanded by my mother, who was trying to pull white socks over my dancing feet and fasten intricate silk slippers. Yet even though I was excited, my stomach was playing funny tricks, and when Feride appeared with a little tray of fruit and milk it revolted in no uncertain fashion. However I was forced to swallow some milk, even though it tasted like poison, then I was taken down to my father. He held me at arm's length and laughed at my timorous face. Hacer and Feride came to inspect and Mehmet, clinging fiercely to Inci's red skirts, suddenly burst into loud howls— whether of envy or horror, I shall never know. He had to be taken away hurriedly for my grandmother's frown of displeasure threatened to make him worse. The salon was full of people. Feride helped my mother dispense liqueurs and bon-bons and there was a great deal of noise and laughter, with everyone drinking my health and crying 'Maşallah'.

It had been arranged that circumcision should take place in our neighbour's house, a Colonel in the Ottoman Army, for his son and half a dozen other children were also to be circumcised. Presently the front-door bell trilled and the Colonel was brought into the salon, very erect and military looking. The mere sight of him and what he represented was enough to unnerve me completely. He chucked me under the chin and boomed in a terrible voice:

'Well, we're all ready for you.'

I felt like a lamb being led to the slaughter-house. My stomach turned over and did a somersault without any help from me at all. It felt as if it were pouring away. My mother came over to me and put her arm about my shoulders.

After the Colonel had tossed off his liqueur in one gulp, having waved Feride and her bon-bons indignantly away, he joined my father. Presently they came and took my hand and we went out with the cheers of the guests echoing after us. My mother stayed behind, for it is not the custom in Turkey for the women to be present at a circumcision.

For fear my silk slippers should become soiled, my father carried me across the little side path which divided our house from the Colonel's. The front of the house was crowded with children and one or two of the bolder ones had even entered the garden to get a better view of the circumcision robes. I would not look at them and buried my face in my father's shoulder.

Inside the Colonel's house everywhere was decorated with flowers and silver streamers. There was the same bustle here as there had been in our house, and as I was carried through the long hall I caught glimpses of the native servants entering and leaving the salon with trays of drinks. I was taken to a small room, which had been especially set aside for the use of the children. There were six or seven other boys there, all a little older than me and similarly robed. They talked animatedly, showing no sign of the burning fear that was now rapidly devouring me. They greeted me in a grown-up fashion and I envied their composure, and my father and the Colonel left us whilst they went to pay their respects to the adult guests. When we were alone the other boys, the eldest of whom was eight, strutted proudly about the room and talked in a very off-hand way and wondered which of us would be the first to go to the doctor.

Then a clown appeared, dancing in and out between tables and chairs and playing a flute. Presently a second one came to join him. This one juggled deftly with oranges, and they both looked so funny with their exaggerated eyebrows, their white faces and red noses, that soon we were all laughing merrily and even I was beginning to forget my cowardice. An orchestra could be heard tuning up in the salon and then a woman's voice broke out in a little plaintive melody that reminded me of Hacer.

Suddenly I began to laugh louder than any and the clowns were delighted and redoubled their efforts to amuse us. But they did not know that I was laughing because I had had a vision of fat Hacer's leaping, merry breasts. More and more clowns appeared and we eagerly crowded round them and they played gay little airs on their flutes and we children jigged lightheartedly about the room. The eldest of us, the son of the Imam, was very fat and pasty-faced and wore huge, disfiguring spectacles and suddenly one of the others snatched a clown's hat and put it on his head. He looked so solemn and funny, with his eyes blinking owlishly behind the thick lens of his glasses, that we roared with spiteful laughter. He looked immeasurably silly and he just stood there quite still, whilst we shouted with laughter until the tears poured down our aching cheeks.

The Colonel appeared in the doorway and told us to go upstairs. Clowns, laughter, excitement were all forgotten and even the orchestra no longer played from the salon. We all held our breaths and looked a little fearfully around us. My father came over and took my hand and we followed the others up the stairs. How slowly I took each stair! And how each one passed seemed to seal my doom inevitably!

The fat boy was just in front of us with the Imam, his father, and he was saying:

'Now there is nothing to be afraid of. You are the eldest boy here, therefore you must be the bravest and set an example to all the others.'

But the poor fat boy only trembled violently and looked slack with fear. The room we entered was at the far end of a long corridor, a large room that overlooked the gardens. I remember that I looked out of one of the windows, across to our garden, and I saw Inci and Mehmet playing together on a rug which had been put out for them. I wished to run to them but there was no escape. My father's hand held mine reassuringly. He had seen my involuntary glance through the window and I think he wanted me to know that he understood.

In the room were eight beds, arranged dormitory-wise, four down each side. Each bed was covered with fresh linen, lace-edged pillows and a blue silk coverlet. In the centre of the room was a large table, loaded with sweetmeats and fruit and glasses for drinks. All the clowns had followed us and were dancing and tumbling all over the floor, playing their flutes, juggling with oranges and throwing their absurd, tall hats into the air. My father showed me my bed, for I was to sleep in this house for a day or two. It was under a window and I felt momentarily happier, for from here I could watch the garden and see Inci and Mehmet at their play. The doctor came in.

Instinctively I glanced away from him and over to the fat boy. His cheeks were wobbling with terror and his knees trembling so violently beneath the long robe that I wondered how they ever supported him at all. His fear communicated itself to me. I wanted to run, to shout, to call for my mother, to feel the comfort of Inci's arms about me. I looked at my father and felt my lower lip begin to quiver uncontrollably. He stooped over me and I still have the memory of his face, that kind gentle face, that lonely, shut-away face I loved so dearly. He was willing me to be brave and his fingers closed tightly over my icy hand.

'It's all right,' he comforted me softly, so that the others should not hear. 'Just be brave for one little minute more and then it will be all over.'

The doctor looked at all of us standing so docilely with our fathers and began to shout with laughter.

'What!' he said happily. 'Eight children in one room and not a sound to be heard!'

He looked at me.

'You are the youngest,' he said, 'so you shall come first.' He took my hand and peered into my face. 'I don't really believe you are afraid,' he said gently. 'There is no need to be afraid, you know! I never hurt good boys and your father tells me you are a *very* good boy indeed. Come!' He insisted to my stubborn, disbelieving face, 'You will see, I shall not hurt you.'

He took my arm and led me to an adjoining room, a small bare room to strike fresh terror into an already terrified heart.

The Colonel stood me on a table, which had been specially placed in the centre of the room. I faced the window, the Colonel on one side of me and my father on the other. The doctor busied himself with a black bag and boiling water and after a minute which seemed a year approached the table.

'Now just be a good child and stand still,' he commanded, but it was unnecessary for him to waste his breath for I could not have moved if I had tried. My legs were rooted immovably to the table and my body icy cold. I turned my head away as I caught sight of a little shining instrument and the doctor said heartily:

'Come, Hüsnü bey! Let us see what sort of a man your son is.'

My father lifted my robe, baring my legs and the lower part of my body.

'Open your legs!' commanded the doctor, his voice no longer sugared but the voice of a man intent upon performing some duty. 'Wider!' he roared.

I tremblingly obeyed. I remember that the Colonel held my ankles from behind me whilst my father pinioned my arms tightly. The doctor came nearer. I closed my eyes and was ready to die. There was a slight stinging feeling and suddenly it was all over.

I had been circumcised and my fears had been groundless. Nevertheless I screamed lustily. Screaming was such an exquisite relief to my overwrought nerves that I continued, long after the need for it was over.

The Colonel carried me back to the large room, meeting the second victim in the doorway. I was put into bed and clowns played their music and turned somersaults for my benefit and I felt proud and important.

I had intended to eat many sweets but Nature had her way with me and very soon I slept.

When I awoke the circumcision was over for everyone and the music of the orchestra came faintly and sweetly from the salon. The clowns had all gone. It was night and the stars looked very near and brilliant in a cloudless sky. Laughter and music and the chink of glasses came stealing up from downstairs and all the other boys slept. I was drowsy and contented and I turned on my side and went to sleep again.

The next morning I awoke to sunlight and peals of laughter. The foot of my bed was heaped with presents and I sat up quickly and began to undo them. The terrors of the previous day had vanished and everyone boasted of his remarkable bravery—all, that is, except the fat boy. And he turned out to have a sense of humour for he told us that when the doctor came over to him, he had neighed like a horse.

In the midst of our laughter a coloured servant came in with a tray of breakfasts. There was the customary white cheese, grapes, boiled eggs and bread and butter, wild cherry and rose jams and tea, served in small glasses with slices of lemon.

She mocked our inability to get up and walk, remarked on our appetites which, she said, were surprising since yesterday we had rejected every offer of food and she had thought perhaps we were delicate children. And all this said with a twinkle in her eye to abash us for the cowards we had been less than twenty-four hours before. After breakfast our mothers visited us, promising that upon the following day we would be taken to our homes. I asked my mother why she had not been to see me the previous evening and she replied that she had but as I had been asleep she had not wanted to awaken me. She said she was proud of me because someone had told her I had been a brave boy. I blushed with shame, trying to explain that I had not been brave at all but she laid her cool fingers over my mouth and would not let me finish.

'Sometimes the weakest of us are the bravest,' she said.

Mehmet had sent me lokum to eat and had cried for me during his breakfast. I was so touched by this that I resolved never again to be impatient with him when he could not follow a game. I kept that resolve for quite three days.

CHAPTER IV

SARIYER

THE MOST BEAUTIFUL present I had received for my circumcision was a big rocking-horse, brought me by my uncle Ahmet.

Uncle Ahmet was my father's brother. He was big and jolly and very good-looking. In his younger days he had been the despair of my grandfather's life but after his marriage, to a young and wealthy girl, he had apparently settled down considerably. I loved him and his wife too, for they had no children and used to spoil me atrociously.

The day after I arrived home from the Colonel's house, Uncle Ahmet and Aunt Ayşe arrived in a horse-drawn cab, laden with presents. They had come unexpectedly but there was a great joy in welcoming them, with we children making most of the noise and refusing to be hushed. My uncle brought many stuffed animal toys for Mehmet and butter and cheese and eggs from his farm for my mother.

Aunt Ayşe was a lovely, shy person, most surprisingly blonde with large dark eyes. I think she was a little frightened of my grandmother for she hardly ever opened her mouth in her presence or expressed an opinion. I discovered later in life that she need not have been afraid, for my grandmother had a great liking for her and her money. Her greatest respect in life was for money.

The day they arrived the house was soon filled with noise. Our squeals of delight, coupled with the loud hearty laughter of my uncle and the orders screamed by my grandmother to the servants, the chattering voices of my mother and my aunt, all served to give a stimulus, a sort of artificial gaiety to the drowsy old house.

My rocking-horse was borne off to the playroom by my uncle, I following slowly and painfully for I was still unable to walk properly. Mehmet was lifted, chortling with joy, on the lovely horse and I was bitterly jealous because I could not yet do the same. My uncle played with us for a long time and promised me that he would ask my father's permission to take me back with him to Sariyer, which was the name of the place where he lived. I loved to stay at Sariyer for it was much bigger than our house and had vast gardens and an orchard and many greenhouses. There was a gardener there too who, contrary to all accepted ideas, loved little boys.

It was the custom for my family to spend three months of every year at Sariyer. Usually we went there during May, when the heat of Istanbul began to become unbearable, but this year my grandfather's death and my approaching circumcision had kept us in the city all through the interminable dust and heat and flies of summer. We had suffocated beneath mosquito nets and insufficient fresh air, for the windows had been fitted with fine netting in an effort to keep the insects away and the shutters tightly barred at night. Yet just the same the mosquitoes found entry, filling the dark nights with their whining music. So that it was the middle of that fateful August of 1914 that eventually brought my parents to Sariyer.

Permission was readily given for me to return, on the following day, with my uncle and aunt—the remainder of the family to leave Istanbul as soon as my father's business activities permitted. I was very excited to be travelling without the restrictive eye of Inci or my grandmother. I helped Inci to pack clothes for me and lovingly stroked my rocking-horse, for this was to come with me. Mehmet's lamentations of grief I ignored and could not be persuaded to leave the horse for my father to transport, being convinced that if it were left after me Mehmet would pull off all its lovely mane and no doubt do other irreparable damage.

Murat, my grandmother's coachman, drove us to Galata Bridge, where we were to board the boat which would take us down the Bosphor to Sariyer.

Murat was a grumpy, miserable old man, who immediately made difficulties over my rocking-horse. My uncle however eventually managed to persuade him that there was plenty of room for it in the phaeton. Murat, in darkest retaliation, prophesied that it would get damaged on the boat. Unlike my uncle's gardener he had no love for small boys and thought it beneath his dignity to drive us to Galata Bridge where, he said, all the riff-raff of Istanbul gathered. He liked best to be seen driving my mother and grandmother, both heavily veiled, around the quiet green squares of Bayazit, to one of the big houses to pay a brief morning call.

Driving across the Galata Bridge, behind the high-stepping, cream-coloured horses, was an adventure in itself. In those days there was even less traffic control in Istanbul than there is to-day—and God knows there is little enough to-day. That morning, horse-drawn cabs, carts, porters carrying beds or other furniture on their shoulders, gipsies stepping out into the road beneath the very feet of the flying horses, peasants riding their mules—all were in danger of being knocked down or overturned, for Murat, with a fine disregard of human life, drove like the wind and was more autocratic than any Sultan.

Boarding the boat was fraught with difficulties, for I lost sight of my horse and in the resulting confusion wailed long and loudly and would not be pacified, despite my aunt's repeated assurances that she had distinctly seen Murat give the horse to my uncle. In the end, however, the horse was discovered to be safe and sound, seated all by itself importantly and looking over the rail of the boat with glassy eyes. Uncle Ahmet bought simit, a sort of crescent-shaped, pistachio-studded bread, and we fed the following, crying seagulls.

The journey took two hours and I was beginning to be bored with inactivity when the boat-station of Sariyer came in view.

It was good to be on land again, to catch a glimpse of my uncle's greenhouses through the trees which enclosed the gardens from the curious eyes of the boats. Servants met us, taking our meagre baggage, and I swung happily along the dusty road, clinging to my uncle's strong hand and keeping a half-fearful look-out for snakes—for which Sariyer was notorious.

That night I slept in a little cool room overlooking the house garden, a wilderness of tangled briars and tobacco-plants with their hot, hurting scent, and roses which were not considered good enough for the famous rose-garden. Jessamine trailed through the windows, and it was very quiet. I missed the sound of the sea, for the Bosphor was on the other side of the house and could not be heard from my room. I missed also Inci's clever fingers to undo my buttons. My aunt had sent an old servant to look after me and she fumbled over my clothes and over my bathing. Crowning insult, she omitted my evening glass of milk and closed the door after her when she had put me in bed. Inci had always left my door ajar, so that I could go to sleep to the sound of my parents' voices from downstairs and to the comforting clatter old Hacer made when she washed the dishes after the evening meal. I lay in my little bed, listening to all the unfamiliar sounds that assail one away from home. Furniture seemed to creak extra loudly and shift itself and the shadows in the corners were alive with fearsome things.

Fidèle and Joly, the house-dogs, padded restlessly up and down the path under my window, sometimes brushing through the shrubs, sometimes stopping to bark ferociously—at some unaccustomed noise perhaps, or merely because they were bored. When they barked, Hasan—the gardener—or Thérèse —the Greek cook—would hush them to cease their noise. Once a big black cat climbed on the branches of a tree opposite my window and my heart leaped in terror, for it seemed so large there, so still and evil in the dusky light. Yet for all my little fears I slept soundly, awaking next morning to the friendly voice of my aunt bidding me get up.

We had breakfast in the garden, my uncle fresh from a dip in the Bosphor. Afterwards I played with my aunt and the dogs, big, lovable Dalmatians, who gambolled on the smooth lawns, chased the innumerable kitchen cats and licked most of the gleaming paint off my horse.

When I had been there a few days, one morning my uncle announced that he was going to his farm, in the hills, and proposed to take me with him. My aunt was bade prepare snacks for the journey for the farm was two and a half hours' drive from Sariyer. The phaeton was brought round and in we climbed, settling ourselves with much laughter amid the cushions, and my aunt's face was covered with a thick motoring veil—a veil that fluttered in the breeze and sometimes tickled my nose. When we arrived at the farm, dogs leaped out to greet my uncle hysterically. They seemed very big and fierce to me and I clung tightly to Uncle Ahmet's coat-tails. The dogs wore great iron collars around their necks and, because wolves always first attack an animal by the throat, these collars were heavily spiked for protection.

We lunched in the farmhouse, in a low dining-room that had a big, open fireplace large enough to roast an ox and an uneven stone floor. The furniture was primitive and handmade but the meal which was served us was delicious. There were roast fowls piled on a mountain of pilaf—rice cooked in butter and chicken-water; swordfish straight from the sea and served with parsley, slices of lemon and various kinds of salads. There were dishes of grapes, water-melons and some kind of heavy sweet made of shredded wheat, butter, syrup and chopped nuts. Wine was served in carafes, and my uncle, answering the appeal in my eyes, poured a little into my glass. After the meal, Turkish coffee was served under the lime-trees and my elders seemed drowsy, lying back in their chaises-longues, their eyes half-shut against the glare of the sun on the grass.

I wandered away to explore. I went into the empty stables that smelled of horses and leather and I discovered seven or eight puppies playing in the straw. They were so soft and fluffy that I could not resist taking one of them into my arms to pet. The rest played about my feet, trying to climb up my legs. Suddenly two large dogs sprang in and I dropped the puppy to run, but the dogs were on me in a thrice and I thought they intended to eat me. I began to scream and a farm labourer came running and I heard my uncle's voice in the distance. My legs threatened to collapse and, ignominiously, I wet my trousers. The farm labourer told me in his difficult, peasant Turkish, not to be afraid. The dogs were the father and mother of the puppies and only wanted to play with me. I mistrusted however their idea of play. The peasant tried to press bread into my trembling fingers, with which to feed the dogs, but before I could take it, the dogs voraciously snatched it from him. The puppies, scenting sport to be had, got joyously under my feet and succeeded in knocking me down into the straw. So there I lay struggling, with dogs and puppies crawling over me and I screaming like one possessed. I was eventually sorted out of the doggy mess by my uncle's capable hands and taken, in flood of tears, to be changed and washed. My aunt and uncle were roaring with laughter, and the louder they laughed, the louder I bawled, feeling their amusement to be adding insult to injury.

After that disgraceful episode, I took care ever afterwards to avoid the stables and was glad when we returned to Sariyer.

My uncle used to bathe every morning before breakfast and I used to watch him from the dining-room windows, running down the garden to meet him when he was returning to the house. Some mornings I was taken with him and he taught me how to swim. We had fun splashing about in the chilly water but would come to breakfast with great appetites. Now my uncle was very fond of grapes. He could eat with ease two or three kilos each morning, and because of this my aunt was miserly about cutting from the house-vine, which spread out over the terrace like a canopy. She treasured those grapes and would tie each cluster in a little muslin bag, to prevent birds or bees from blemishing the fruit. And she never gave my uncle enough of them—at least in his estimation. Instead, dishes of market grapes were set on the table, which would cause heated words between them, he saying that one of the few pleasures of his day was to reach up to his own vine and cut as much as he wanted. He would come on to the terrace each morning, eyeing with disgust the market-grapes arranged so temptingly but so futilely for him.

'H'm!' he would remark disparagingly, ringing a little silver handbell for the parlour-maid, who would timorously emerge from the house knowing full well what was to come. 'What are these grapes doing here?' he would demand, to which she would reply sadly:

'Bey efendi, it was not possible to get any from the vine this morning. . . .'

And stand there before him, looking down at her feet, her face and neck slowly reddening. Before my uncle could any further embarrass her limited intelligence, my aunt would appear to ask what was the matter.

'The grapes, hanim efendi——' the parlour-maid would begin.

'These grapes, Ayşe——' my uncle would interrupt, waving to the parlour-maid to go away. 'Why cannot we have our own grapes instead of these half-dead-looking specimens?'

Then he would stick out his lower lip, looking charmingly at my aunt, and maybe she would sigh and proffer the grape-scissors without another word.

Having got his own way, my uncle would be instantly re-pentant, contenting himself with one outsize bunch and one meagre one, calling upon my aunt to witness his amazing economy. But victory was not always so easy. The results largely depended upon my aunt's mood and she could very easily turn her face to all cajolery. So my uncle formed a plan. I was shamelessly instructed to pamper and pet my aunt and when her mood was judged to have been softened sufficiently look appealingly to the house-vine and beg for some of its grapes. This I did and my aunt responded in the way my uncle had prophesied but I sometimes wonder how much she guessed of his villainy. For he would come to the table buoyantly, his face wreathed in smiles at the sight of his favourite grapes and my aunt would now and then look thoughtfully at him, then turn towards me as if wondering how far she was being made a fool of between us.

I used to spend most of my days in the gardens, my aunt sitting sewing under a magnolia-tree and keeping an alert eye on my activities. I loved the magnolia-trees with their shining green leaves, the thick, creamy texture of their flowers and sometimes I would pluck one, giving it to my aunt, who would place it behind one ear, looking suddenly exotic and strange. There was a pool in the middle of the grounds and I would peer into it for hours, watching the lazy goldfish with Fidèle and Joly panting beside me. They had adopted me as their own property, following me everywhere and howling dismally if I left them to look for Hasan. They were forbidden the rose-garden and the kitchen-garden but lived in the hope that one day an unsuspecting human would leave one of the wall doors open for them to slip through. Hasan would let me pick up the over-ripe apples that had fallen to the ground and on rare occasions he would give me peaches to eat, warm from the day-long sun on the southern walls. Once I let the dogs come with me and it was the only time I saw Hasan really angry as opposed to his not infrequent grumblings. He fussily hunted the two dogs off the carrots and onions, beat them from the raspberry canes and swore luridly when they trampled his strawberry beds. I took to my heels and ran, Fidèle and Joly flying after me, having had enough of sport—and Hasan's curses filling the air with vengeance.

My uncle had a rowing-boat and in the cool of the evenings he used to take me fishing. I used to look down into the Bosphor, into the clear blue waters and watch for fish, my uncle amused by my exclamations of delight. He used the line and we some-times hooked mackerel or small tunny and great would be my excitement to see them flapping and gasping on the floor of the boat. Once I saw a school of dolphins and watched breathlessly as they leaped through the air. Then homing in the twilight, with stars beginning to prick the green evening sky, with mackerel or tunny at our feet and my uncle telling stories. Riding the Bosphor effortlessly, hearing and yet not hearing the voices of the shore people and the sirens from the big boats. They were good times for an almost six-year-old to remember, times that have lived on in the memory long after the pleasure has died.

One afternoon, during siesta time, which was taken in long, cushioned chairs on the veranda, I awoke to laughter and heard my aunt saying:

'You must be tired, travelling in this heat.'

And my mother replying that it had been quite cool in the boat and that she was not tired. I jumped up and ran into the hall, and there stood my smiling family, in various attitudes of arrival. I was so happy that I could not speak for a moment or two but just stood there fingering the soft stuff of my mother's dress, going redder and redder with suppressed emotion. My mother unwound her veil and stooped over me.

'How brown you are!' she exclaimed, kissing me, and suddenly my feelings were loosed and I started to chatter.

I flung myself on Inci and Mehmet, only realising at that moment how much I had missed them. Immediately the comedian Inci started to roll her eyes at me and I roared with laughter, turning somersaults to show my appreciation. My father restrained my high spirits and put his hand on my head. He seemed quiet, unlike himself, and I was too young to know or understand that Germany and England were at war. Too young to know the difference that these far-off countries would make to Turkey and my own life.

We sat on the veranda, where the vine sheltered us from the afternoon heat of the sun. Extra cushions were arranged, a maid brought glasses of iced water and Turkish coffee and I climbed on my father's knee. He was absent-minded and did not take any notice of me, intent upon discussing with my uncle the manner of school I should be sent to. My uncle was opposing the whole idea, saying I was still too young to be sent to school in these troubled times, and here a secret look passed between them, which puzzled me but meant nothing. The subject was dropped and they began to talk of other things. I was too young to follow their meaning but in after years my mother pieced together the most of it for me.

That night, lying in bed in a bigger room which also held Mehmet, I could hear the voices of the grown-ups as they talked together on the veranda. There seemed to be a difference in their voices, an argumentative note not usually discernible. There was less laughter, more urgency—which was odd when the ladies were present. I crept from my bed and leaned out through the open window. I looked down on the thick matt of the vine-leaves, which looked pale green in places where the light of the lamp shone through. It was very still and I could hear every word of the conversation. My father appeared to be attempting to persuade my grandmother to sell our house! He said there was war in Europe and that none knew the day our country would be in it too. He said anything might happen and that, in view of the poor way of his business lately, we ought to cut down on expenses.

'Nonsense!' came my grandmother's voice crisply. 'Why should a war in Europe make any difference in our lives? All my children were born in that house, Hüsnü, and two of yours. I came to it when I was only thirteen and I would rather die than leave it now.'

Here my uncle interposed:

'Hüsnü is right. The house is too big for you now. It has been too big for years but when our father was alive it was not our business to interfere.'

'I should hope not indeed,' said my grandmother but her voice did not sound so harsh—perhaps this was an old argument. 'We have enough money,' she went on. 'And Hüsnü has your father's business——'

'I have told you I am selling it,' came my father's voice, sharp with finality.

There was a silence and I shivered in my thin nightshirt, although the night was so warm. I felt the tension in the air. I could not have explained my feeling or defined it in any way, but it is a fact that I was aware of a strangeness, an alien influence hanging over my family.

Years later when I began to record family events in diary form, my mother most faithfully reconstructed that night at Sariyer—the night when a small, inquisitive boy first discovered the cold breath of insecurity.

My mother was the first to break the little silence.

'Selling the business?' she said, bewilderment in her voice as though powerless to understand what strange force was driving my father.

'It is necessary to sell it, if we are to survive at all. When my father died I had hopes of reviving the business on a large scale but, as you all know very well, events were against me. Oh, it is impossible to explain all these things to you and make you understand. There are so many difficulties, labour, export, bad representation abroad; now the war in Europe writes finis to all my hopes of markets there. If Turkey comes in— and in my opinion she will—I shall have to go. Ahmet will go and who will look after things here? It is better to get rid of it now, and if one day I come back—well, with our name it is easy to build the business again.'

Again there was that frightening silence, a grim, uneasy sort of silence that paralysed me. These conversations were the first hint of the changes that were to come. I was tearful standing there, insecure and wishing passionately for life to stay as it was now—no, not as it was now, but as it had been yesterday when I had gone fishing with my uncle, helping pull in the mackerel and we had rowed home singing, under an evening sky.

This time it was my grandmother who broke the silence, obstinate, wayward, still indomitable.

'Because you may be called to the war, Hüsnü,' she said—'and I must say the possibility seems remote to me, although no doubt you think me a stupid old woman—it still seems drastic to sell your business. Your father and your grandfather built that business and surely this war which you talk about cannot interfere with the selling of our carpets to Persia and Europe. There must still be people left in the world who appreciate beauty.'

She was answered by a shout of laughter from my father, strange laughter that sent little shivers down the spine. He said:

'Mother, I kiss your hand and have a great respect for you and I know you will forgive me if I say you are talking nonsense. When Turkey is in this war nobody will care about our carpets or the business my grandfather built so diligently.'

'Very well then, Hüsnü,' declared my grandmother, unexpectedly capitulating. 'I do not understand why this war can make so much difference but you are a man and know these things better than I, so sell your business if you wish but leave me my home, if you please.'

My father sighed heavily, the sound ghostly and distinct through the vine. Perhaps his eyes appealed to my uncle, for presently I heard the deep voice of uncle Ahmet saying:

Hüsnü is right, mother. You must let him sell that barn of a house and find a smaller one and you must get in supplies of food. Prices are rising, the peasants beginning to hoard their wheat. It is better to provide now against the day when the shops may be empty and you and my sister Şevkiye have to look after yourselves.'

'I wish I knew why we are all so gloomy,' said my grandmother, 'and why we have to look after ourselves. Where will Hüsnü be?'

'God knows,' said my uncle feelingly.

'Even if he goes,' continued my grandmother, determined to be fractious, 'he will be an officer and will be able to send us many things. He will surely not see his family hungry.'

My father said quietly:

'The Ottoman Army has too many well-trained officers already. They will not want more officers, they will want good material to feed the guns.'

I did not know what he meant but apparently my mother understood for she made a little moaning sound of protest, and my grandmother was silent for once.

I could hear my mother softly crying and my heart began to pound and my skin to prickle uncomfortably. What had happened to my mother and my jolly father? What was all this queer new talk of war, and what was 'war'? I was wide awake and suddenly sleepless. I would like to have called down to the little group sitting so still under the protective old vine that listened to their tragic secrets. I did not know why I was afraid but I was old enough to realise that I had eavesdropped on a conversation not meant for my ears.

The next morning after Inci had dressed me I ran impatiently downstairs, anxious to know what change there would be in my parents. They seemed perfectly normal. My mother calm as ever and my father smiling-eyed. I felt a great relief. Perhaps the night and the darkness had played tricks with my imagination and I had never heard their conversation at all.

My uncle greeted us merrily and cut great clusters of grapes from the precious vine, with a fine disregard for economy. All that day I seem to remember that my father sat idly in the gardens, sometimes throwing sticks for the dogs, or playing with us children. He asked me if I would like to go to school, and when I enthusiastically replied in the affirmative he said he would make arrangements when we returned to Istanbul.

I timidly asked him if we were going to leave our house and he looked startled for a moment and I thought he would ask me where I had learned this, but he did not, only sighing a little and saying that perhaps we would have to leave.

Before going to bed that evening I sat playing alone on a corner of the veranda. My father and my uncle sat sipping wine and talking quietly together. I listened idly to what they were saying and heard the strange, new word 'war' repeated over and over again. The word appeared to dominate all thought lately and cropped up with unfailing regularity whenever the men were alone together.

My father was saying:

'The German officers are not training the Turkish Army for the sake of their black eyes.'

'But,' my uncle was inclined to disagree, 'if we go into this new war we are finished as a nation. Already we have lost our Empire and have just come out of the Balkan war, defeated and belittled. Surely Enver's conceit is not so great that he will see his country in ruins?'

'When a man is trying to create history about his name there is little he will not do, and the Sultan is powerless, which is perhaps just as well, since there is little to choose between the two of them.'

'What treasonable talk is this?' enquired my grandmother's voice sternly, and I looked up at her, as much surprised by her silent approach as the two men.

'Treason is a word that has very little meaning these days,' replied my father and his eyes caught mine, for I was watching him intently. 'Where is Inci?' he demanded. 'Why is this child sitting here with us at this time of the night?' and he violently rang the handbell.

After that I heard no more disturbing talk of 'war', or of anything else, for my parents were most careful to see that I was fully occupied, or safely in bed and asleep before they began their unsettling conversations.

Those days at Sariyer passed swiftly and we children grew brown beneath the sun. My father began to fish with my uncle during the evening and idle in the gardens during the day. The ladies would go for short drives, pay calls on the one or two big houses in the district and sip Turkish coffee in the cool of the afternoon under the spreading branches of the magnolia-trees.

They looked so gay and elegant there, seated in their chaises-longues, chattering like magpies, the sun washing their vivid silk dresses to shades of pastel. Sometimes I used to stand at a little distance from them, watching them embroidering or lifting the coffee-cup to their lips with white, languid fingers that flashed fire as the sun's rays caught the gleam of their rings. Perhaps the parlour-maid would come across the lawn to them, her apron dazzlingly white against the sombre darkness of her dress and I would feel nostalgia clutching at my heart, for I knew not what. Vague fears would begin to tremble formlessly in the mind and I would want to catch and hold that brilliant, vivid scene for ever. But at last the day came for us to leave Sariyer and returning home to Istanbul and Feride and Hacer was filled with its own excitement.

My aunt parcelled quantities of food for us and Hasan presented my mother with a bouquet of roses.

As the boat passed the bottom of the garden we waved gaily to my uncle and aunt and all the servants, who had gathered there with them, and we none of us knew that we were saying good-bye to a life that had gone from the world forever.

My aunt waved her scrap of pink handkerchief and I did not know that in after years, whenever I saw just such a pink wisp of cambric, it was to bring that day before my eyes again. I did not know of the long years of poverty ahead or that one day this I, this happy boy, would eat the grass because he was hungry.

CHAPTER V

THE NEW HOUSE AND OTHER THINGS

MURAT, WITH THE phaeton, met us at Galata Bridge, less bad-tempered this time about my rocking-horse and travelling at a sedate pace, because my grandmother was with us. On this occasion incautious pedestrians were quite safe from the hooves of the horses; but I was bored, longing for speed.

Once home, life very quickly resumed its normal tempo again, our holiday a thing of the past and already beginning to lose its bright shape in the memory. No more talk of 'war' threatened to disturb our peace of mind. It was arranged that I should start at the local school and several days were taken up with the preparation of new clothes, and a smart leather satchel was purchased. Hacer made tray after tray of lokma, a heavy, syrupy sweet, for it was the custom, thirty-five years ago, for newcomers at school to provide sweets for the other pupils. I was taken to the school by my father, full of importance and pride. We were met at the entrance by the hoca, a teacher who looked very fierce—or, at least, it seemed so to me. How-ever, he patted my head kindly enough and my first impressions were somewhat allayed. He wore a large black beard, a black robe to match and a white sarik bound about his head. We followed him into the school, which consisted of one classroom. There were no desks, no chairs, no books, indeed no evidence to connect it with any scholastic activities. Twenty or thirty children were seated cross-legged on cushions on the floor. The hoca sat on the floor also but on a bigger cushion and away from the children. The trays of lokma were brought in by Murat, who gave a sour look at the hoca, who peered into the trays, took a few lokma between his fingers and popped them into his mouth. He chewed ecstatically, his eyes raised to heaven, then bade Murat place the trays on the floor, whilst he himself arranged the children around each tray.

I was told to say good-bye to my father and kiss his hand, which I did, feeling vaguely uneasy for I did not like the hoca and did not think he was liable to improve upon closer acquaintance. I was given a place on the floor with the others and listened disconsolately to my father and Murat driving away. I was soon called to attention, however, by a smart rap on the head from the hoca's large stick. It was about ten feet long, which enabled him to chastise any child without moving from his cushion. I cannot remember any lessons from that day and am inclined to think that there were none, save occasional readings from the Koran. I best remember my horrible fascination as the stick of the hoca descended on some luckless pupil's head. It descended on mine too, frequently, and no matter how hard I tried to dodge it, the hoca was always quicker than I. Other refractory children were put in the various corners of the room and made to stand on one leg, with their hands in the air. They looked extremely funny but I was afraid to give way to my mirth, for fear the hoca should stand me there in similar position. He used to preface all his remarks with 'Padişahim çok yaşa'—('Long live my Sultan')—and we had to chant it after him.

That evening my father closely questioned me about the school, appearing to have been suffering from the most terrible misgivings all day. I described it to him and I noticed the glance he exchanged with my mother. My grandmother was highly indignant that the ignorant hoca should dare to beat her grandson.

'Ahmet was right,' declared my father firmly. 'He must be sent to the French school at Gedik Paşa.'

So ended my first and last day at the district school, Inci lamenting the trays of lokma which she evidently considered far too good to have been eaten by the hoca and his pupils. Arrangements were made with the Principal of the French school, a smart grey uniform ordered for me and primers and notebooks put into the leather satchel. In September of 1914, one month before my sixth birthday, I started school again.

The French school was totally different from the district school. In the first place there seemed to be an abundance of teachers and many classrooms. I learned to say 'Bon jour, m'sieu' or 'Bon jour, mam'selle' as the case might be and to count to ten in French. I made many new friends at the school. The majority of the pupils were Turkish, from families in the same social strata as my own, but quite a few were French or Armenian. I soon learned to go to school by myself and would meet my friends on the way. We would bow to each other and affectedly say 'Bon jour, mon ami. Comment allez-vous?' for it was the fashion to ape our elders and to speak French in public, a rather grand and adult thing to do.

Sometimes my new friends would visit me at home and I began to grow away from Mehmet and Inci. I would refuse to play babyish games with Mehmet and when he used to stagger into a room where my friends and I were gathered, would peremptorily ring for Inci and tell her to take him out of the way.

One evening, after I had returned from school and was sitting in the salon telling my mother about my day, my father arrived home with a porter from the market-place who was carrying several large tins. They were given to Hacer, and my father afterwards explained that these things must be filled with storable foodstuffs.

'The situation is serious,' he explained to my grandmother's wooden face. 'I shall go myself to the market to-morrow. Palace gossip suggests that our country will go to war. Enver and Talat Paşa are strongly pro-German, and if I have to go away I want to feel that everything possible has been done for your comfort.'

My mother's face grew serious and I knew that a discussion was imminent. I half expected to be sent away but my father said I might stay, adding:

'When I am gone you will be the only man in the house, therefore you must know how to guard your women-folk, eh?' and he playfully pulled my ear.

He stood leaning against a console table, and for the first time I felt him to be old. I did not know he was only twenty-six and, perhaps if I had, I should still have considered him old, for twenty-six is a gigantic age to a child. That evening he looked white and tired. Had my father been born in this age, in another country, he would not have fought in any war. He was essentially a man of peace, a good Muslim who feared his God with an awful fear and believed in an after-life. A man who was appalled by the poverty of his people and who, in his own small way, attempted to alleviate it. The carnage and brutality and utter senselessness of war tore his heart for the ordinary man who was caught up in the military machine. I have no picture of him and his face refuses to clearly emerge from the mists of time, but my mother represented him as a thinker, a bit of a dreamer if you will, a man more fitted for the leisured life than the life he was afterwards to know. He had sure knowledge of Turkey's muddled politics, the schemings of the peacock Enver, the treachery and greed of his subordinates, the weakness of the Sultan and the lack of organisation, the unpreparedness of Turkey for a new war.

That evening, I remember, he told my grandmother that he had received an offer for our house, too good he estimated to refuse. She looked thoughtful and said:

'I do not know how we shall manage in a smaller house and there are the servants to be considered too.'

'Hacer must go,' declared my father—and one wonders how it must have hurt him to talk like this to his womenfolk, he who only wanted to heap fine gifts on them. 'Feride,' he continued, 'must take over the kitchen. You must arrange these domestic problems yourself but Hacer is to go.'

'Oh dear!' said my mother, 'is it really necessary for Hacer to go?'

'Yes,' said my father. 'One day gold will buy nothing for you. Whatever amount of stocks we get in now will only last a certain time—so the less mouths there are to feed, the better. To-day the Colonel told me that all the Army are buying so fast that the shops are emptying. Murat and the horses must go too, there will be no place in a new house for a phaeton.

'No!' said my grandmother violently, standing up so quickly that she knocked over a bowl of roses which stood on a little bureau, 'I refuse to part with Murat.'

Fascinatedly I watched the water from the overturned bowl spreading darkly on the carpet.

'This is no time to think of grandeur,' said my father. 'You have not seen the poverty outside your house or the bewilderment on the faces of the soldiers, with their patched uniforms and their worn-out boots. You cannot be expected to understand politics or know that our country is under the heel of the Germans. We are riddled with German influence and capital, even though we may appear to be only sitting on the fence.'

'I don't understand a thing you say,' grumbled my grandmother. 'And if you only want Hacer to go because of the food she eats . . .'

But though she paused, nobody enlightened her. My father had done with explanation.

After that, quantities of food would arrive at the house for storing and the kitchen became alive with the sickly smell of jam-making and Hacer was told she would have to go. My mother moved through this activity serenely and calmly, never to my remembrance betraying her feelings. But my grandmother remained stubborn and intractable, spending most of her days paying calls—as though suddenly making up for a lifetime of neglected duties.

She would sit proudly and coldly in the phaeton, ablaze with jewels and hauteur. She would have to give in to my father but she intended to go down fighting. A new house was found and bought, at a higher price than had been anticipated. The prices of everything had risen and many of the shops remained closed for long periods of each day. More and more men were taken to be soldiers and presently one saw mainly women in the streets. Servants and mistresses and prostitutes, they all had to eat and would spend their days tramping the streets in search of an open shop. Bewilderment, resignation was to be seen in all their faces but no resentment. That came later.

The new house seemed very small after the large, rambling old Konak where I was born. No longer had I a room to myself but shared one with Mehmet. There was no playroom and we children had to use the dining-room if our parents required the salon to themselves.

The garden was large and had many fruit-trees and a pocket-handkerchief lawn, with a lime-tree standing in the middle of it. When my grandmother first saw it she snorted with disgust—if one may use such an inelegant term in connection with my grandmother. She demanded how she could be expected to live in a house that size and wanted to know where all her furniture would go. She made it quite clear that she had no intention of selling any of it.

When I first saw the house my father said to me:

'I hope I shall see you here as a grown man, my son, and myself as an old man. But if anything happens to me, then you will have to take my place. Perhaps many times it will be difficult for you but it will be your duty to look after your mother and your grandmother.'

I could not bear to hear my kindly father talk like this and I threw myself on him, weeping as if my heart would break. The house stood on a hill and from the upper windows we could see the Marmora, but faintly from this distance and more grey than blue. A laundry had been built on the side of the house by a previous owner, a haphazard after-thought. And a fig-tree grew in the middle of it. There was no proper roof on the laundry, only a sort of terrace built of wood with a hole left for the fig-tree to triumphantly emerge, so that in summer it could spread its glory outside the bedroom windows. In winter rain must often have come through but because it was only a laundry no one seemed to care. Only in Istanbul could such a lovely, enchanting thing be found. Later on, after we moved there, Inci would spread a carpet across the terrace and my mother would lie there with us on cushions, watching the sun through the leaves of the fig-tree, now and again stretching upwards to pull the ripe, purple figs with a stick which had been specially made for that purpose.

But before we moved in, men erected chicken-coops at the end of the garden and furniture was arranged, to the satisfaction of none, for the smaller, darker rooms looked unbearably overcrowded with my grandmother's unwieldy furniture. She never liked that house and seemed a different person for the short while she lived there. The day before we moved in my father bought a ram, for this is a tradition still observed in Turkey to-day. Its horns were painted gold, its woolly coat red and gold and a large red ribbon was tied about its neck, the bow sitting coquettishly under one ear. That night I could not sleep for I was excited and at the same time sad for the poor beautiful ram which would be killed on the morrow. Next morning a butcher was called and, with my father reading extracts from the Koran, the ram's throat was slit and as the blood poured down into the street, a great shout went up from the watching crowd.

'Hayirli olsun!' they cried, meaning, 'let this house be lucky for you!'

My father turned to us and said: 'Bismillahir rahmaner rahim,' which can be very roughly translated as 'I go into this house in the name of God.'

Then the little ceremony was over and the ram taken away to be cut up for distribution amongst the poor people. The same evening after sundown my father went to the Mosque to give thanks for the new house.

So into the new house we went and strange indeed it was that first evening. There was the garden to be explored and the joy of discovering ripe pears and quince on the little trees, to open the garden gate which led to a path to our neighbour's home and to a big field that was just waste ground, dotted here and there with a few stunted fig-trees. Strange it was too to see Feride in the kitchen, to know that never again would one hear Hacer's laughter or see her fat buttocks straining under her skirts. Strange to play in the dining-room for the last half-hour of the day before bed, although we discovered that a satisfactory 'house' could be made beneath the table. And then to go into the salon, with its tall, narrow windows fronting the hilly street, to see my mother and grandmother there, thoughtfully looking round them at the clumsy, heavy furniture made for a roomier house. And strangest of all it was to go up the stairs and see Mehmet's little bed alongside mine—strange, but comforting nevertheless—and to hear Inci's breathing all through the night, knowing she was there within call in the little scrap of room that opened off ours and was barely wide enough to hold her bed or the cupboard for her clothes.

The newness wore off and we became accustomed to the sight of Feride in the kitchen and I still continued at school. One evening when I returned from school I saw that my mother had guests. I flung my satchel on the hall table, washed my hands and went into the salon, where my greater years or the slight relaxation of discipline now gave me the right to enter freely.

A very elegant-looking lady was seated on the sofa, drinking Turkish coffee, and two children, about my own age, sat demurely with her. My light-hearted entrance was somewhat checked by their presence, for I had not realised children would be there. My mother, however, introduced me before I could turn tail and run to find Inci.

'This is our neighbour, Madame Müjgan,' she said and I had to step forward and kiss her hand. 'This,' continued my mother, bringing forward the girl, 'is Yasemin and her brother, Nuri.'

I bowed to them both, then retired a little shyly but my mother rang for Inci and we were told to go into the garden and play together.

Once out of the presence of our elders, our shyness melted
and we talked to each other freely. Nuri, I discovered, was two
years older than me and Yasemin one year younger. From then
on we frequently played with each other, our friendship being
smiled upon by our elders. Nuri was very jealous of his sister
and seemed to resent the quick friendship which sprang up
between her and me. He would suddenly leave us in the middle
of a game and go stalking off by himself to sulk. He was a
heavy handsome boy, unable to bear the sight of his sister
hero-worshipping somebody else. One day he and I had a
fight and arrived at our homes with bloodstained noses and a
couple of ripe black eyes. Our outraged parents forced us to
apologise but, although we were civil enough before them, we
continued the feud in private for many weeks.

One other day stands out in the memory. Yasemin and I
were playing alone together in our dining-room. We were
playing the age-old game of 'husbands and wives' and I was
proudly returning from my 'work', greeting her with a passionate kiss when a sharp slap on the backside put paid to that.
Inci had discovered us and went to inform my mother, who
apparently blushed deeply, locked me in my room and escorted
a tearful Yasemin to her own home. It appears that the two
ladies talked long and earnestly, later informing their husbands
of this dark deed, and the upshot was that Yasemin and I were
separated and forbidden to play with each other again.

So Nuri got his sister back again. I would see them playing
in their garden together, and if Yasemin were to catch sight of
me she would give a little precocious, flirting tilt to her head,
ignoring my placatory smiles.

Life was full of resentments for me just then. I was very hurt
and puzzled by my parents' attitude towards the kissing of
Yasemin and angry that nobody would give any reasonable
explanation as to *why* I should not kiss her. I became suddenly
troublesome at home and at school, being surly with my
teachers, who promptly reported this behaviour to my father.
One other night I refused to eat my dinner, demanding that
Inci should serve me with the sweet course first. When she
refused, I bit her hand and, knowing that trouble would arise
from this behaviour, added insult to injury and pinched her
hard. She howled with pain and rushed to tell my mother. My
father was very angry. He beat me with a stick then sent me to

my room without anything to eat. In my room I angrily kicked all the furniture, hoping thereby to damage it. I tentatively used some of the swear words I had picked up from the other boys at school, half expecting that the house would fall on me with the wrath of God. When nothing happened, I used the words more freely, shouting them aloud to the empty room and, to make matters worse, I could see Yasemin and Nuri playing in their garden, uncaring of my misery.

I was so hungry I wanted to cry. After Mehmet and Inci slept, I debated with myself whether I dare go downstairs and raid the larder. Before I could summon enough courage however my grandmother crept stealthily into my room with a slice of bread and white cheese and a glass of milk. I ate ravenously and she whispered that she had been unable to bear the thought of my hunger, but that I was not to tell my mother that she had given me anything. I promised fervently and soon went to sleep.

I had been at the French school a little over two months, when one morning upon arrival all the pupils were told to go into the music-room, instead of their classrooms.

We were very curious, especially as all the teachers were also gathered there, and wondered if we had done something awful. Presently the Director of the school arrived, going to the dais and looking sternly down at us. At least we thought he looked stern.

We said: 'Bon jour, Monsieur le Directeur,' and he replied in kind.

Then he spoke in Turkish, which was very unusual, but he wanted to make sure we all understood him. He said:

'My children, this country is at war. This is a French school and my country and your country are now enemies. This school will be closed indefinitely. You may all go home now and God bless you.'

His voice cracked and his little goatee quivered mournfully. And that day too my father told my mother that a pact had been signed between Turkey and Germany and our country was now in the war.

Thus ended an era for us, quietly and soberly and with no indication that these times would never come back again.

About this time I became acquainted with Bekci Baba. There is still a Bekci Baba in Turkey, but the 'Baba' has been dropped and his duties are less onerous than they were in the old days.

Every Bekci Baba is attached to a police-station, and thirty-five years ago many and varied were his tasks. During the day he would bring vats of drinking-water to the houses and during the night he became our guardian and our watchman.

He used to carry a large, thick stick, the bottom of which was bound with an iron rim. This was very useful when he wanted to beat a miscreant, or knock him unconscious until the police arrived. It was also Bekci Baba's duty to beat the drums during Ramazan, or any other religious Bayram. He had to announce important tidings or give warning if there was a fire in any part of Istanbul. This latter warning was the signal for all the young men in the district to leap from their beds, hastily collect the one and only pump allotted to each street and rush madly and with wild cheers to the scene of the fire.

I had never seen Bekci Baba, for during the day, when he called with the water, I was never allowed into the kitchen, and at night, when he turned watchman, I was generally in bed and asleep.

But one night I was lucky for I was lying in my little bed, wide-awake, looking out at the evening sky. The pale light from the street gas-lamp shone faintly into the room and there was a great stillness everywhere. Not a soul seemed to stir in the streets and only now and then could be heard the faint, far barking of a dog. Suddenly a noise came out of the quietness—a heavy tak-tak-tak. . . . The sound grew nearer and I heard a voice crying something but it was too far away to distinguish what it said.

My father came out into the hall. He was calling back to my mother and grandmother in the salon:

'Bekci Baba is coming. He's shouting something but I do not know what he is saying. There must be a fire somewhere.'

I began to feel excited up there in my little lamp-lit room and I sat up in the bed to listen. The noise of Bekci Baba's stick was nearer now. It went tak-tak-tak on the cobblestones, and the old man shouted: 'Fire! Fire! There is a fire in Beyo-ğlu——' spacing out his words carefully and clearly, so that none should misunderstand.

I jumped out of bed and ran to the window.

Bekci Baba was coming up the road, a fearsome-looking

figure with his dark cloak flapping out behind him and his stick thumping the ringing stones. He stood for a moment under the gas-lamp in front of our house, and to my heated imagination his face looked ghastly.

The poor, wavering light from the lamp leaped and flickered over his face, now lighting, now shading the prominent cheek-bones and the cadaverous eye-sockets. My father called out to him:

'Where is the fire, Bekci Baba?'

'Beyoğlu!' the old man rasped and was off again on his way, his cloak still flying out behind him and his stick going tak-tak-tak far into the distance.

For a long time after I ceased to hear his voice I heard the echo of his stick coming back to me, ever fainter. Probably Bekci Baba was still shouting of the fire in Beyoğlu.

CHAPTER VI

THE CHANGING SCENE

The end of 1914 and Turkey at war.

How little that meant to me then or to my family, save perhaps my father, who had the gift of vision and foresaw things more clearly.

Just at first there was no change in my home. It is true I no longer went to school but the events of the house continued without change.

One evening our neighbours were to dine and, war or no war, food must still be served, wine decanted. My grandmother took an active interest in this little, quiet dinner-party. She felt she could not trust Feride to do everything properly and lamented the loss of Hacer.

One of the dinner dishes she particularly wanted prepared was lahana dolmasi—stuffed cabbage-leaves—of which she was very fond, and she spent the entire morning complaining to my mother that Feride would ruin them. Eventually she marched into the kitchen herself, tied a large overall over her black satin dress, deposited her many rings in a safe place, and started to prepare the lahana dolmasi. She explained to Feride that although she had never *actually* cooked them, she nevertheless knew perfectly well how to do it.

Apparently Feride watched her noisy preparations with a great deal of misgiving, and found difficulty in getting on with any other work, since my grandmother continually got in her way.

I was allowed into the kitchen to watch. I was continually directed to do this, that and the other—all the dirtiest jobs incidentally.

She called Feride to her side and gave a demonstration of how onions should be chopped, looked up directions in an old cookery-book, then disagreed with them. She chopped onions with great gusto, calling upon my mother and Inci to witness her handiwork. Whilst my grandmother busily explained to us how capable she was, Feride was frantically trying to interrupt to tell her the cabbage leaves were boiling over and what should she do with them? My grandmother disregarded her. My mother said thoughtfully that it did seem to her rather a lot of rice was being prepared, surely too much for a quiet dinner-party of a few people? My grandmother airily disregarded her too and proceeded to wash and drain the rice. She then proceeded to mix her finely chopped onions with it, and poor Feride, unable to stand the strain any longer, burst into loud tears. My grandmother paused in the mixing, looking with astonishment at the violently weeping Feride and asked what was wrong. Poor Feride gasped between the paroxysms that shook her that the onions had first to be cooked with şam fistiği, nuts in olive oil, *before* being mixed with the rice.

My grandmother paused uncertainly, then demanded from my mother what the cookery-book said. The cookery-book, unfortunately, said the same as Feride.

My grandmother looked down at her messy fingers, the piles of wasted rice mixed with the wasted onions, then rinsed her hands under the tap declaring she was finished cooking. Amidst a great silence she untied her overall, put all her rings back on her fingers again and told Feride that she could make the dolma herself—the way the cookery-book advocated. She declared she would never set foot in the kitchen again, having expected a little gratitude from Feride, not tears. She then went haughtily out to sprinkle eau-de-Cologne on her hands. Afterwards she complained of the smell from the cabbage leaves and was all for having them thrown down the drain and vine-leaves substituted. My mother restrained her and led her to the salon still grumbling. She then began a long tirade, pointing out the shortcomings of Feride and the merits of the absent Hacer.

That evening, despite my grandmother's poor opinion of Feride, a dish of beautiful lahan dolmasi appeared on the table and my grandmother told everyone she had made them herself. When she caught my astonished eye she stared so haughtily at me that it was I who was forced to blush and look away first. Indeed she half convinced me that she was right.

Our guests arrived early and were taken to the salon, where a bright fire crackled merrily in the white china stove and Inci served little dishes of lokum.

Yasemin and Nuri were on their politest behaviour and very demure. In the dining-room they sat with Mehmet and me at a smaller table in a corner whilst our parents ate at the big walnut table in the centre.

During dinner my grandmother talked vivaciously, even being prevailed upon to sip a little raki, which brought the colour to her cheeks.

Just as dessert was being served—slices of yellow water-melon in a silver dish surrounded with ice—there came a strange, odd noise which sounded like drums. Everyone at the big table was suddenly stilled. I, noticing the silence, looked at them and saw the colour ebb from my grandmother's face and my mother's hand unsteadily reach out for a fruit-knife.

My father said:

'They are playing the drums to-night—that must mean an announcement of some sort. Let us hope it is good.'

Our neighbour, Orhan Bey, replied:

'They play the drums during Bayram or Ramazan but to-night is neither. What can it be?'

'They play the drums for war also,' said my mother faintly, and we all looked at her, surprised that she should intervene in a masculine conversation.

'Şevkiye hanim, I hope you are wrong. I sincerely hope you are wrong.'

He spoke jerkily, fussily, unable to entirely hide his own fear.

The faint drums beat on and we finished our dessert almost in silence. The grown-ups toyed with the melon and my grandmother peeled a tangerine, cutting firmly with her knife into the bright skin, making it stand out around the fruit like a flower. She quartered it with deft fingers, then put it on her plate and sat looking at it with far-away eyes as though wondering how it got there. The drums came nearer and I started to tremble, the fear of my elders once again communicated to me.

They left the table, the ladies huddled by the window and my father and Orhan Bey going into the hall and opening the front door. I crept out after my father and stood beside him in the darkness. The drums were nearer now. They sounded their doom, their terrible message, and even to this day I cannot bear the sound of drums.

We could hear Bekci Baba calling something but he was too far away for us to distinguish what it was he said. My father put his arms around my shoulders and I pressed against him,

feeling intolerably cold and miserable. Then the figure of
Bekci Baba turned the corner of our street, a man beside him
beating mournfully on the big drum. They came nearer, the
drum beating ceaselessly. Dan-dan-da-da-dan-dan cried the
drum and Bekci Baba came under the lamp before our door, to
shout his shattering news.

'Men born between 1880 and 1885 must report to the recruiting centre within the next forty-eight hours. Who fails
to do so will be prosecuted.'

And dan-dan-da-da-dan-dan went the drum and my heart
echoed its melancholy.

Orhan Bey shouted:

'What does it mean, Bekci Baba?'

And the reply was: 'War! War! Don't you know your
country is at war?'

Bekci Baba moved off, and the old, old man with the drum
followed him, to spread their news farther.

We went in to the ladies. There they stood by the window,
like three flowers blown in out of the black night, their silk
dresses spreading about them and their faces pale to the
lips.

Madame Müjğan started to speak, then swayed uncertainly
and fainted in my mother's arms. Yasemin and Nuri ran to
her, shouting 'Anne! Anne!' and Inci was despatched for eau-
de-Cologne with which to massage the wrists and forehead of
Madame Müjğan. Whilst my mother was busy with her, Orhan
Bey put his arms about his two children and said:

'I was born in 1885——' and broke off, too full of tears to
say any more.

He pressed his children closer to him, so close that Yasemin
cried out that he was hurting her and then he released them,
looking at them for a moment or two with the eyes of a sleep-
walker—the eyes of a man who no longer saw two frightened
children before him but the long, dark, stinking nights in the
trenches and the gun-flashes to now and then lighten the sky
and finally the long dark night of death.

Presently his wife recovered. He took her on his arm and
with great dignity thanked my mother for her evening and for
what she had tried to do for his wife.

He bade us good night. My father went with them across the
garden, the two children tightly clutching his hands. Mehmet

was taken away to be washed and I stayed in the salon with my
mother and my grandmother.

'Ahmet was born in 1885,' said my grandmother.

She repeated it softly over and over again like a litany.

The next day my father left home early for he was going to
Sariyer to see Uncle Ahmet.

All that long day the house was a dead house. I tried to play
in the garden with Mehmet but I was bored and uneasy, sensing
accurately my elders' alarm. There was no sign of the children
from next door and the first hint of there being anything out of
the ordinary about the day came with the arrival of the cook of
Madame Müjğan. I was on the back porch at that time and
heard her asking Feride if the bakkal (grocer) had been with
the bread. Feride replied that she too was waiting for him,
since she had no fresh bread for luncheon. They talked for a
few more minutes in whispers and although there seemed to be a
great sense of urgency about their talk, I could not distinguish
anything. I was just left with that queer, empty feeling of
there being something wrong but I could not put a name to
what it was. The morning wore away. Inci set the table for
luncheon but still no bread appeared. Feride eventually told
my mother, who treated the matter lightly, saying that no
doubt bakkal had forgotten us this day and gave permission for
Feride to go out to buy bread. We waited over an hour for
her to come back, my mother growing more and more impatient
but when she did come wearily back she had no bread.

'What is wrong?' asked my mother, very surprised.

'There is no bread anywhere, hanim efendi,' replied Feride.
'Since I left here I have been standing in a queue, with the
people killing each other and breaking each other's heads to
get near the baker's door. Some of them were buying twenty
loaves at a time. Every family in the district is there, with all
their children and their servants and all of them trying to get a
loaf each. The baker had sold out before it was my turn.'

So we sat down to our meal, grumbling that we had to eat
the previous day's bread. We did not know that one day we
might be glad to eat bread a week old.

During the afternoon Feride again went to hunt bread but
again returned with empty hands. This time she reported that
the shop was shut and that, although the queues were greater
than ever, nobody knew when the shop would open. Nerves

were uneasy that day and tempers broke easily. My grandmother sat reading the Koran, decorous and pious-looking in
her black dress and her face pale. My mother sat most of the
day in front of one of the windows, watching for my father's
return and her hands strangely empty. What a difference
there was already in them! Looking at my grandmother,
reading the Koran so soberly, it was difficult to find in her the
amusing old lady who only yesterday had made us all laugh at
her culinary efforts. My mother was very white, a fact em-
phasised by the dark stuff of her dress, and her busy hands were
twining and untwining all the time in her idle lap. Once she
asked Inci to fetch her a glass of wine and the request was so
unusual that, momentarily, Inci forgot all her good training to
stare at her in wide-eyed surprise.

My father returned in the middle of the afternoon, having
been unsuccessful in finding my uncle. My aunt had told him
he had left that morning, early, for the Recruiting Centre and
she did not know where he was now. She was, my father
observed, very distressed.

He had called at the Sariyer Recruiting Centre on his way
back to the boat-station but all had been confusion and uproar
there. Harassed officials roared instructions and civilians were
herded like cattle, hungry, hopeless and apathetic. No one
had been able to give news of my uncle. In fact no one, it
appeared, had had time to listen to my father's questions and at
one time he had been in danger of being herded with the other
conscripts. My mother mentioned the incident of the bread
and he laughed tiredly. The streets, he said, were full of panic-
stricken people, all looking for something to buy and store.
News of Turkey's entry into the war had swept fear into
Istanbul and rioting was taking place in some quarters.

He went out himself to seek bread and returned after many
hours with one small, hot loaf in his hand. He looked ineffably
weary and dispirited and there was a long scratch down one
side of his face, inflicted by a panic-maddened woman who had
tried to snatch his bread.

Dinner was a sober affair, with us children being urged to
hurry and our elders silently making a pretence of eating.
Gone were the leisured, laughter-filled nights of good eating
and good conversation, with my grandmother tossing off
sparkling, malicious epigrams and my silent, shy mother only

offering her grace and beauty as a contribution to the dinner-table.

The next morning Uncle Ahmet came to say good-bye to us. Mehmet and I greeted him quietly, no noise, no fuss this time, for our parents' faces set the pattern for our behaviour. He had brought boxes of bon-bons for us and we were sent into the dining-room, whilst they discussed the serious business of war in the salon.

Some things in life stand out sharply in the memory, making a picture so vivid, so clear-cut, that the mind's eye retains them indelibly forever. Such a precise memory I have, of that November day my uncle visited us for the last time. Sharp and cold was the morning, with sunlight playing behind the scurrying clouds. The house was peaceful and still as if great things were not happening all around it. The odd-job man was sweeping the terrace of the last fallen leaves. Feride was creating a good, appetising smell from the kitchen and Inci was pegging out the washing in the little side yard. The washerwoman sang lustily in the laundry, uncaring of the draughts which swooped moaningly from all about her. What cared she for war? And what cared Feride or the young Inci for war? Everyone that morning had something to do. I stood with my nose pressed against the window-pane and looked out to the windy, rustling garden that held its own wild, winter beauty and Mehmet played busily on the floor.

My father came into the room to decant some wine and, perhaps because I looked dejected or perhaps because Inci was not there to guard us, he told Mehmet and me to go to the salon and play there.

In the salon my uncle was drinking Turkish coffee, looking unhappy. Nobody took any notice of us so I sat down in one of the chairs and my mother looked at me, perhaps wondering why I was there. My uncle was talking about my aunt, saying that her health seemed to be getting worse. There was a peevish, worried note in his voice. Then he mentioned the farm, saying that most of the men had registered with him and who would look after things in future he did not know.

My grandmother sat very silent. She sat looking at Uncle Ahmet as if her eyes could never see enough of him, her eldest born. She was an unemotional woman but that day the tears were seldom far from her, only her fierce, high pride beating them back. I suppose she was realising for the first time in her life what war might do to families. For the first time, I think, she saw herself as a defenceless, ignorant woman who knew nothing of events outside her own small world, the world which held only sociability, women's gossip and formality. And the last two men of her family were going from her. I am quite sure she did not pause to consider my mother's or my aunt's feelings. Naturally cold and a bit of a despot she only ever saw things in relation to herself. She was losing her sons, might lose them forever, but my mother and my aunt were only losing their husbands.

And although my grandmother had a high opinion of husbands she had a higher opinion of sons. It is trite to say that little escapes the eye of a child, but nevertheless it is a fact and I knew my grandmother better then, if more inchoately, than she would ever know herself. She had no time for self-analysis and the Freudian theory had not yet burst over Istanbul. My mother too I knew and the latent streak of hardness there was in her, so that in after years, when hardness had become her chief characteristic, I was not taken by surprise, having all along recognised its deep-down existence. I could not write a true picture of them today, were I not looking back with the eyes of a child to pictures I had thought dead. But just as today these pictures bring back so vividly places, scenes and conversations that are gone, so too do they recall in part the *sensations* I felt as a child.

That November day, for instance, I *knew* as if she were screaming her thoughts aloud what was going through my grandmother's head. When she asked my uncle to stay for luncheon I knew she was prolonging the fatal moment of good-bye and when he refused she seemed to shrink into herself, looking small and lonely in her tall chair. He said he had many things to attend to in Sariyer and was anxious about my aunt and all the time he carefully avoided her eyes, perhaps feeling if he looked at her too closely he too would break down.

Presently he stood up to go and I can still see his tall figure dark against the windows.

'I shall be leaving tomorrow,' he said and when my grand-mother enquired for where he shrugged his massive shoulders and replied that he did not know.

He leaned over his mother, kissing her hands, and she

murmured a prayer over his bent, dark head and one hand escaped from his kiss to tenderly stroke his cheek. Uncle Ahmet swung Mehmet on his shoulders, took my hand in his and went out to the hall. My father said he would accompany him to Galata Bridge and my uncle beat his foot impatiently whilst Inci helped my father into his overcoat. Then they were ready and we were kissed. My uncle put his hand over my hair and I saw his mouth suddenly quiver and my inadequate heart longed to comfort him. Down the short path they went to the street and at the corner they turned to wave to us, then they were hidden from our view and we went back into the house again, Mehmet and I—two small boys who knew of no way to relieve the partings.

That evening Orhan Bey came to bid us farewell. He too was off the next morning to a place he did not know. We drank his health and wished him well, Mehmet and I holding our glasses high with the others. And down the street the drums beat for someone else. For in those days going away to the war, any war, was a brave and noble thing to do and as the young men left a district so the band would play outside each of their houses, the Turkish flag being handed to the newest recruit. And all the youth with their wild, wild hearts leaped and danced and shouted, the better to drown the noise of the women's weeping. When they were leaving their homes the band played a song of unbelievable sadness and everyone started to sing:

'Ey gaziler yol göründü
Yine garib serime
Dağlar, taşlar dayanamaz
Benim ahu zarima . . .'

('Oh wounded ones I am coming to take your place and my heart is crying because I am leaving my beloved ones. The mountains and the stones cry with me. . . .')

Orhan Bey bade us farewell and left for his own home and in the street the band still played.

Again the next day my father hunted for bread and once again tried to see my uncle. He came home very late and my grandmother immediately asked if he had seen him.

'Yes,' replied my father, 'I caught a glimpse of him as they marched him away.'

'And did he look well in his uniform?' demanded my grand-mother eagerly.

My father said gently:

'He had no uniform. All the men wore their own clothes and carried bags on their shoulders. They had no marching boots and armed soldiers kept between them and the crowd. And all their wives and mothers and sweethearts were there. I followed with the crowd and they were put in a building in Sirkeci. We all waited, hoping for a sight of them but nothing happened and in the end the soldiers guarding the building sent us away.'

My father ceased talking and his eyes looked bitter. He had seen Uncle Ahmet ordered and pushed and prodded by the butts of the guns of the peasant soldiers. He had seen a soldier kick one of the men but he did not tell these things before my grandmother.

The next day my mother prepared a bag for my father, made like the bags the other men had been carrying across their unaccustomed shoulders. Nobody mentioned anything about his going but we all knew the day would come. So my mother sewed a bag for him, a coarse white linen bag which she sewed with exquisite stitchery. And I think she sewed her heart into that bag too for after my father had gone we who were left saw nothing of her heart.

My father's business had been sold and now he spent the days at home, awaiting his turn with horror and impatience at their delay. It seemed as if the Government would never call him and now that he knew he would have to go he wanted to be away, to be done with the waiting that tore the heart and whitened the cheeks.

But the day came at last. The same drum beat out its poignant message, the same Bekci Baba stood under the same lamp and delivered his ultimatum:

'Men born between 1886 and 1892 must report to the Recruiting Centre during the next forty-eight hours. Who fails to do so will be prosecuted. . . .'

And dan-dan-da-da-dan-dan mocked the drum.

My father had been called at last and we thought that nothing worse than this could ever happen to us.

He went the next day to the Recruiting Centre and all the remaining young men of the district seemed to go with him.

When he returned I was in bed but I was not sleeping, even though I could not hear what they talked about. It was a grey day when he left us, a grey, cold day in early December, and because so many others were leaving with him, the band was going to play them all out together, from the lives they had always known to the bleakness of the battle-field. Feride packed the coarse linen bag with cakes and pies and other delicacies she had prepared for him. My father stood in the middle of the salon, already gone from us in spirit and he looked about him for the last time. His face was secretive and closed, an alien, soldier's face that had no right in this elegant, smiling room. My mother stood close beside him and she too had that alien, shut-away look. But my poor, huddled grandmother, who could not go to where these two had gone, sat in the windows and listened for the drums that would take away her youngest son. Inci brought in Turkish coffee, Feride following with the packed linen bag and Mehmet ran to pull at her skirts, not understanding what all this fuss was about or that his father was going away. I went to my father and put my arms around him and he lifted me up in his arms.

'You will be father from now on,' he said and I pressed my head against his face and felt a tear drop on my cheek. Whose tear was it, mine or his? Perhaps it fell from both of us for tears tormented both of us. Feride and Inci burst into loud wailing, their soft hearts inexpressibly touched but my mother stared dry-eyed. She had, I think, shed all the tears she would ever shed in some more private place than this. And now her frozen heart was able to look on this farewell scene with almost-tranquillity.

My grandmother prayed without stopping and then she began to mutter:

'My eldest son and my youngest son. My eldest son and my youngest son. They have taken you both.'

The distant drums began and my father put me down, drinking his coffee quickly. He said:

'Şevkiye! Don't look like that! Smile for me. I shall come back again——'

And my mother's frozen face relaxed to give him her old, dazzling smile and my father said to her:

'You would make a better soldier than I.'

They stood there facing each other, smiling their brilliant

smiles, not touching each other yet indissolubly merged into each other. The band came nearer and now we clearly heard the drums and the zurna and the shouting of the following children.

My mother's eyes flew away from my father's and the lovely miracle was broken. She picked up his heavy bag and handed it to him and they kissed like strangers, those two who had no need of kissing. My grandmother held out her hand for his gesture and Feride and Inci then came forward to pay their tribute to him. They were crying bitterly and he patted their heads, as if they were children again, like Mehmet and me. He swung his bag over his shoulder and went to the front door and the crowd that waited outside. The band played softly and mournfully and my father kissed us children, then said his good-bye with lips that were wooden and stiff.

An old man came forward and handed him the Turkish flag and the people all shouted 'Padişahim çok yaşa' and my father stepped into his place, amongst the other recruits. The waving and the cheering went wildly on but there was no need to drown the weeping from our house, for the women did not weep. They stood there gently smiling and the band played for my father:

> 'Ey gaziler yol göründü
> Yine garib serime
> Dağlar, taşlar dayanamaz
> Benim ahu zarima . . .'

Then they turned the corner, out of our sight, only the sound of the cheering and the singing voices and the noise of the band, coming ever fainter back to us.

CHAPTER VII

WEEK-END LEAVE AND THE NEW BRIDE

We did not know where they were taking my father, and although we asked Bekci Baba, he could only say that the Recruiting Centre might have some information.

The next day Feride was sent to enquire and came back to tell us that my father's age-group were at the Hasan Paşa Mosque, waiting to be sent away. My mother was excited and bade my grandmother get ready to accompany us to the Mosque, as perhaps we would be able to catch a glimpse of my father before he left. We made our way through the crowded streets, my mother and my grandmother heavily veiled, the latter volubly protesting at having to walk, and lamenting loudly for the vanished Murat and the phaeton.

Hasan Paşa Mosque was built in a garden, high above the street. When we got there there were many other women and children, also come to try and see their menfolk before they left Istanbul. Crowded in the garden were the soldiers, looking down at us and searching for their loved ones. One of the soldiers shouted down to us, calling my grandmother by name and telling us that my father was somewhere in the garden. We looked at the soldier wonderingly, for who was this rough-looking person who dared to call my grandmother by her name? Suddenly my mother recognised him, telling us that it was the man who lived opposite us. I could hardly believe her. That soldier in his drab, grey uniform, with his hair cut close against his head, could surely not be the elegant gentleman from across the way—who had so proudly carried his wife on his arm each evening, when taking her for a stroll? It was impossible: where was the similarity between this soldier and the frock-coated, fezzed man from across the street?

Tension increased as I saw my father walking to the edge of the garden. There was quite fifteen feet between us and the garden stood so high from the ground that it was not possible to see each other clearly.

My grandmother called to him, asking if there was anything he wanted but he shook his head and said, sternly:

'Take the children home and do not come here any more.'

So we waved our handkerchiefs to him and left. There was nothing else to do. We could not wait there all night and we could not bring my father home again. A few days after this we learned he had been moved to Selimiye, on the Anatolian side, for training, and one day my mother took me there with her, hoping to see my father. But it was impossible and we returned wearily home. When we arrived home, we found that Madame Müjgan and her children were with my grandmother and my mother begged them to stay for dinner, for I think she felt their presence would help us forget our father's absence. It seemed odd to have guests without my father being there, and to see my mother sitting in his place, at the head of the table. The talk was naturally about the war and their absent men-folk. My grandmother inclined still to grumble over changed conditions. She was horrified by the war-lust manifest in the bloodthirsty youth of the district, the only youth she ever saw and those only from her window, for she could not be persuaded to go out on foot. And she was piously indignant that the Sultan and his Government should be so inconsiderate as to leave all the women without their men to protect them.

But we others were growing accustomed to the idea of war, and even to the absence of my father. My mother seemed a different person without him, more competent now that she had not his shoulder to lean on, more decisive and less inclined to sit doing pretty, useless embroidery. She made an effort to instil some scholarship into me, since there was no school to which I could be sent, but it was not a success. She had not the teacher's patience and I no inclination to learn from her. She was very affectionate with us, but curiously detached, and it was not possible for a child to want to run to her or sob against her shoulder his small fears. We children appeared to be the merest incidents in her life and my father a sort of god.

One day Aunt Ayşe came to visit us, bringing a tall, gaunt maid with her as chaperone. She looked very thin and was distressed at having to travel without my uncle, saying that the noise and confusion in the streets frightened her. She asked for news of my father and my mother told her where he was and she replied that Uncle Ahmet was outside Turkey altogether.

Then sat twisting her hands, as though that knowledge was a fearful knowledge to hold and to be outside his country the most terrible thing that could happen to Uncle Ahmet. During dinner that night she ate little, although Feride had been at pains to prepare all her favourite dishes. She sipped a little red wine and coughed continuously, apologising blushingly, saying that she had had this cough for many months now and that it would not go or respond to the various herbal treatments her cook had recommended.

During dinner Feride appeared with a letter for my mother. It had been brought by the batman of a certain captain, whom we knew very well. He said that my father was well but unable to write, for he was undergoing a very rigorous officers' training which for some reason or another made it impossible for him to communicate with my mother himself. The Captain went on to say that at the end of the initial training period, probably by the coming week-end, my father would be given a few days leave.

Feride stood by whilst my mother read this out to us and she was as excited as the rest of us and there and then began to plan what my father would be given to eat. My aunt smiled wistfully. But my grandmother triumphantly held out her glass for more wine and said:

'You see! They will make him an officer. Did I not tell you that always?'

Then we all drank my father's health and felt proud and happy. Inci was despatched to tell Madame Müjğan of the good news and to request that she should come and drink coffee with us. Mehmet and I were taken to bed but the women sat long in the salon, their happy voices floating up the stairs and my mother's laughter now and then ringing out purely—just as in the days when my father had always been with us.

Aunt Ayşe left for Sariyer and we had two more days to prepare for my father's arrival. In those days the Muslim week-end was Thursday and Friday and no cleaning could be done during that time. Thursday morning dawned clear and cold and Inci had no time to waste with Mehmet and me. Once we were dressed we were severely cautioned not to get ourselves dirtied, but a twinkle lurked behind the severe voice for to-day was a happy day, not to be spoiled by tears. That day the house was enchanted. Clean curtains were hung in the main rooms, a great orgy of polishing went on and silk cloths and lace cloths were put everywhere—just as at Bayram. But this was better than Bayram for our father was coming home.

Many neighbours called and my mother drank endless cups of Turkish coffee with them. My grandmother held a sort of court among them, all five fingers of one hand decorated with exquisite rings and jewels blazing about her neck. She was her old, arrogant, despotic self again and commanded royally.

Feride and Inci worked like slaves. Flowers were found and arranged, glasses polished until they shone with a thousand eyes and silver made a note of glory against the mellow walnut of the great buffet. Morning slipped by into afternoon and still my father did not come. Mehmet and I waited for hours in front of the door, until finally the raw air drove us shivering indoors. Everywhere in the house was a sense of expectancy. The hall was all a-glitter with the sheen from the freshly polished floor and with the reflection of the giant silver trays in the patina of the table—an English table my great-grandfather had once brought back from his travels. A copper mangal—a sort of brazier—gave off heat to thaw a cold and weary voyager and the chrysanthemums from Sariyer glowed brightly in a corner. The house waited for its master and nothing more remained to be done. But still the afternoon flew until it was evening and time for Inci to light the six tall lamps in the salon and the smaller ones in the hall.

Mehmet and I were disconsolate. Would our father not come after all? We opened the front door, for a last peep into the evening gloom, letting in such a gust of cold air that Inci sharply ordered us to close the door immediately. But I had seen a soldier turning the corner and I thought it was the Captain's batman come with another message and I shouted to my mother to come. The soldier called to me and then I knew it was not the Captain's batman after all, but my father. I ran to him, throwing myself with violence into his outstretched arms and Mehmet came flying after me. We went into the house together and there was my mother in the hall, all a-tremble with happiness and flushed rosy red, wearing a wine velvet dress and rubies to glorify her neck.

Such laughter and tears there were suddenly, such excited question and answer, for the master of the house was home again, and the old house creaked in its joints and sat back content to shelter such radiance.

My father looked drab in his uniform and said he only longed for a bath and a change of linen, for the coarse Army under-linen chafed his skin.

He was gay and talkative, glad to be home again, hiding his unhappiness at being in the Army. He said he would be training for several more months, adding that that was all to the good since it meant he would remain at Selimiye and might occasionally be permitted to come home. He mentioned the Commanding Officer, a man who had been a great friend of my grandfather's but he only touched lightly on him, saying that one could not expect favours in the Army. German officers were attached to the Unit, Prussian upstarts he called them, adding that there was no love lost between the Turkish officers and the strutting Germans.

My mother shone quietly for the two days he was at home but on the last evening I wandered into the salon on a conversation that was to puzzle me for a long time.

'. . . anything may happen,' my father was saying earnestly, adding, 'but if I am not here at that time, I would like the baby to be called Muazzez—or Arif, if it is another boy.'

Here I saw the ever-alert Inci look across to them—she was pouring coffee at a side table—and I was intensely curious, wondering what baby they were talking about. I had not the courage to ask questions and, in any case, the subject was abruptly dropped since my father noticed the proximity of Inci and my own staring face.

When my father left to return to his unit everyone was cheerful, for this time we knew that he was only going as far as Selimiye and might soon be again with us.

'Au revoir,' my mother called gaily to his handwave and Mehmet and I remained to watch him out of sight.

Then we went back to Inci and daily routine and we none of us knew that this was the real good-bye.

Some weeks later a letter was brought from my father. My mother kept that letter all through her life and it is in my possession to-day—almost the only souvenir left from those times:

'. . . so you see we shall be leaving Selimiye almost immediately. Our training is not finished and what they intend

doing with us nobody knows, so for the time being we march
with the rest. We shall leave by train so come to the railway
track tomorrow morning. I cannot give you a time but I
would like one more glimpse of you before I go. Let the
children come too. There is nothing more that can be said
here, but I pray God all goes well with you. I leave you and
my unborn child in the hands of God and kiss from your
eyes. . . .

My mother cried over this letter but my grandmother was
offended because my father had not mentioned her and sulked
a little for the ingratitude of all sons when they take a wife.
Mehmet and I were excited to be going to the rail-tracks.
They ran across the bottom of the big waste field behind our
house and although they could not be seen from the house,
very often one heard the rumble of the infrequent trains. It
seemed very romantic to us that our father should travel in such
a fearsome monster as a train and we bitterly envied him.
Inci said to me that day:

'Perhaps soon you will have a baby brother or sister; shall
you like that?'

'No!' I replied, appalled by the thought of a new baby in
the house for perhaps some subconscious memory lingered
from Mehmet's babyhood, when I had been continually hushed
into silence.

'But perhaps it will be a lovely baby sister,' persisted Inci
until she finally aroused my curiosity.

'Who will bring it?' I wanted to know.

'One of the pigeons in the garden, one of *your* pigeons, will
bring it from your father.'

'This morning?' I asked, 'or tomorrow when we go to the
tracks to see my father?'

'No, silly!' said Inci.

I lost interest immediately, uninterested in the arrival of
such a remote baby.

'Did my pigeons tell you?' I asked finally, not quite able to
entirely dismiss the subject, and when Inci replied that they had
I sat and thought about her words, then dragged Mehmet off
to the garden to look for the knowledgeable pigeons. They
strutted at the bottom of the garden and thought we had
brought bread for them. And to all my questions they only

answered 'Coo-coo', in their soft, throaty voices. Mehmet maddened me by rushing at them, his arms flapping, and they took fright and circled irritatingly above my head.

'Tell me!' I shouted at them, and they replied, 'Coo-coo', 'coo-coo', curving and diving and circling and I sadly decided that Inci must have some very special knowledge of pigeon-language.

Next morning we were wrapped in heavy overcoats and scarves and taken with my mother and my grandmother to the bottom of the waste field, where we could see all the passing trains. It was bitterly cold and many trains passed that day, all of them overflowing with soldiers who shouted and sang and waved to us but my father was not amongst them. Trainload after trainload passed us and still he did not come and after two hours we children were almost crying with the cold, stamping our feet in an effort to keep warm.

'Perhaps he had already gone,' said my mother, her voice despairing. 'Perhaps he passed this way when we were still sleeping.'

On came the thundering trains bound for Edirne and God knew what hell afterwards. On the other line we saw a Red Crescent train come in and I felt my mother shiver beside me, as she said to my grandmother:

'An ambulance train, mother! I wonder if they are sick or wounded soldiers?'

And my grandmother replied:

'Stop tormenting yourself like this.'

The Red Crescent train slipped past with its weary travellers and then another train, coming in the opposite direction, caught our senses. With such suddenness that we were almost startled, we saw my father's face at a window and his white handkerchief waving to attract our wavering attention.

'Look!' Mehmet shouted. 'It's Baba!'

My mother waved to him and threw reckless, last-minute kisses, half laughing, half crying in her excitement. As the train roared past, my father leaned far out of the window and shouted:

' Good-bye! God bless all of you!'

And my mother cried back to him, 'Not good-bye, Hüsnü!'

But the train had passed on so perhaps he never heard what it was she said to him, those last, poignant words which she did not know were to be her last words to him.

One little moment more we saw his outstretched hand and the waving, waving handkerchief, then that too was gone and he was gone and the cold morning seemed suddenly colder. We returned home to a warm fire but the chill that was in our blood took a long, long time to thaw.

But life had still to march on and the slow, agonising days of waiting for news to be lived through. Then other problems began to present themselves, creeping insidiously into the normal pattern of life and disrupting it. Firstly arose the problem of food. For weeks past Feride had been using our reserve stocks and my mother became alarmed by the rapidity with which they ran down. Six of us to be fed several times in a day made great inroads on flour and sugar and rice. Feride spent more time hunting open shops than she did in the kitchen. Our bread consumption was cut to the minimum. Sweets with luncheon became things to be remembered and fresh milk was scarce and costly. When it could be bought, it had to be boiled for several minutes before it was safe to drink and was almost half water. The odd-job man was dismissed, since formerly he had always had all his meals in the house. The washerwoman was, for the moment, retained since she only ever came once a week and she was deemed a necessity.

My grandmother professed to take no interest in these domestic problems but many times I heard her grumbling voice declaring that in her time six servants had been necessary to run her house and that now my mother expected to get the same results with two and a washerwoman. My mother ignored her. She had ceased to be a lady of leisure and was frequently to be found in the kitchen these days during Feride's shopping expeditions. Prices had suddenly become fantastic, and when food could be bought, treble its normal price was asked. But in those days our trouble was not one of money. When my father had sold his business he had brought all the money home to us, in notes and in gold, and it was decided to keep this large amount in the house, since banking systems were deemed to be too intricate for my mother to understand. So the undefended money lay in the house, many thousands of liras dangerously reposing in a flat wooden box in my mother's bedroom. And none realised the danger of that arrangement.

My grandmother had no money of her own. My grandfather, according to old Turkish custom, left everything with my father, merely stipulating that my grandmother should be cared for all her life. Since this was the usual manner of leaving possessions or property, my grandmother felt no resentment. She had many fine pieces of jewellery and the lack of ready money was no drawback to her. She had never been allowed to handle money in her life, rarely went out anywhere and had no knowledge of the value of anything. She got impatient if my mother complained of the dearness of things and could not be made to understand why no sweets were nowadays served with luncheon. She had a great appetite for the heavy, syrupy Turkish sweets, made with butter and eggs, and accused my mother of trying to starve her, now that there were no menfolk in the house to defend her. She would imperiously demand fruits or bon-bons and sulk when she was told she could not have them. And she complained that her Turkish coffee was not sweet enough and took to secreting little packets of sugar about her person, tipping a little surreptitiously into her cup when my mother was not looking.

As the winter grew more severe she became more and more cantankerous and would sit huddled over the fire in the salon, wrapped in numerous shawls. She was morose and irritable, her appetite insatiable and she found fault with everything. One morning she threw us all into a flurry by announcing over breakfast that she was going to Sariyer, where she insisted she would get more to eat than she was getting with us. She demanded that Feride should accompany her, remaining with her during her stay with Aunt Ayşe. My mother indignantly opposed the idea, asking what she was expected to do without her treasured Feride. My grandmother grunted, implying tacitly that she neither knew nor cared. She wanted Feride and that was all there was to it. However, in the end it was all arranged to everyone's satisfaction. Feride would accompany my grandmother but would return to us that same evening. We bolted our meagre breakfast and Feride tore herself in little pieces, trying to do too many things at once. But at last we got them off, my grandmother having her last little grumble because she had to travel to Galata Bridge in a hired cab.

Mehmet and I followed my mother into the kitchen, where she was going to take Feride's place for the day. She wore an apron over her pretty dress and we were set to work to help her. I was put to peeling potatoes, a job I loathed only a little less than I loathed the taste of potatoes. Mehmet was given the easiest things to do and happily staggered about, taking the dried cutlery into the canteen in the dining-room, hanging cups and managing to break a few.

'Times are changing,' said my mother to me conversationally, briskly shaking out the freshly washed kitchen-cloths. 'Perhaps there will be many things you will both have to learn to do until this war is over. When your father comes back again everything will be all right but until that time we must all learn to look after ourselves. Your grandmother is old and she does not understand things, therefore we must have patience with her.'

She sounded hard and a bit impatient and I wondered why she spoke of my grandmother like this. She felt me watching her and said:

'She is a very good woman but she will not accept the fact that there are many things we cannot get nowadays. All those little luxuries your grandfather used to bring her——'

And she broke off, pondering on the changed conditions. Her hands looked red and ugly and I was horrified to see that they looked like Feride's or Inci's. All their smooth, cool white-ness seemed to have disappeared. She caught my look and smiled at me, then glanced back to her rough hands and seemed proud of them. I thought she was very brave. She was only twenty-two at that time, well born and accustomed to the sheltered life that only the well-born women of old Turkey really knew. Yet she had taken on her shoulders the responsi-bility of us children and my grandmother and was so sensitive to the welfare of her servants that she shared their work willingly. She could not sit idle whilst two servants did the work of four and, despite the fact that she was a shocking cook in those days, was always ready to help in the kitchen, humbly learning from the experienced Feride.

During my grandmother's sojourn at Sariyer we received a letter from my father. He was somewhere near Edirne, was well but worried because no letters were being received from us or from Uncle Ahmet, to whom he had repeatedly written. He wrote of his longing to be with us and of the appalling misery of the Turkish soldier. It was the first news we had had for many weeks and it was like a tonic for my mother and we heard her lilting, singing voice again about the house.

My grandmother brought back news that Uncle Ahmet was at Şam, in Syria, and that my aunt was worse than we had suspected. Sariyer, she said, was in a shocking condition, all the young men having gone to the war and only the old ones left to look after the estate, with no supervision to guide them. She brought back eggs and chickens and fresh butter, eagerly saying that Feride could now make for us some nice, heavy, sticky sweets. My mother was going to indignantly veto any such idea but perhaps the old lady looked pathetic, for she suddenly relented and let my grandmother have her way. The visit to Sariyer had done a lot of good for my grandmother. I think the state of things there had depressed her unutterably for now she took to doing small things about the house and stopped complaining, appearing genuinely glad to be back in the sane, healthy atmosphere of our house.

One day the wife of the local Imam paid us a surprise visit. She was a vast caricature of a woman with treble chins and a bosom that shot straight out like a board. She sat very upright in the salon, obviously not wanting the presence of Mehmet and me. My mother apologised for us, explaining that Inci had so much else to do that she could not be expected to look after us exclusively. The Imam's wife nodded gravely and said she quite understood, but her hard eyes raked us with positive dislike and I felt quite sure she did not understand at all. She settled herself comfortably near my grandmother, beginning to talk in a penetrating, sibilant whisper. She was telling her that a certain well-known gentleman of our slight acquaintance, a rich, eccentric old gentleman, was looking for a wife! She put a world of meaning into that one word.

'Why?' demanded my grandmother blankly and with such astonishment in her voice that the Imam's wife huffily sniffed that she did not know but that it was no unusual thing for a gentleman to want a wife. Energetically my grandmother replied that it was highly unusual for the gentleman in question. The Imam's wife made no comment and then my mother came in with coffee and for a while the subject was not discussed. But as though drawn by a magnet the visitor could not keep away from the matter for long. This time she came straight to the point and propounded the amazing suggestion that my grandmother should marry him herself. We were all flabbergasted. And taking our astonished silence for approval

she continued by saying that the old man had himself
expressed a great preference for my grandmother! He only
waited for her to give her decision before formally declaring
his intentions when, we gathered, he would eagerly like
a young man leap into the arena and carry her off for
himself.

There was an astounded, disbelieving silence when the
Imam's wife had finished speaking. I sat on the floor gaping
foolishly until my mother—an exasperated, angry note in her
voice—told me to go out of the room immediately and to take
Mehmet with me. I rushed in search of Inci to tell her what I
had overheard. Her reaction disappointed me for she sagely
nodded her crinkly head and said that she knew all about it.
I could not believe her but she assured me that every servant
in the neighbourhood knew for they had been informed many
weeks ago by the old man's cook—who was too astute to let
much pass her ear.

I could not imagine anyone wanting to marry my grandmother for she seemed incredibly, unromantically old to me
though Inci pointed out that she was still several years short of
fifty and a recognised hostess in the district. What this had to
do with her marriageable qualities I did not know but Inci
assured me they were both very important.

I heard no more about the matter for several days for my
mother would not discuss anything of such a delicate nature
before us. Neighbours took to more frequent visiting, to my
usually hospitable mother's annoyance for she had to provide
coffee for them and sugar was short. Madame Müjgan breathlessly arrived to give her advice. She pointed out what an
excellent match this would be since the old man was fabulously
wealthy, owning many coal depots and wharves and heaven
knew what else. And—best of all in their opinion—he had no
tiresome relatives to interfere saving a nephew who could be
trusted to behave. My grandmother noticeably weakened and
my mother grew more and more tight-lipped, seeing the whole
situation as a farce.

'Have you lost your senses?' she demanded one day in
exasperation. 'What do you suppose Ahmet and Hüsnü will
say to such a marriage?'

My grandmother replied that Ahmet and Hüsnü had their
families around them and that she had nobody to care about

her and that she did not wish to grow old and lonely and a burden to all about her in this house.

My mother turned her face from such reasoning and a coldness blew shatteringly between the two of them. Mehmet and I were insatiably curious for knowledge, anxious to know the outcome of such an odd, unorthodox courtship, but little enlightenment came our way. Then one day my grandmother defiantly announced that her mind was made up and that she was going to marry her rich old man. Mehmet and I wriggled with excitement but my mother received the news coldly, merely saying that she would immediately set about listing my grandmother's furniture and belongings, as she supposed she would be taking them to her new home. Never was a marriage arranged with such lack of warmth, such formality. New clothes were prepared for everyone and Feride drew again on our precious food stocks, for a reception was to be held in our house.

On the marriage morning, Madame Müjğan, the Imam—who was going to perform the ceremony—and his capacious wife and several neighbours gathered in the salon to await the arrival of the bridegroom.

My grandmother looked pale and composed and utterly magnificent in grey watered silk, a material all the rage at that time in Istanbul. The old man arrived in his carriage, his nephew assisting him into the house for he was very gouty. The Imam read from the Koran and after a few minutes my grandmother became a bride again for the second time in her life. Congratulations, false and unreal as a winter's sun, broke out, liqueurs and bon-bons were distributed before the more serious eating really began. My mother drank to the couple's health but looked forbidding and was nothing more than politely formal to my grandmother.

Later in the day the bridal pair were handed in to their elegant carriage, and my grandmother, looking suddenly lonely, drove away to her new home.

In the evening three porters from the old man's house called for my grandmother's furniture. For the next hour or so they were busy removing it and things kept shifting in the salon and in the dining-room until I had a fearful thought that nothing would be left for us.

Last of all they stripped my grandmother's room and that,

for me, really was the end of her, for when the room was empty
I peeped inside and saw that nothing of her was left there. The
patterned curtains swung in the little breeze I made with the
open door, and so little impression had my grandmother ever
made on this house that it seemed to me as if she had never lived
here at all. The empty room echoed gently when I said
'Grandmother' and I shivered and ran to find Inci, who was
always at hand when a small boy needed comfort.

CHAPTER VIII

MUAZZEZ MAKES HER DÉBUT

AFTER MY GRANDMOTHER'S marriage the house seemed larger and, it must be admitted, more peaceful. The remaining furniture was re-arranged and I moved into her empty bedroom.

Occasionally during the afternoons my grandmother would visit us, for she still lived quite near Bayazit, but she never mentioned her husband and my mother never enquired after him. By tacit agreement, his name was taboo. Later on in the year, in the fine Spring weather, Mehmet and I were given permission to visit her. But this we did not like doing, preferring to see her in our own house, for her husband had no affection for small boys and, in particular, he disliked Mehmet and me. Another time my mother paid an afternoon call with us but the old man stayed in his own little sitting-room the whole time we were there and made it so abundantly clear that we were unwelcome, that my mother decided never to set foot in his house again. We were also forbidden to visit there but, nevertheless, when the days were fine and we were supposed to be playing safely in the garden we did sometimes manage to escape.

My grandmother's new home was very beautiful, with exquisite old tapestries and Chinese vases, which we were told were very valuable. He was a bit of a connoisseur in his way and loved beauty. The gardens were expansive and well kept but my grandmother had a temporary look in that house, as though she had rested there but for a moment. The servants were all old retainers who had been there for years and knew their job so well that she had no conceivable right to interfere with them. This restraint, this lack of freedom in her kitchen, made her feel lonely for Feride and Inci and the other long-departed servants she had trained from childhood. As I have remarked before, the old man did not like Mehmet or me. He was very jealous if my grandmother gave up any time to us, resenting us in some queer, illogical way, and telling her over and over again that she must give up her visits to our house. He said our family were dead for her, that she had married him and that he required some attention from her. All of this I learned many years later but when I was a child I only saw him as a cantankerous, horrid old man—totally unlike my own beloved grandfather. One other thing I learned later in life. He had expected from his marriage that she should share his bed with him and, upon her adamant, astonished refusal, informed her that he could, if he wished, insist on this right. She, apparently, sharply and coldly reminded him that as he was well over eighty years old, he should be contemplating his death and not setting himself up as an amoureux. This plain speaking had considerably affronted him and huffily he had warned her that if she were to continue in this attitude she need not expect any benefits from him. Since my grandmother *was* hoping for benefits from him, she thought it better thereafter to hold her peace, though still continuing in her firm refusal to become part of his bed. Later, a bitter quarrel took place between them and he refused her permission to visit us. And a husband's will in those days was not to be lightly disregarded.

My mother did not know of this quarrel and Mehmet and I were sent to find out what was wrong. We met the old man in the street, almost at his own door so to speak. He was carrying a large stick and asked me where I was going. Tremblingly I replied that I was going to see my grandmother and he lifted his heavy stick to bring it down on our shoulders. I quickly dodged out of his way, dragging a surprised Mehmet after me and the stick dropped shatteringly to the ground from his fingers. Nimbly I picked it up and ran away with it in the direction of our own home to breathlessly pour out the story to my mother. She grew white as she listened. She banished the offensive stick to the kitchen and later on a servant of the old man called for it, bringing with him an insulting message that we were to be kept out of his master's way. Never have I seen my mother in such a passion. She put on her veil, asked Feride to accompany her and leaving us in Inci's care, went off to my grandmother's house.

When she told me the story in after years—with a good deal of laughter for things so far behind her—it appears that she had marched boldly to the old man's room, ignoring alike the alarmed faces of my grandmother and the servants. She thrust open the door of his private sitting-room, leaving the terrified Feride outside to wait for her, and had told him what she thought of him—and a good deal else beside, I gathered. He had been as astonished as the rest of his flurried household and had listened, unwillingly, to most of what she had to say before reviving sufficiently to ask her to leave his home.

Naturally this dispute did not make relations any less strained between the two families—if anything it widened the breach. Once my grandmother secretly managed to visit us but she was in such fear of being discovered that my mother asked her not to come again.

I thought she was hard with her, not listening to her complaints, not giving a word of comfort and I felt near to tears as I saw my grandmother hurrying furtively away from our house—a little lonely old woman she seemed to be without a word of comfort in the world.

In Turkey in the old days there used to be a month called Aşure Ayi.

A ure is a sweet cooked with wheat, sultanas, figs, dates, dried beans, what you will, the whole being boiled for several hours until the result looks a little like aspic jelly. The legend of a ure is that when Noah in the Ark found himself running short of supplies, he ordered all the remaining foods to be cooked together for one last gigantic meal. This was aşure—or so we were told. During the days of the Ottoman Empire a month used to be set aside each year for the making of aşure in all the houses of the rich, who afterwards distributed it to the poor. When my grandfather was alive it used to be made in our house, fat Hacer being an adept at it, but latterly my mother had discontinued the habit, for Feride was uncertain of the recipe and my mother too cautious nowadays to waste any precious food. But it was made in my grandmother's new home, and a huge silver pot of it sent to us. Feride was immediately ordered to give it to the poor and my mother sent a message to my grandmother not to send any more to us. If my mother had anything to do with it, the breach between them would never heal.

After that I remember Ramazan. None of us kept the fast, although in my grandfather's day Ramazan was the signal for the entire household to fast and pray the prescribed five times

in a day. With the ending of Ramazan comes the Şeker
Bayrami, when all manner of sweets are distributed, especially
to the children. This particular Bayram was unbearably sad
for us, and perhaps that is why I remember it so well. My father
was no longer with us, my grandmother had re-married, and
my mother was, although I did not know that, pregnant with
her third child. And she was alone in this great, empty house
with two small children and her faithful Feride and Inci. That
Bayram morning Inci dressed us in new clothing—for new
clothing is as necessary to a Bayram as are the sweets and the
celebration. We were taken sedately downstairs to the salon,
where my mother sat alone, in a pretty silk dress and all her
rings sparkling on her reddened fingers. A few neighbours
called to congratulate the Bayram then went away again and I
saw my mother quietly crying to herself. . . .

What an emotional, unhappy Bayram to remember when
only happiness should have been present.

Later that same week we were taken to Madame Müjğan's
house to stay for a few days for we were told our mother was not
well. We were inclined to be tearful but I remember that Inci
whispered that perhaps when we came home again the new
baby would have arrived. So that made us feel better and we
proudly boasted of this to Yasemin and Nuri, who were bitterly
jealous that they had no new baby to boast about.

The last evening we spent in the house of our neighbour
Mehmet was inclined to be fretful, calling for Inci but was
eventually persuaded to sleep by Madame Müjğan's upstairs
maid.

I lay there in my little narrow bed, listening to the street-
sounds drifting in through the window. Somewhere I could
hear Bekci Baba crying his news of a fire and sleepily I remembered the night I had seen him for the first time. Then I
remembered the shivering, mournful beat of the drums the
day they came to take my father away and I felt suddenly
lonely, lying there in an unfamiliar room. I wondered if the
pigeons had brought the new baby yet and finally drifted into
sleep to the sound of Bekci Baba's voice. He still cried of a fire
that raged somewhere in this city but a fire was not exciting
to me, for I had never seen one and I did not know that the
wooden houses and konaks of Istanbul were a heaven-sent
opportunity for enemy spies. I did not know that one day I

should see my beloved Istanbul burning, burning to the empty skies.

The next day Inci arrived to take us back home. On the way across the gardens she said to me:

'Your pigeons have brought a lovely baby sister for you. Aren't you pleased?'

I was uncertain until I had seen the wonderful baby, so reserved my judgment, and Inci thought I was sulking and laughed at me.

Upstairs in my mother's room all was arrayed as if for a wedding. Lace pillows supported my mother's dark head and a satin quilt dropped almost to the carpet. Mehmet and I stood awkwardly in the doorway, uncertain whether or not to advance into such grandeur but my mother smiled and called us over to her. Excitedly we ran for her kiss, my grandmother fussily warning us not to jump on the bed.

'Where's the baby?' we wanted to know and my mother pulled back a lacy sheet and we looked down at a little dark head and a red crumpled roseleaf of face.

Mehmet said:

'Why doesn't she open her eyes?'

And my mother laughed and replied that she was sleeping. She put her hand against the baby's dress and drew out a long white box.

'Look what she has brought for you from your father,' she said and we took the box in delight, discovering chocolate bonbons inside, a rare luxury nowadays. We were happy that the baby had not come empty-handed and disposed to regard her more kindly.

The days passed by, those sunny May days of 1915, and one day my mother was downstairs with us again and we became accustomed to seeing the baby sleeping in her white cradle on the terrace. Mehmet and I would peep at her curiously, anxious for her to open her eyes and smile at us. She was so quiet, lying there, such a remarkably docile baby that we quite grew to love her, for no matter how much noise we made, she still slept on. We were never hushed for her sake and I think our love for Muazzez dates from that time.

About this time too my grandmother started to disobey her husband and visited us whenever she pleased. One day she helped my mother compose a letter to my father, telling him of the birth of his daughter but we never knew whether he received the letter or not. Neighbours began to alarm my mother, hinting that his long silence might mean that he was dead and advised her to go to the War Office for information. But this she would not do, perhaps fearing to hear what they would say.

Aunt Ayşe paid us a visit from Sariyer, eager to see Muazzez. She looked so different that I could scarcely recognise her, so gaunt and white and with cheeks sunk in. She started to cry when she saw Muazzez and I remember that I fascinatedly watched her. The tears poured down her face and Mehmet plucked uncertainly at her sleeve, distressed to see such sorrow, his small brown face looking unhappily at Aunt Ayşe. When her tears ceased she began to cough, in a sickening sort of way, and my grandmother, who sat out on the terrace with us, looked impatient and tapped her foot, as if she abhorred such a display of emotionalism.

I stood there, pondering about crying. Everyone seemed to cry nowadays and for no reason at all, in so far as I could see. Rebelliously, I wished my father back with us again. I had not thought about him for weeks, perhaps for months, yet suddenly there he was before my eyes and my heart ached with longing to see him come striding on to the terrace, to hear him call out to us, in the old way. And I felt rise in my throat a great lump and I did not know that crying was infectious. Afterwards I heard my aunt say that Uncle Ahmet had been blinded somewhere in the desert and she could not understand why the authorities did not send him home to her. Her unhappiness nagged at the heart, even phlegmatic Mehmet noticing it and trying to climb across her knee to console her. My mother told her we would all come to Sariyer later in the summer, when Muazzez was a little older and in a better condition to travel. And my aunt sighed and asked if we remembered last year there.

I listened to her soft voice, rising and falling, but in my eye was a picture of Sariyer. I saw the old house set amongst the trees and heard again my uncle's merry laughter. I went fishing with him on the Bosphor and slept again in the little rose-scented room above the tangled old garden. I heard the ships' sirens as they passed in the night—and yet I never left the terrace. But the memories were so clear and insistent on the brain that for a split second in time I had been back again in Sariyer.

When my aunt left us to return home I felt sorry that she had to go. She looked so little and lonely that I yearned to protect her from the world she found so hard now that my uncle was not beside her.

She did not kiss us, I remember, but stood fondling our heads, reluctant to leave yet anxious to return to Sariyer, where news from Uncle Ahmet perhaps awaited her.

'We shall come in June,' said my mother confidently, as if nothing might happen to disturb that promise.

Aunt Ayşe left and I never saw her again in my life. I never saw Sariyer either, for many years afterwards when I visited it nothing remained but a tumble-down house and a garden choked with weeds. The Sariyer I knew and loved was no more, vanished like its long-dead owners. Yet that Sariyer still shines clearly for me to-day, just as Aunt Ayşe's face emerges out of the mists of time, and shines too. There are some things in the heart that do not die and the loves of early childhood are the strongest loves of all.

CHAPTER IX

A LONG FAREWELL

MUAZZEZ MUST HAVE continued to be a quiet baby for I remember next to nothing about her from those days. Looking back, I find it is easier to remember all the strange, unquiet things that happened. I suppose all memories need only a little shaking-up to restore again places and things and people. Certainly I have had little difficulty in delving back into the past. Letters and photographs and later-day conversations have brought all these long-dead days before the mind's eye again, in some cases with startling clarity. For instance, I still recall the day my grandmother came to take Feride away from us.

It was high summer and we played in the garden, under the eye of my mother. She was sewing clothes for Muazzez, who kicked on a rug, Inci being inside in the house working. Feride's singing voice drifted out from the kitchen and a great peace lay about us. It was a cloudless, blue, shining day and I had a surge of happiness for no reason at all. Never had my home looked prettier, standing there squatly and compactly in its green lawn, the flower-beds a blaze of colour, the house blindingly white where the sun's long fingers touched it, blotched with grey, lacy patterns where the leaves of the vine and the fig-tree sheltered it. Recalling that scene now, did an uneasy peace linger in the sky above it, I wonder, making the tranquillity stand out all the more sharply by contrast—because of the things to come? That morning remains etched on the mind, one of a series of pictures that will never die whilst I live.

My grandmother called towards noon, coming across the grass to us, severe in her high-necked gown.

Inci followed her almost immediately with a tray of iced sherbets—cooling, effervescent drinks that tasted of roses.

My grandmother sat down in the chaise-longue my mother pushed forward for her, unveiled her hot face and held her hand to us children to be kissed. She was disposed to be gracious, praised the looks of the baby, gave my mother some entirely unwarranted advice regarding her embroidery and was altogether so charming that I felt she must want something. For my grandmother was never known to waste her charm on us.

She lay back in her chair, talking animatedly and fanning herself with a little ivory fan which she carried everywhere with her. My mother sewed tranquilly, replying to the other's rapid questions in her light, low voice which seemed to blend so well with the dreaming mood that was upon the house that magic day. My grandmother finished her sherbet, then came to the main point of her visit. Her husband, she said, was giving a very big dinner-party that night to some business acquaintances and she was distracted to know how she would manage, since her cook was in bed sick and the other servants did not know how to cook any of the elaborate dishes she wished to give the guests. Here she paused, eyeing my mother uneasily, but the latter never betrayed by as much as a flicker of the eyelids what it was she was thinking. She sewed peacefully on and Mehmet, thoroughly bored by this woman's talk, commenced to pull grasses from which to suck the sap. I hovered uncertainly behind my sister's rug and my grandmother began to display the faintest trace of irritability.

'Well, Şevkiye!' she demanded in her old bullying voice, all the sweetness gone. 'Did you hear what I was saying, or have you been dreaming all this time?'

'Of course I heard,' returned my mother, looking at her steadily. 'But I cannot suggest anything. Perhaps your cook will be well enough to get up and prepare everything and then go back to bed again.'

'Don't be silly!' said my grandmother waspishly, the control beginning to go out of her face. 'Well, I suppose I shall have to manage something. You could not spare Feride, could you?'

'No,' said my mother very gently and I marvelled at such control and discipline.

My grandmother's mouth folded obstinately.

'But only for the one night,' she begged. 'I shall send her back to-morrow morning.'

My mother did not reply and my grandmother talked on and on, putting forward all sorts of reasons why she should have Feride with her.

In the end, worn out by such volubility, such unceasing persistence, my mother gave in but on the condition that Feride was returned to our house that same evening.

Sulkily my grandmother agreed to this but she could not afford to be too sulky, since my mother was quite capable of changing her mind. But I think my grandmother had hoped to retain Feride until her own cook was well again. It mattered nothing to her that Inci and my mother should do all the work of the house between them—although if you were to ask my grandmother to do anything she would be highly indignant and explain to you that she was not a servant.

Once she had gained her own way she hurried off, refusing to stay for luncheon but stopping on the way to tell Feride what had been arranged for the afternoon.

My mother sighed after her but made no comment to us.

After she herself had gone to the house Mehmet and I continued to play listlessly for the sun was very hot. The grass was burning to my hand, the pigeons cooed sleepily and the whole romantic little scene was so peaceful that it might have been something in a dream. I think too the mood for dreaming was heavy upon me that day or was I only weighty with prophecy? It is a fact though that I remarked to Mehmet, or so my mother in after years assured me, that it would be a pity if all this peaceful life were to be swept away. Mehmet it is to be assumed would have only looked at me drowsily, his black eyes uncomprehending, and perhaps it is also to be assumed he would have asked me what I meant. And if he had I could not have explained. There were no words yet in my vocabulary to express my only half-formed, inarticulate thoughts. The white house, the green lawn, the brilliant flowers all seemed threatened with annihilation but where were the words to tell this picture? The dark flash that had for a moment lit my imagination would have been dismissed as a silly, childish fabrication. With Mehmet's drugged eyes holding mine I might have forgotten the threat that had hung in the bright air, the dark hand that had hovered over me.

Little things stand out from that day, all of them unimportant then but having their own sad value in after years. Luncheon was hurried, Feride anxious to get away, and Inci was sent to look for bread for she had a way of insinuating her lithe body between the crowds in a manner the more solid Feride could never emulate. Madame Müjgan came across from her garden in the middle of the afternoon, Yasemin and Nuri trailing hotly after her. My mother and she sat idly talking until evening crept into the brilliant sky and Madame Müjğan was begged to stay to dinner. My mother was loath to eat alone these days and welcomed the little diversion her neighbour made.

Madame Müjğan talked of the war and her husband but my mother I thought seemed anxious to discourage this trend in the conversation. She rarely mentioned my father even to Mehmet and me; she spoke of him seldom so that after a while his face would rise before us the face of a stranger or the face of someone well loved a long time ago, now only vaguely seen or recognised. For long periods at a time we forgot him altogether and could not imagine him ever again in the house. The squat white house he had bought for his family now seemed a woman's house and it needed an older imagination than mine to give it back my father's lounging figure or my uncle's laughter. My grandfather had receded far into the distance. He held no place in this house; he had never known of its existence. Their male figures were dimmer now and every day they dimmed a little more, waving their ghostly hands in farewell.

The day would no doubt come when they would be back with us again—as Inci not infrequently reminded us when we were disobedient—but in the meantime they had lost their authority with us.

The sun dropped lower down the sky and the faintest breeze blew through the long grass. The ladies drew little cashmere shawls about their shoulders and Inci came to take Muazzez to bed. Mehmet and I gathered our playthings then took our guests, Yasemin and Nuri, to wash before dinner. Yasemin splashed cold water across her face and her reflection glimmered palely in this place of uncertain light. She said, catching sight of herself, 'How odd I look!' and there was a doubtful note in her muted voice as if not recognising herself.

The dining-room was filled with a lucent, tender green light and all the windows stood open to the empty garden. The snowy table set with damask and glass and silver, with plates of cold food, looked cool and remote, a dish of black and white grapes making a sombre mark in the centre, like a bruise on a white face—like Yasemin's face so lately seen in the mirror, her eyes like bruises in the pallid ivory of cheek and nose and forehead. Wine chilled in a cooler and we children were allowed for this once to sit at the big table.

Inci appeared from upstairs, her day with Muazzez finished, and my mother told her not to bother about waiting at table but to eat her dinner quickly then go to collect Feride. She was so anxious to have the absent Feride back in the house again that she told Inci the table could be cleared the following morning. Never had I known such a thing permitted before, she being most punctilious in having the house in order before she retired for the night. After Inci had gone we few were alone in the house and a great, waiting silence seemed to descend upon us even though wine flowed in the glasses and the ladies' laughter tinkled.

Dinner over we left the salon—leaving the débris on the table, which looked a little vulgar now as tables always do after a meal has been eaten. My mother made coffee on her little silver spirit lamp and we sat there in the lengthening dusk that shadowed the salon, a little tired now that the day was over. Presently we would go yawning to bed and the square white house that held us would creak and grumble and mutter before settling into sleep under a summer sky. Yasemin and Nuri were petulant with tiredness and Mehmet nodded by himself in a big chair. It was nine o'clock and long past bedtime. Madame Müjgan gathered her children and we roused ourselves to walk with them across the garden to the little gate between the houses. We bade them good night and came back again along the white path glimmering in the dusk and a little bit of a moon was rising in the clear sky. My mother waited for us in the french windows of the dining-room. She looked unreal and ghostly standing there, like a figure in a play, so pale she was in her pale clothes. The house by night looked withdrawn and secret, a little frightening in its tall shroud of trees. We went in to my mother, who tightly shuttered the windows and the dirty, littered table looked like a table in a dead house. I helped to fasten doors and windows and then we went up to bed together, a tall, golden candle lighting our way. The house seemed incredibly quiet without Inci and Feride.

'How will they get in?' I asked.

'Who?' asked my mother, puzzled.

'Inci and Feride,' I replied and she laughed at my anxious face, telling me that they had the front door key and then Mehmet suddenly said that he wanted Inci and started to cry.

My mother put her arm around him and he sobbed that he was frightened.

'But there is nothing to be afraid of,' said my mother amusedly.

The image of Mehmet's fear had imprinted itself on the dark air and I too began to feel vaguely uneasy. When my mother kissed us good night, I begged her to leave her door open as well as ours. She seemed so reluctant to give in to our fear that Mehmet started to weep again and her own face began to reflect his terror. I do not know why we were so unaccountably afraid that night. Perhaps a little bit of the future impinged on the consciousness. Or perhaps—— But I do not know. I only know that having slept contentedly in the dark for years, that night both Mehmet and I were unwilling to see the candle go out of our room and across the landing to my mother's. Before she left us she stood a few moments at the window and the tak-tak of Bekci Baba's stick could be heard coming nearer to us. My mother sighed imperceptibly.

'Bekci Baba is a great comfort,' she said, adding, 'I wish he could stay outside this house all night.'

Then she recollected herself, closed the window a little and went across to her own room, where Muazzez slept peacefully. I lay sleepless for a long time after she had gone. Street noises drifted in, two cats were fighting in the gutter, hissing and spitting at each other with cold, rapacious felinity. The house was very still, the bedroom door a dark cavern, and as the street noises gradually died, I had an odd sense of waiting. I waited and the house waited and the empty staring sky waited but I do not know for what it was we waited. But I grew tired first and slept and wild dreams threshed to and fro in my brain. How long I slept I do not know. But I remember waking to a terrible crying from my mother, or was the crying only part of my dreams? Someone was shaking my shoulder, telling me to get up quickly and run—run.

My tortured mind could only absorb the one word 'run', so still enmeshed in violent dreaming was my mind. Mehmet whimpered like a little animal and I caught his hand as he ran blindly past me, swinging myself from the bed, bemused, bewildered, wondering if this horror was still part of a nightmare. My mother was screaming, no control left in her voice, but what it was she said I shall never know—only guess at perhaps

—and the unendurable nightmare persisted. In the dark door-way clouds of thick, acrid, eye-smarting vapour caused me to choke but my mother, with Muazzez wailing in her arms, inexorably pushed Mehmet and me on before her. Down the dark stairs with the hot, thick vapour burning our throats. Blindly we stumbled, terror-stricken and half stupid with sleep. A great, dark-red lick of flame belched upwards to meet us.

'No! no!' screamed Mehmet, hesitating and dragging on my hand to impede progress.

'Fire!' I shouted, suddenly wide-awake and comprehending, but my mother pushed me on and I dragged Mehmet after me, his feet slithering reluctantly on the stairs.

'Run!' commanded my mother in an awful voice, a voice to freeze the blood in the marrow, and she forcibly impelled me onward, with such force indeed that Mehmet fell on one knee, letting go of my hand. She swooped down on him, frantically tearing him by the shoulder, shouted to me to hold her skirts and ran like the wind down the narrow pathway through the flames. For a moment that seemed an eternity she wrenched at the overheated front door, swinging it open for us to fall into the daylight of the street. Oh to remember that night, when the enemy spies set fire to the wooden houses of Istanbul, when they burnt like matchwood under a summer sky! The street was daylight for all the houses on both sides were a lurid, blazing mass.

'The garden door!' my mother was saying piteously, but we had not been able to get to the garden door, for the flames in our house had been worse in the back. Did we stand foolishly in the flaming street for one petrified moment? Who knows? Memory has shut down on that for I can only coherently remember running along the street, clutching my mother tightly, whilst she sought a way to turn off, to reach the waste field that lay at the back of our house, at the bottom of the garden. The street was full of humanity gone momentarily mad. Maidservants, old men in their night-shirts, screaming, petrified children and tumbling down on us, great, fiery rafters from the derelict, deserted houses. One fell in my mother's path and I heard her give a sort of gasp of horror, a moaning, inhuman gasp. Pitter patter pitter went our bare, running feet on the hard cobblestones and our breaths emerged harshly from our chests and all the time the fires crackled merrily.

Down a dark street this time, with no falling rafters to block our path. Frantic men and women at their doors, wondering if the fires would spread to threaten them too.

'God save us! What a terrible night!' said their grotesque faces but we panted on to reach the open fields.

Waste ground at last, soft grass under our bleeding feet and mass hysteria to greet us under the fig-trees. Mehmet and I fell on the ground, sore and bleeding, our hearts thumping to bursting-point, our thin nightshirts bound with perspiration to our shivering bodies. My mother laid Muazzez across my lap and leaned against a stunted little tree in a posture unendurably touching and desolate.

'My money!' she said over and over again, 'and all my jewellery.'

And suddenly like a mad thing, and indeed I believe the dark, feathery wing of madness touched her brow eternally that night, she darted away from us on her weary, bleeding feet.

'An-ne! An-ne!' I shouted in a fresh paroxysm of terror. 'Don't leave us, oh don't leave us!'

And then I started to cry in a weak sort of way for I had no energy left to put into crying.

But my mother ran unheeding of my crying voice, stumbling a little, falling over, picking herself up to forge ahead again. Muazzez lay on my knee, wrapped in a little lacy woollen shawl, and I bent over her, wearily trying to hush her whimpering. Mehmet plucked at my sleeve, wanting sympathy too, and I put an arm about him and drew him against my shoulder. We watched the fires and our own house burning with the rest and our brains were numb, no longer functioning properly. Even fear and tiredness had dropped away to leave us mercifully empty. All about us, children were crying and women were wailing but these were only external things, having no power over us. Even the knowledge that my mother had gone back to that burning house could arouse no emotion, revive no terror. We just sat there, Mehmet and I, and the fig-tree stretched above us and now and again Muazzez softly whimpered.

Before us lay our garden and farther back was our home, our home that had been our comfort and our childish security. The district tulumba had arrived and were trying to find water, and their frantic shouts echoed to us across the gardens. We could see them running from place to place, trying in vain to stem the fires. They had only one pump but at least ten houses were burning and on the other side of the street, which we could not see from here, as many more burned. So they ran and they shouted, throwing ineffectual buckets of water and the fires roared triumphantly. I was watching for my mother to come back but there was no sign of her for a long, long time. Then I saw her running to us down the garden path, for it was as light as day, and I plainly saw her night-dressed figure and the thin, white, delicate feet running, running, running. . . .

She came to us and flung herself down, utterly exhausted. Her hair hung wildly about her face and in her mournful eyes was a glare, a brilliance, which knew nothing of sanity. She looked towards our house and I looked too and the last bit of the roof came down into the greedy inferno that waited for it. Our house, like all the others, had blazed up like matchwood, like a piece of paper, and now only its ghostly shell remained to remind us that once we had been happy there.

Still, thirty-three years afterwards, I have only to close my eyes to be back again to that night and see our home burning. It is as clear before me as if it happened only yesterday.

A woman came with a crying child and threw it on the grass beside us, then ran off again to God knows where. Surely she did not hope to go through that hell to salvage anything? My mother stared before her with dilated eyes and my heart turned over in fear, so still and pale she looked. She said very loudly, as if to make sure I quite understood,

'Everything is lost. Everything—do you understand that?'

And she fixed me with that hard, brilliant stare, her nostrils quivering, then suddenly she heeled over in the thick, soft grass, oblivious to the sounds about her or her ruined, blackening house.

How long she lay there, how long we children sat there, I do not know. I think perhaps Mehmet cried himself to sleep and even Muazzez at last gave up her whimpering. Dawn was breaking over the desolate scene and the fires had died down, only a pall of thick, black smoke lying over the empty shells of the houses and there was the chill of early morning in the air. Presently in all that dead, exhausted place I discerned my grandmother with Feride and Inci coming over the fields, looking to right and to left, as though searching for us.

'Grandmother!' I called but my voice was no voice at all, only a thread of sound, a croak that could not disturb the silence.

I placed Muazzez carefully on the wet, dewy grass and stood up stiffly, walking towards the three who were searching for us. I walked haltingly, for my feet were badly torn and the blood had dried between the toes and the soft dawn air whipped through my thin nightdress like a gale.

They saw me and ran crying to me and put their kind arms around me and my grandmother warmed me with her coat. I stood looking at them as if they were strangers and in a sense they were strangers, for they came to me out of another life, a gracious, easy, friendly life that might never come again. I told my grandmother my mother was safe, and my brother and sister too, then led her across the grass to them.

Feride knelt down beside my mother, taking off her own warm cloak and wrapping it tenderly around her. I saw her force cognac down my mother's throat and heard her cough and choke a little with its burning rawness. Then she opened her eyes and looked at us for a moment, uncomprehendingly. She looked at each of us in turn, then picked Muazzez up in her arms.

'If you had not taken Feride,' she said to my grandmother, 'something would have been left of my home. I could have saved the only money I had, or my jewellery—if you had not taken Feride.'

Then her stiff body relaxed and the hardness left her eyes. She looked at me, at Mehmet, and at our poor, cut feet and smoke-blackened faces, at our quivering, unsteady mouths and she put out a hand to draw us to her.

'But I still have my two big men,' she said and we fell on her and shed the tears that had been dammed up inside us for too long. Then my grandmother got busy with hot drinks, which she carried in a sort of flannel bag, and we were taken to her home.

And of all that little group perhaps it was I alone who said a long farewell to my burned home, that had smiled so brilliantly in the sun, only yesterday.

CHAPTER X

TRYING TO BUILD AGAIN

So to my grandmother's house, where we were bathed and fed and put into warm beds, whilst Feride was sent to buy clothes for us.

My mother became very ill with a fever and the doctor called many times each day and we were constantly told to keep quiet. My grandmother's house held an alien quality for us, more than the quality of strangeness. We used to sit out in the gardens with Inci, feeling unwanted in that childless house, and we rarely saw the old man. As a matter of fact we were so terrified of him that if we ever saw him coming we used to run like the wind in the opposite direction. Nobody knew how long we were going to remain in this house, my grandmother only saying that when my mother was well again something would be arranged. Mehmet and I felt cut adrift, not being allowed to visit our mother, never seeing Yasemin or Nuri for they had moved to another part of Istanbul, their house having perished with ours. Changes began to take place. One morning Feride bade us good-bye for my grandmother had found another situation for her, knowing we could never afford her again. Inci left too, with many tears, for she had never known any other service but in my home. Now she was being sent as a nurse-maid to a strange family, even she would be separated from her mother. Saying good-bye to Inci frightened me for I did not know what we were going to do without her. It was almost like losing a limb, a part of one's self. One morning we were allowed to visit my mother, who lay in her big bed looking like a doll. Her appearance shocked me. Her dark curls had all been combed flat against the sides of her face, her cheeks were pinched and taut from the fever. Although she reached her hands to us there was no welcome in her face and her eyes were expressionless. She looked as if coming back to life was too much of an effort for her and that given the slightest opportunity she would slip loose.

As I grew older and came to a better understanding of things

I realised that my mother was a woman predictable only if things went her way. Poverty she had to face but many people in the world face poverty, if not with contentment at least with resignation. She was unable to do this, yet unable also to escape. The sight of her burning house was a far greater shock than my father going to war, the loss of her possessions the worst blow. With money she could have built a new life, without it she was unable to accept what other people did for her. It was not so much pride, although that entered in too. It was more an incapability to deal with life on any other terms than with money behind her. I think she had hoped to die the night of the fire. The thought of having to rear three children and one of them an infant was almost too much for her simple, inexperienced mind to bear.

She was sick of a fever for days and emerged from it quite another person. She had always been quiet but now her silence was a fearsome thing. She had never been known to lose her temper, now she flared into easy rages that were all the more alarming because of her usual chilling quietness. The shy beautiful young woman came out of her fever with a different personality. When she was able to get up, she would sit in the gardens, looking at nothing and seemingly unaware of her surroundings. She never once asked for Feride or Inci and would gaze speculatively at the infant Muazzez, who was being looked after by a wet-nurse.

One day my grandmother told her that the old man was willing to give us rooms in one of his many houses. My mother listened to her and agreed to accept the offer, but my grandmother had to urge her almost forcibly before she would give her decision. She had one good diamond ring, which she had been wearing the night of the fire, and she asked the old man to sell it for her. I remember she held it out to him disdainfully, between her finger and thumb, and the sun touched rays of fire from it. As he took it from her, her eyes flickered uncertainly. When he returned and handed her the money from its sale she thanked him and said she would be glad to move into the rooms he proposed to give her as soon as possible. The old man replied, but with courtesy, that nothing would please him better and his cold eyes raked Mehmet and me with such an expression of active dislike that I was quite breathless with astonishment. This old man had centred all his dislike on us children. He had hoped that his marriage would give him children, sons, to carry on his name and his business. I think my grandmother's refusal to share his bed had damaged some part of his pride to such an extent that he could not bear to look on us, the fruits of her life with my grandfather.

To my grandmother, I never saw him anything else but coldly polite. She was an obstinate, self-willed woman with a wounding tongue and I imagine his pride suffered badly beneath her hands. Looking back, it amazes me to what extent she over-rode him since he could have, in those days, thrown her penniless from his house by simply saying: 'I divorce you', three times in the presence of witnesses. Many a wife, thirty years ago, was a good wife simply because she lived under the threat of those words. With the Atatürk régime all this was done away with so that nowadays, in Turkey, the divorce system is so complicated that many couples effect a reconciliation long before the slow-moving, intricate machinery of divorce goes into action.

Servants were sent to the house we were to occupy, or, more accurately, the rooms we were to occupy. I was permitted to go with them. The house was behind Bayazit Square, two-storied and so old that one wondered what it was that continued to hold it erect. There was no garden and it fronted the narrow, dreary street, all its windows covered with kafes—closely latticed harem shutters always used in old Turkey to prevent passing males from catching glimpses of the women who moved within the house.

The upper floor was to be ours. It consisted of three large, very dirty rooms, a big square landing with no light save the greyish haze which filtered through the unclean skylight. All the rooms were dark and airless, because of the kafes covering the windows. My mother told one of the servants to tear them off but he trembled with horror to attempt anything so revolutionary, without the old man's permission.

My mother knew it was useless to insist. She looked impatient and the servants started to scrub the floors, and she took my hand and we went back to my grandmother's house. She seemed very determined and I had difficulty in keeping up with her hurrying figure. These odd, inexplicable moods of hers tormented my heart and gave me a feeling of insecurity. Too much seemed to be happening at once and I had mental indigestion trying to keep up with events. Lately I clung to her passionately, watching her face anxiously for signs of storm, learning of the coldness of the world before my time. My mother represented love and stability and, to be trite, children are conservative.

When we arrived at my grandmother's house, she asked to see the old man and finding I would not be dissuaded from her side impatiently allowed me to enter his room with her. He sat in a big chair in front of the window and looked irritable, for it was a day when his gout was giving him its own particular hell. My mother, with remarkable docility, asked if the kafes might be removed from the windows of our new abode. He sat looking at her for a moment or two, she staring steadily and coolly at him, and surprisingly he agreed to her request. He added that he would instruct his men to paint the rooms for her and hoped that she would be comfortable there.

His voice was quiet and formal but I think he liked my mother in his own way for he liked so few people. He probably felt a certain understandable pity for her distress but her relationship to my grandmother alienated her.

My mother was pleased with her victory and hummed a little air, a sure sign that things were going well with her. I was overflowing with thankfulness to have her back with us again, even if it was only for a short time. For ever since the fire she had been unapproachable, far away from us, and several times I had caught her remote eye fixed on Mehmet or myself, as though she asked herself what we had to do with her. I smarted under this unawareness for she was all that we had left, having lost so much from childhood.

When my mother told my grandmother what she was doing about the kafes, the latter was appalled—in much the same way as the servant had been earlier in the day. She told my mother she must not do such a thing, that she would be stoned as a prostitute if she exposed herself in this shameless fashion. My mother laughed at her and afterwards, when we were returning to the house, she disdainfully refused the offer of a maid to accompany her, saying that in her new station in life she could not afford the luxury of a maid.

At the house, the scrubbing had been finished and clean, naked floors gleamed wetly. A man was busy removing the offending kafes from the windows, whilst another mixed distemper in a bucket. They were very polite to my mother but it was plain to see they thought her very odd to want the kafes off the windows, to let the unaccustomed daylight into these depressing rooms. She was very gay all that day. Her gaiety transformed her so that one could see she looked twenty-two again, beautiful and high-spirited but husbandless. And the men servants were probably prophesying amongst themselves her downfall. She was an odd contradiction, one moment spineless and the next bounding with immense vitality. In one way, her own unobtrusive way, she was the forerunner of Kemal Atatürk—for she emancipated herself years before his time. That the people in her new life would talk about her she did not care.

She had always lived in houses which admitted fresh air and she intended to do the same thing here, and if there was no garden to protect her from eager scrutiny—then she would have to get used to the peculiar ways of mankind. But fresh air she intended to have even at the cost of her reputation. So she snapped her fingers at the gossipers and acted the lady in her three mean rooms and lamented the loss of her diamond ring. Now that she had found a home again, her vitality was boundless, colour seemed to return to her cheeks, the flesh to the delicate bones. To Mehmet and me her courage was terrific and we still think so to-day. We cannot help but admire her colossal struggle, her intrepid spirit and even as children we were aware of this courage. We could forgive the lapses into depression and bad temper, the seeming ruthlessness when she banished her children eventually. To-day we see these things in their true perspective and can only see the wit, the bravery and the gaiety which transformed three mean rooms in a mean street into a formidable bulwark against the rest of the world.

My grandmother arranged to let us have the most of her furniture, the cumbersome, handsome walnut furniture she had moved from our house upon her re-marriage. From her vast stocks she provided curtains and linens and rugs and tapestries which had once graced our salon in my grandfather's house. The three rooms and the dark, square landing took on a joyous air, as if they had been waiting for just such a transformation. The windows stood wide open to the world and if the neighbours gasped at such audacity in their midst, my mother I am sure was totally unaware of it. Naturally they knew her story, for gossip has a way of travelling in Istanbul as rapidly as it has in any other part of the world. No doubt the good neighbours thought she had brought these 'fast' habits from her former life.

The first evening we were established in the new house we discovered that, so much else having been thought of, we were without lamps or food. My mother went down the naked stairs to the widow who lived beneath, thinking perhaps she could oblige. Their conversation must have been pathetic. The grand lady in her fine silk dress and the poor, wretched trollop, shunned by the neighbours because of her reputed 'goings-on'— she must have thought it was the Sultan himself, no less, who had descended upon her to request the loan of a lamp! Unfortunately she had no lamp, or if she had was far too flustered to search for it, but she produced a scrap of candle. This my mother triumphantly bore upstairs, to place in a silver candlestick on the buffet. So much had been lost and was irretrievable but a silver candlestick was a necessity. Nothing less would have done, not glass or china or even just plain, honest tin, nothing but a silver one was good enough, for ladies only used the best. . . . The room in the candlelight hid some of its secrets and the cracks in the ceiling might have been gold-encrusted ornamentations in that kindly glow—if you had enough imagination, and I had plenty. Well, there we were in our new home, in our new clothes provided by my grandmother—and we ate dry bread and a handful of black olives to still the ache in our stomachs. Then we settled to sleep, far away from the murmur of the sea or the scent of the flowers from an almost forgotten garden and for me, at least, it was as comfortable as the Dolmabahçe Saray. It probably was too, for the white, iced-cake-looking Saray with its echoing dungeons had no great reputation for comfort—or so I heard afterwards.

And I wonder what my mother thought that night, as she lay down in my grandfather's exotic bed—the one where I had once played 'lions'—and the legs of which were placed in glass bowls of water, to prevent the bed-bugs from becoming too adventurous? Did she thank God for safe deliverance into a new home, however mean, or did she pray for guidance for the future? Perhaps. Perhaps not. She was never a religious person, being too impatient to accept the Muslim teaching of Fatalism, and with a mind so hurrying that God must have just flitted through it with barely a hurried nod in her direction. She had been born in Albania and her unorthodox views of life and religion derived perhaps from some far-off Christian ancestor who slept uneasily in her blood.

The next morning, şütcü—the milkman—awakened us by his violent assertions that his milk was the best in Istanbul. Mehmet and I leaped from our shared bed and rushed to the window, to see this remarkable apparition who had dared to disturb our dreams. Always before, şütcü had decorously called at the back door and in a series of sibilant whispers conducted his business with Hacer or Feride, never dreaming of loudly crying his wares for fear of waking the sleeping occupants of the house. This was a great change. In our new life, people şet their day in motion with the arrival of the milkman and sütcü himself had no false illusions about his value, and firmly believed in thoroughly arousing any sleepy heads who still remained in bed.

He saw us hanging out of the window and his jaw dropped in surprise because the kafes were gone. He was long and lean and bronzed and wore patched clothing but it could not disguise the smooth rippling of the muscles under his shirt. He had a several days' growth of beard and this fascinated us very much. His voice was the voice of Doom.

'Milk!' he barked at us fiercely. 'Do you want any milk to-day?'

'No, thank you,' we said politely, in chorus, and he grinned sourly and stood back to get a good look at us, the paragons of good behaviour.

Just then the widow opened the front door, thrusting forward a saucepan which the şütcü silently filled. Then I heard my mother's pattering feet taking the stairs and she also held out a receptacle to be filled. She bought yoğurt for us too, a sort of sour junket which we loved with sugar.

With the coming of şütcü, the street came to life. Doors opened and saucepans were thrust forth and Sütcü did a roaring trade.

My mother called to us from the landing, which had been made into a kitchen, that it was time for us to get up. We began to pull on our clothes, fumbling over buttons and tapes. Mehmet exasperatedly started to cry and said he wanted Inci, and my mother swept impatiently into the room. Suddenly buttons and tapes became docile things under her experienced fingers. She showed us both how our clothes should be put on, how held together—which was the most important so far as we were concerned. She explained that for the time being there was no Inci to help us and that we must learn to do these things for ourselves. She was particularly scathing with me, declaring that a boy almost seven years old should at least be able to pull on his boots, even if he were incapable of lacing them. I hung my head in shame for every word she said was painfully true and I simply had not the remotest idea of which boot went on which foot. No doubt we benefited from her instructions for I certainly never remember another occasion of being helped into our clothes.

Later that day when I was sitting in the so-called salon I saw my grandmother coming up the street. I recognised her by her veil for all the women in the street wore the çarşaf—a sort of black scarf tightly binding the forehead and hair and with another piece of material, a peçe, covering the lower part of their faces. They looked unbearably ugly and drab and I was thankful that neither my mother nor my grandmother wore such things. I called to her from my little window and she waved her hand to me and I rushed down to open the door for her. She instructed me to leave the door open, as two of her porters were to arrive with more furniture for us.

My mother greeted her, then mocked lightly:

'But what is this to-day? No chaperone?'

And my grandmother self-consciously replied that she saw no reason why a poor old woman like herself—she was about fifty—could not walk the daytime streets unescorted.

My mother's emancipation seemed to be affecting my grandmother too, although of course she would never admit that, holding firmly to the argument that whereas perhaps *she* might be rash enough to venture out alone, by reason of her age, my mother could not do the same thing and for the same reason!

Porters arrived with a sewing-machine that had formerly been used by Feride for the household mending. A large console table followed, a little inlaid Moorish coffee-table, a wooden chest containing God knew what and monstrous arm-chairs that would crowd everything else out of the salon. My mother's face was a study as she watched all these things hauled up the narrow stairs and heaved pantingly into the rooms.

When the porters had departed she asked my grandmother where she thought everything would be put and my grandmother looked taken aback for, naturally, such a thought had never entered her head. In a sudden burst of generosity she had given this furniture to us and expected pleasure as our reaction and not pointless questions as to where they should all be put. She looked around her, having to admit that the rooms were already overcrowded but she told my mother she ought to be grateful for that. She felt affronted and took no pains to conceal this. I think she saw nothing incongruous in this lovely old furniture adorning these poor rooms, or the silky Sparta and Persian rugs strewn across the uneven floorboards, broken in places. She had wanted to instal her daughter-in-law and her grandchildren in a fine home and hey presto! had she not done so? Why then was the daughter-in-law looking round her so doubtfully, as though ungrateful for all these lovely things? She must have given up struggling with the idea for she abruptly dismissed the subject of the offending furniture and proceeded to unpack the wooden chest, feeling certain that these treasures would be appreciated. She brought forth curtains, to be hung immediately, she stipulated. Table- and bed-linen was dragged out to trail on the floor, heavy silver cutlery, to be used presumably for our dry bread and our black olives. Hammered brass lamps, which would require a gallon of oil a day to keep them going. A silk-embroidered bed-set which, she proudly informed Mehmet and me, had been given to her when she was a young girl for her wedding to my grandfather.

My mother looked at all these old treasures and her eyes filled with tears. They reminded her too vividly of my grandfather and my father and the houses where she had been happy and I felt she did not want them here, in this house that held no memories. She said nothing, although the tears began to drop on to her cheeks. Then she recovered herself and bade me blow the mangal, so that coffee could be brewed. I went out to the landing, where lurked the mangal, a table, crockery for everyday use and several buckets of water. There was no water in the house, although fresh drinking-water was supplied each week by Bekci Baba. All other water had to be fetched from the local pump, the meeting-place for all the ladies of the district, and only that morning I had staggered twenty times or more with small tin cans to be filled. I could not bear to see my mother do such menial work as this. The darkness hid what was on the landing but the unlovely smell of cooking filled the house perpetually. Cooking facilities were primitive. Charcoal was burned in the big copper brazier, the mangal, an iron tripod placed over it and the pan containing whatever had to be cooked stood on it. After several slow hours a meal was either cooked to perfection or ruined beyond redemption, depending on the sort of cook you were. In those first days with this cooking arrangement much of our food was uneatable for my mother was *not* a good cook. She liked good food but had no patience and could not be bothered to do everything the cookery book prescribed. Many years later she became quite an expert but only when she had already ruined our digestion.

That morning she made coffee for my grandmother, handing it to her on a thin, very old silver tray and, if one turned one's back to the window—ignoring the view—one would have thought that Inci had just left the room and that we were back again in the house that had been burned. So firmly was ritual in her blood that my mother saw nothing odd in the fact that she should continue to serve coffee on a silver tray that would have graced a collector's possessions. She who had nothing left in the world, who was poorer by far than the widow who lived under us. We saw no incongruity in my mother's gesture either, but remembering that moment so long ago can bring a smile to me to-day. There they sat, those two elegant ladies, in a slum room and they sipped coffee from a silver tray. The old order was established once more and presently my grandmother would forget herself and look for the bell to ring for Inci to clear away. . . .

That day, before she left, she pressed gold money into my mother's hand, the latter protesting that she was not in need of it since she still had the money from the sale of her ring. My mother had very little knowledge of the value of money and absolutely no true knowledge of food prices. If she wanted something she had to have it and if it seemed to cost many gold coins—well, unfortunately that was life and we were in the middle of a war. Consequently, traders robbed her, demanding exorbitant prices for their wares. She was always too shy to argue with them, feeling it beneath her dignity but I had begun to notice that the other women in the market-place paid much less for their foodstuffs than she did. If I remonstrated with her, she would hush me impatiently, but there came a time when she began seriously to worry about her money. It was inconceivable that my grandmother could continue to support us. We had already heard that her husband had been almost insane with fury when he discovered she had moved all her furniture without consulting him. Still food continued to be our biggest problem and one gold coin seemed to have very little purchasing power—especially if one patronised the Bourse Noir, which my mother did.

About this time in my life I became initiated into the purely feminine mystery of acting nursemaid. My mother had formed the habit of shopping alone, usually after the morning's meal was over. She would leave Mehmet and Muazzez in my charge, to my disgust, for I hated to be held responsible for everything they did. My duties mostly consisted of saying 'don't' but occasionally I would give Mehmet an exasperated slap, which would make him roar so loudly that once the widow rushed up to see what was wrong and afterwards complained about me to my mother. When my mother remonstrated, I was resentful, blind and deaf to everything save my intense dislike of looking after the younger ones.

One particular day my mother had found more difficulties than usual in getting bread for us. Latterly our whole world revolved on the one word 'bread'. She had spent most of the morning at the baker's, returning weary and empty-handed. She went out again in the afternoon, with the same result. Towards evening she set off again, telling Mehmet and me not to make too much noise since Muazzez was sleeping. For a while we played quietly, then Mehmet became tired and fretful, and we gathered our toys together, putting them into a cupboard on the landing and went back to our favourite corner seat to watch for our mother's return. It was getting duskish and my mother seemed to be away for an unusually long time. The street was deserted and presently we heard the widow go out, closing the front door conspiratorily after her. We watched her black, dumpy figure disappear down the street and we became uneasy, knowing there was now nobody in the house save ourselves.

Perhaps some memory of the darkness which had preceded the night of the fire came up to catch us by the throat, causing us to talk in whispers and look, now and then, furtively over our shoulders into the darkening room. Mehmet was sleepy and begged to be allowed to go to bed but I was loath to part with his company. I longed for my mother's return. I wished the lamps were lit but dared not touch them, on my mother's orders. We continued to sit there and still she did not come and the room grew darker and the street was silent as the grave. There was a little Mosque near the house and from our corner window we could see it quite plainly, its one, slender minaret piercing the gloom. More clearly to be seen, and within one of its windows, was the tomb of a holy man, with a candle—lit by some pious aspirant—burning steadily in a glass holder. Muezzin had mounted the lonely minaret and was calling the people to prayer, but we could not see whether anyone was entering the Mosque or not for the entrance faced in the opposite direction to us. Muezzin's voice was mournful and mysterious, the liquid Arabic notes rippling from his tongue like strange music. When he had finished reading Ezzin and had left the minaret the night seemed stiller and blacker than ever. Only the candle still winked brightly on the holy man's grave.

Suddenly I began to be afraid. Fear and hunger and tiredness combined, loosened my tongue . 'Dead man is coming! Dead man is coming!' Mehmet looked at me in the semi-darkness and his lip started to quiver. He looked in the direction of the candle and began to howl with fear too. We rushed from the window and over to the sofa, which was draped with an old Persian praying-mat, and this we pulled over our heads, whimpering in terror. We whipped up our fear to a greater frenzy, telling each other that the holy man had got out of his grave because he was cold and lonely there and was coming to take us back to his grave, so that we should keep him warm. We shivered and our teeth chattered and scattered remnants of Inci's ghostly lore kept coming back to keep our terror at fever pitch. We lay clasping each other in desperation, muttering that the holy man must be very near to us now. We pushed each other in our extreme agitation, pulling the too small praying-mat first over his head, then over mine. In the midst of all this I heard footsteps, slow, furtive footsteps.

'Here he comes!' I yelled, panic-stricken in earnest this time. The footsteps drew nearer and nearer, entered our front door and mounted the stairs—slowly, wearily, heavily, just as I supposed a long-dead holy man would walk. My heart was ready to stop forever and I lay under the praying-mat, with Mehmet screaming his lungs out, and a stern hand pulled the praying-mat away from our faces.

'What is this?' enquired my mother's voice.

I was so relieved to see her that I was totally unable to reply but Mehmet managed to stutter 'D-Dead man!' and then went off into a fresh paroxysm of wailing. My mother strove to make him cease, sorting him out from beneath me—where he had wriggled—and trying to wrest the corner of the praying-mat, which he tightly clutched, from his fingers.

When she had finally extricated him, it was discovered that he had wet his pants a couple of times, and looked as if the slightest cross word from my mother would cause him to do the same again.

CHAPTER XI

THE END OF SARIYER

LIFE WAS BY no means dull in our street. From the arrival of the first, early morning şütcü, to the departure of the last evening Yoğurtcu, there was noise and bustle and arguing and laughter. I used to sit in my corner window, a pile of cushions placed on my chair so that I could see the better, and watch the street vendors leading their lazy-looking mules up and down, up and down, crying their wares and shouting insults at each other. There were the aubergine sellers, the tomato-sellers and traders with great, glowing heaps of lemons. And, in their seasons, the water-melon sellers and grape-sellers. They would lead their mules drowsily, enormous baskets strapped on either side of the beast to display the aubergines and the tomatoes and the tender, young French beans. They would cry hoarsely to the listening houses that no finer vegetables than theirs were to be found in any part of the world. A shrill housewife would demand the price and, upon hearing the reply, would commence to abuse the seller. Perhaps even a battle would ensue, the trader and the housewife each vieing with the other for the honours of the slanging match. Sometimes other housewives would join in, defending their representative. A few of the other traders would listen sceptically, and after a while the battle of words would reach such a pitch that the combatants had to search deeply into the opponent's antecedents, in order that fresh fuel might be added to the fire. There was never any danger of either side running out of words, even if it meant reiterating the same ones over and over again. It was nothing to hear one of them informing the other that he was a son of a donkey or that he was the husband of a prostitute or the father of innumerable illegitimate children. These were mild epithets against the stronger ones that could be used if the housewife really got into her stride. She usually bested the trader, for she almost always had grown sons, ready to defend her honour should he reply to her in like manner. And of course there were always the other housewives, who would think nothing of setting about the poor unfortunate seller, beating him with whatever came to their hands, whilst their children would rifle his laden baskets, lying across the back of the phlegmatic mule.

There were a great number of children in the street, dirty-nosed, underfed children who were tougher at seven or eight than many a man is at forty. Mangy cur dogs roamed the dustbins, which were left outside the houses, for we were no respecters of authority in our street. Thousands of cats, in all stages of growth and development, ranged the rubble-heaps and chased the rats from the sewers, and were even capable of eating each other when their hunger became maddening. Through all this wretchedness and dirt and poverty, my mother walked with her proud, firm step and the other women eyed her suspiciously and murmured against her because she thought so little of their censure, that she had torn the kafes from her windows and walked amongst them as shamelessly as a prostitute. And the small boys threw stones after her and the men leered into her veiled face and she passed through their malevolent ranks like a queen. She would not allow us to play in the street, for despite her destitution she retained her snobbishness. Our daily exercise depended on the amount of time she had left over from her shopping expeditions. She rarely bought from the street-sellers, having no bargaining capacity and rendered shy before the cold, appraising scrutiny of the other women, who auto-matically crowded their doors to see what she bought and how much she was foolish enough to pay for it. She bought in the local market-place, a street urchin—always to be found in the markets—to carry her wares in a basket slung over his thin shoulders. She would walk home before him, direct him upstairs to the smelly landing, tip him and send him away.

Mehmet and I were always given the job of sorting the vegetables into their respective places, for in those days she soiled her hands as little as possible. She hated the street and its inhabitants, their coarse humour and their impure speech. She had an almost academic passion for purity of speech. Once home, she would remove her veil, sink into a chair and look about her at the treasures of my grandfather's day. Gradually peace would creep back into her face again. She lived always in the past, emerging unwillingly for the daily routine. Each night saw her tranquilly sewing in a deep chair, where the lamplight caught her hair, or tending her nails, the curtains drawn and her face composed, as though no hostile strangers lurked outside in the mean street. Her habit of going back to the past, of turning her mind ever inwards would become perilous in later life but none of us knew that then. She roamed around always in her memories, refusing to recognise the ever-encroaching future of penury.

Money was very scarce but still she spent what we had like water. If she thought she was going to start worrying about it, down came the shutter over her mind and the thought was pushed into the uneasy background—along with all the other unpleasant thoughts she did not want to recognise. When my grandmother frequently remonstrated about the way money was slipping from our grasp, my mother would turn the subject aside, perhaps showing my grandmother some piece of embroidery she had just completed and the discussion on money would be dropped almost as soon as it had started. And my mother would talk vivaciously about many things, eagerly switching the conversation if money threatened to crop up again. She acted the part of a fashionable young woman of position and began to talk of my father's return from the war, and after a time a disquieting note crept into her talk for she began to forget that there was any war at all and took to mentioning names of men long dead. She would not accept defeat but defeat crept up behind her like a stab in the dark. She planned a visit to Sariyer, animatedly promising Mehmet and me a long holiday there, but now and then a little shadow would cross her face as though she knew she was talking nonsense but preferred her nonsense to the unsavoury truth. The more contact she had with the outside world the more she turned her thoughts inwards, the more extravagant became her plans.

I never remember her to be demonstrative, clasping her children to her or kissing them in moments of nearness. We never had any moments of nearness to her but, nevertheless, she remained our only bulwark against the world, our one security. The touch of her cool, remote hand, the rustle of her skirt or the sound of her light, emotionless voice was enough for us. These things could still all our fears or soothe away pain. As time passed, she grew more cordial to the widow below us, although my grandmother did her best to discourage this.

But my mother genuinely liked the widow. She had a sort of sure instinct for human nature, ignoring the outward pattern and swooping down to discover the heart, with a beautiful compassion.

The rest of the street shunned the widow, hinting that she was no better than she should be. My mother, shunned and shunning, had a deep sympathy for this. She would ask the widow to come upstairs and drink coffee, ask her mature advice on the method of making clothes for Mehmet and me, or how to cook such and such a dish. The widow became very grateful for these little attentions from my mother, these subtle flatteries, and rapidly became the devoted slave of the family. She would sit with us and amuse us when my mother was out, wash us and feed us and dandle Muazzez for hours on her capacious knees. She was a sort of unpaid servant, an Inci and a lewd Hacer rolled into one and was, no doubt, very useful to my mother. She even took to preparing all the food for us but this my mother put a stop to, for the widow's hands were seldom clean and she had a habit of scratching her sparse, grey hairs so that some usually fell into whatever it was she was cooking. My mother's passion for cleanliness was as great as her passion—an odd one in the old, vanished Turkey—for fresh air. One morning there was a great knocking at the door and I heard someone asking for my mother. I called out to her and she ran down the stairs, then her voice cried:

'Hasan'!

And whilst I was wondering whom 'Hasan' might be she thanked Bekci Baba for having directed her visitor here. Then I suddenly recognised the voice of the mysterious 'Hasan' and he was no mystery any longer for he was the gardener from Sariyer—the gardener who must be commemorated forever because he liked small boys.

My mother and he came up the narrow stairs and into the salon. Hasan greeted Mehmet and me then with the privilege of a very old family servant, looked all about him and said querulously:

'What is this dreadful place, hanim efendi?' and before waiting for any answer shook his old white head sadly. He peered at my mother with his near-sighted eyes and said uncertainly:

'I went to your house first. Such a shock I got!' he grumbled.

'I did not know it was like that, hanim efendi; the news has not reached Sariyer.' He paused for a long minute, still grumbling into his beard, then continued; 'It was Bekci Baba who directed me to this house. Eh dear, dear! To think of you in a place like this!'

And to my acute embarrassment large tears dropped from his eyes, spilling down his ancient coat.

'Now, Hasan!' said my mother, reprovingly, much as she would speak to one of us children if we too easily gave way to tears.

Hasan wiped his eyes with the back of his hand.

'Ah!' he said deeply and darkly, 'things are altering, hanim efendi. Nobody knows from day to day what will happen next, but to see *you* in a house like *this*——' and he paused, trying to find the right words.

My mother covered the gap by asking swiftly:

'And what news of Sariyer, Hasan?'

The old man's eyes filled with tears again, the weak, easy tears of a very, very old man but I could feel the laughter bubbling up in my throat, like water from a spring well. My mother's eyes reproved my levity, which made me worse, so that I got quite red in the face with the effort to contain myself. But my laughter flew before Hasan's next words, which were so unexpected that they hit my brain like a little series of electric shocks.

'The master is believed dead, hanim efendi——' he said, then broke off to cry bitterly, unable to contain himself any longer and my mother looked over his bent head, blindly and with a face that might have been carved of stone.

'Dead!' she said. 'Ahmet dead!'

And frightened of her white face, I began to cry too and Mehmet followed and pandemonium was let loose in the room. I am sure I did not cry for Uncle Ahmet, being still young enough not to fully appreciate the meaning of the word 'death'. And I did not cry because I would never go to Sariyer again, for that I did not know.

I cried, I suppose, because Hasan cried, because my mother had turned to stone and had gone far away from us and this still, summer room. I cried on and on, bitterly, not knowing why I was crying but liking the noise I was making. Even when the tears had stopped flowing I still cried on, broadcasting my woe to the house-tops and never wishing to stop. There is something so elemental, so primeval about human tears that the sound of them causes ripples and tremors to course up and down the spine and through the blood-stream and my own tears that day had just that effect upon me. It was my mother's sharp, stinging hand on my cheek that made me cease, bringing me up short in the middle of a particularly heart-rending sob.

'Stop!' she cried so imperiously that stop I did immediately, my mouth still foolishly open but no sound emerging. Mehmet and I were sent to the sofa, in the far corner of the room, where we gulped and sniffled our way back to sanity.

'Hasan,' I heard my mother say gently, 'tell me all about it. How did your mistress discover?'

The old man made a valiant effort to recover himself and after a moment or two, began to speak.

'My mistress has been worrying for many months and last week she sent me to the War Office to ask if they knew anything about my master. But they knew little there. At last a Colonel was found who said my master was believed dead. They know nothing else about him. Nothing!'

'But that is terrible,' said my mother in an odd sort of voice and was my father's image in her eyes, I wonder?

Hasan continued:

'My mistress took the news very hardly, hanim efendi. She has not eaten for three days now and her cough does not get any better. Last night she had a hæmorrhage.'

'Poor Ayşe,' said my mother. 'Of course we guessed she had consumption——'

'Do not tell this news to the old lady,' warned Hasan, the 'old lady' being my respected grandmother, who would have been most indignant had she heard this term applied to herself.

'Certainly I shall not,' said my mother. 'But she is sure to find out. Oh, Hasan, the terrible things that are happening. All the doors are closing one by one and all the happy families dying. Oh, Hasan!' and she covered her face with her hands but she did not cry.

This was another thing to be bottled up, to be pushed into the back of her mind and not to be thought about, until one day the top would come flying off and all these fearsome things leap out at her with a snarl.

'It is the will of God,' said Hasan simply, and my mother uncovered her face and said:

'A hard will, Hasan.'

'Do not say such things!' cried the old man, forgetting his sorrow, so thoroughly scandalised was he that a woman should question the will of God.

My mother ignored his remark and said instead:

'Do not tell your mistress of the fire, not just yet anyway. She has enough trouble now and the fire is over and my house gone and talking will not bring it back. We are comfortable enough here——'

Her eyes ranged round the room uncertainly, as though seeking reassurance of comfort.

The old man got ready to leave, placing a basket of food on the table and my mouth began to water as I saw the contents being emptied. My mother thanked him and he looked sad and doubtful, as though reluctant to leave. But he bowed to her and spoke a few more words, then went shuffling down the stairs and we could hear him muttering to himself all the way down.

My mother sat in a chair, looking as if she wanted to cry but habit was too strong in her and she held back the treacherous tears. She sat looking into space and presently a little smile touched her lips and I wondered what memory it was that had the power to over-ride her sorrow for Uncle Ahmet, so strong to bring light to her eyes and awareness of Mehmet and me, who sat watching her.

'You must not say anything to your grandmother,' she warned sternly and we replied that we would not and then she left us, to continue with the work which Hasan's visit had interrupted.

Mehmet immediately forgot why he had been so recently crying and went back to play, his thin, brown face sharp with anxiety because a certain brick would not stand up on top of another. I watched him for a moment or two, then said:

'Let me show you,' and I took the bricks from his docile, clever fingers. 'There!' I said, when I had finished, 'that is the way you must build them.'

He looked at the edifice I had erected, then patiently, one by one, he pulled down all the bricks again and commenced to build them his own way. The gaily painted bricks toppled and swayed in their insecure positions and fell to the floor and

Mehmet sat thoughtfully back on his heels, jabbing at them with his fingers, his little face still sharp with anxiety.

I left him to it and went to examine the precious things which had been sent from Sariyer. There was a mountain of rice, a fat chicken, butter more golden than shop butter could ever be, large brown speckled eggs and home-made bread. I pulled a brown crust from the bread and began to eat it with appetite. Sorrows there might be in the world and in my family but childhood's especial world revolves around a crust of fresh bread.

It was inconceivable that my mother should imagine my grandmother would not find out about Uncle Ahmet's death. I prefer to say 'death' and not 'supposed death' for two reasons. Firstly, his death was afterwards officially confirmed. Secondly, the War Office of that time was in such a state of flux, so confused and incapable in fact, that alive but missing soldiers were not infrequently listed as dead, even though they might turn up afterwards. But the War Office never rectified their mistakes, perhaps feeling that in the present state of things most of the so-called missing soldiers would eventually be dead anyway. It became fairly obvious to the people then that anyone listed and notified as supposed dead was as dead as he would ever be.

But to return to my grandmother. Hasan had not long left us when she came angrily into the house, demanding coffee and the reason for Hasan's mysterious visit. My mother looked astonished and enquired how my grandmother could possibly know of his visit.

'I heard it,' snapped my grandmother, furious because Hasan had not paid his respects to her and suspicious that my mother had been told something she had a right to know as well.

My mother said, rather faintly for her, that Hasan had merely brought a basket of food for us. And having said that much, she sat looking at my grandmother, as though the old lady was displaying almost supernatural powers in having known at all that anyone out of the usual had called at our house that day.

My grandmother sat stiff as a ramrod in her chair and demanded what news there was of Sariyer.

'Oh, everything is very well there,' said my mother rather hurriedly but going red and white by turns, with such rapidity that my grandmother must have wondered what on earth was wrong with her.

Mehmet strolled over to my grandmother and with three-years-old unconcern, lisped:

'Sariyer,' and I was terrified that he would remember something of this morning's conversation, some isolated word perhaps, that would tell my grandmother everything. Perhaps I looked anxious for she suddenly said to me:

'What is wrong?'

And I sulkily replied that nothing was wrong and Mehmet, with infinite baby cunning and perhaps scenting that something out of the ordinary was in the wind, plucked at her sleeve, reiterating insistently:

'Mehmet cried! Mehmet cried!'

And when she would not take any notice of him, for she did not know the dangerous thing he was trying to tell her, he pulled at her skirt in a gust of temper.

'Cried!' he said to her but she freed herself from his grasp and my mother's arrival with coffee distracted everyone's attention.

My grandmother drank her coffee as if it were poison and kept making obscure references to Sariyer and Uncle Ahmet, until I thought my mother would faint with the effort to suppress the truth. Once she almost gave herself away for she indiscreetly mentioned that she was thinking of going to the War Office to see if they could give any news of my father. Naturally, my grandmother pounced on this, demanding to know who had been putting such ideas into my mother's head. The latter replied rather vaguely that nobody had said anything, that she had just thought of the idea herself. My grandmother looked at her fixedly.

'Şevkiye,' she accused, 'you are keeping something from me.'

Her perception seemed to us uncanny and even though my mother protested that she had nothing to keep back from anyone, still she warned me with her eyes to take Mehmet to a corner where we could play and from where he would not be likely to give away any secrets. For he was determined to attract my grandmother's attention and would not leave her side and, when she was leaving, beamed proudly at her, saying very distinctly: 'Dead! Dead!'

But my grandmother, strangely enough, had no idea of the frightful thing he meant and my mother interrupted Mehmet's words so smoothly that their gruesomeness was unnoticed.

But perhaps she remembered their message later for we did not see her for a few days and then, when she did come, there was such a wailing and a gnashing of teeth as there never has been in the world before. Her visit did not start like that, of course. In fact it started remarkably normally, with my grandmother sweeping in to demand coffee, very controlled even though a little red about the eyes. My mother just looked at her incredulously for a moment or two, then said:

'You have been to Sariyer.'

And then everything happened at once. My grandmother's face crumpled and she began to cry, but not silently as Hasan had done, but noisily and desperately as though a great well was suddenly finding release. Her tears and her ugly, working face frightened me and I held tightly to my mother's hand, for never had the world seemed so full of tears as latterly. These last weeks had been steeped in tears. The world had become a grim place where people lost their homes and died in unknown places, where women struggled and grew irritable and wept, wept, wept. The appalling sorrows of the moment weighed me down and I started to cry too. When peace had been more or less restored, by the application of sharp words from my mother and still sharper slaps, Mehmet and I were sent to our corner and commanded to play! As if we could play when the pandemonium of my grandmother's tears filled the room! She wept unceasingly, as though she shed tears not only for her own son that day but for all humanity. After a long time she stopped and my mother pressed cognac on her, forcing her to drink it. There was little affection in my mother's attitude towards her, for these two were never to know affection. Yet that day they clung very closely, each depending upon the other for strength to bear these blows from life.

At last my grandmother said:

'My son is dead and my daughter Ayşe is dead and I have nobody left in the world.'

'Ayşe?' asked my mother, in a disbelieving voice and perhaps feeling affronted that my grandmother had regarded her as nobody.

But my grandmother could not answer. She only rocked her body to and fro in an extremity of grief for her eldest born, who was dead. She was almost incoherent with her great grief,

Aunt Ayşe's death appearing a mere incidental in the face of this larger, more suffocating grief.

But eventually my mother extracted the whole story. It ran something like this. My grandmother had left our house dissatisfied with my mother's explanation of Hasan's visit. She had brooded over it all day, finally recollecting Mehmet's abortive attempts to tell her something—something she became sure which was connected with Sariyer. After a sleepless night she had arisen the next morning, determined to go to Sariyer immediately. She had informed her astonished husband of this, taken a maid as chaperone—for whereas she might visit us unescorted, to journey alone as far as Sariyer was quite another matter—and had feverishly hurried to the boat.

Upon arrival at Sariyer she had been met by red-eyed servants, the sight of whom had further increased her alarm, and they had told her that Aunt Ayşe had died early that morning. My grandmother bore up reasonably well under this news and thought her deep, urgent sense of premonition had come from this. She had liked Aunt Ayşe but after all she was only a daughter-in-law, and the women of old Turkey did not attach a great deal of importance to such a relationship. Nobody, at that time, mentioned my uncle, and as a consequence, not knowing of the greater shock that lay before her, my grandmother, although feeling sorrow at Aunt Ayşe's untimely death, nevertheless was able competently to take charge of the situation. My aunt had died as the result of a violent hæmorrhage, which a doctor, had he been available, would have been unable to check.

All this was explained to her by the doctor who had been afterwards called by the terrified servants and who had waited in the house for my grandmother's arrival. He had been startled to hear that no message had been received by her from Sariyer and that her presence here now was pure chance, due to her alarming premonition that something had been wrong. They had sat and talked in the silent, sun-drenched salon that looked out over the gardens of Sariyer, now at their most beautiful. The salon had affected my grandmother unbearably for it looked so ready for occupation, as though it awaited the step of its mistress. Great jars of white lilac, gathered by Aunt Ayşe the day before, stood about on little tables, overpowering the still room with its cloying, sweet perfume.

Later in the morning a notary arrived, to explain that
Sariyer and all its land and farms now reverted back to Aunt
Ayşe's family, to a brother who was a Cavalry officer away at the
War. He had patiently explained to my grandmother's mis-
understanding face that Aunt Ayşe had died intestate and *after*
Uncle Ahmet, therefore according to law the property would
go to any members remaining from her family. This was the
first intimation my grandmother had received that her beloved
son was dead and she had promptly fainted. But when she had
been revived, although still stunned by the terrible news, she
had been able to arrange about the burial of my aunt, dismiss
servants, all of them bewildered and wondering where to go for
they had preferred the servitude of Sariyer to the doubtful
freedom of being alone. She had arranged that all the furniture
should be shrouded and had finally, that same afternoon, seen
Aunt Ayşe lowered into her lonely grave—for burial is swift in
Turkey, the summer climate being unkind to the newly dead.
Then she had bade farewell to Sariyer, lovely under the June
sun, empty now and tenantless with only the fading memory
of our laughter to echo now and then in ghostly fashion. And
my grandmother had returned to Istanbul, seeing no beauty
now in the lovely, sweeping lines of the Bosphor's shores,
anxious only to come to my mother to cry her heart out. So
she sat in her chair all through the day and rocked herself to
and fro, and when the great tide of grief was exhausted the
sun was far down the sky, the first evening yogurtcu coming up
the street. My grandmother moved her stiffened, weary body
and prepared to go to her home. Her face was grey and brittle-
looking and I do not think that anything else in life ever hurt
her again as much as this, the loss of her favourite, her best
beloved.

Mehmet at Kuleli

The author, aged 17

The author, aged 22, at Harbiye. 25th December 1930

Bedia and Mehmet, with the author's grandmother
19th October 1939

CHAPTER XII

DISILLUSIONMENT OF AN AUTOCRAT

Death.

The world seemed suddenly full of the word and the noise of women weeping. All down the street news had begun to arrive of sons and brothers and fathers who had been killed at the front. There were no heated arguments now with the street sellers. The women wearily bought what they could afford, the young boys went off to join their fathers in the fighting and the street was given over to the dribbling babies and the dogs and the ever-ravenous cats. Each waking day brought fresh news from the front, of the appalling casualties we were suffering, and the Red Crescent trains came faster and thicker than ever, bringing the wounded and dying to Istanbul. There was not a woman in the little street but had someone at the front, even the widow downstairs, whose only son was away. Food was scarcer than ever, even if one had the money to buy it, and the Bourse Noir flourished unchecked and people dropped in the streets for lack of nourishment. My grandmother had been in the habit of sending storable foods to us but she too stopped this practice. My mother would make soups for us from a handful of lentils or dried peas, or serve plain, boiled haricot beans, conserving such precious items as rice and flour or olive oil for the leaner times just around the corner. Still she spent weary hours at the baker's, sometimes returning with bread, more often empty-handed. And we were always hungry, always longing for fresh, crusty slices of the bread we could not get.

During the mornings I would be left alone with Mehmet and Muazzez. Mehmet was docile enough but Muazzez used to drive me into a frenzy of exasperation and fear for she would cry so lustily that she became quite purple in the face with rage. She cried if I rocked the cradle, she cried if I did not, her eyes tearless and her screams shrill and unceasing. My mother would leave a bottle of milk for her, wrapped in a piece of material to keep it warm, and this I would thrust exasperatedly at her, trying to quiet her but it had no effect. One morning she was so terrible that by the time my mother returned, I was in tears myself. I told her what was wrong and she lifted the now docile Muazzez, dandling her and calling me over to look at the pretty thing.

'I hate her!' I burst out passionately, stubbing my toe against the foot of the cradle, and the moment she heard my voice Muazzez, the little tyrant, commenced to wail loudly again.

My mother was upset by my truculent attitude and, perhaps as some sort of reward, sent Mehmet and me into the street to play, telling us not to move from the front door. But when my grandmother, later in the day, came down the street she was so scandalised to see us playing like street urchins, to quote her, that she was quite cool with my mother for the rest of the time and accused her of bringing us up very badly.

She was in a gloomy mood that day, complaining that she could not remain long with us as the old man was not too well and had, latterly, taken to demanding her at all impossible hours of the day and night and had renewed his command that she should no longer visit us. She watched my mother's efforts to make clothes for us on the sewing-machine and interfered so much that she quite upset my mother, who in the end was unable to do anything more so long as my grandmother remained.

That evening she made an odd sort of dummy for Muazzez. It was made of muslin and filled with cleaned sultanas and she told me to, in future, stick it into her mouth when she commenced to cry and I was alone with her. She also taught me an old Turkish nursery rhyme, which she not only forced me to sing to her but called up the widow to listen to my voice. I was sure the rhyme would be worse than useless to quiet Muazzez but my mother, lamenting for Inci, looked so sad that I promised her I would try. This was the song:—

> 'Dan dini dan dini das dana,
> Danalar girmiş bostana
> Kov bostançi danayi,
> Yemesinler lahanyi. . . .'

which defies translation but means something to the effect that the little water-buffalo are in the garden and an injunction to the gardener to push them out before they eat all the cabbages! The soft, soothing words brought back memories of

Inci crooning it over Mehmet's cradle. So far as I could remember, the soporific effect on Mehmet had been remarkable and I hoped it would be as successful with my sister. I had the opportunity of judging this the next day and was so relieved when it actually worked that I did not know whether to laugh or cry and was afraid of doing either for fear I should re-awaken the sleeping angel. So the daily round continued, with my grandmother continuing to supply money and my mother growing accustomed to marketing. My father seemed to have dropped entirely from our minds, so little was his name mentioned, and if my grandmother were to say his name it hit the senses like a little shock—as though she spoke of someone a long time dead. He had become a dim, far figure, not easily remembered and so sentimentalised by my grandmother that it was not easy to recognise my flesh-and-blood father from the overdrawn, romantic figure she painted.

The street too had grown used to us and had even begun to nod to my mother. Sometimes they would beg her to do some little thing for them, perhaps decipher a letter from a Government office, reply to one or merely how to write a letter to their loved ones. Whatever it was they asked her, she did with unfailing good humour and tact. She became so well known for this latter characteristic that in the end Bekci Baba would ask her to impart the bad news that he had no heart to face. He had had so much bad news since the war had started that the imparting of it should have inured him to the grief of the women, but he was old and tender-hearted and tears struck deep into his heart, and he never delivered a War Office message without inextricably entangling himself in the toils of the recipient's woe. So he ranged himself alongside my mother, often asking her advice before presenting himself before a fateful door. She became greatly loved in the street. In time, as I grew older, I have seen the women of that street showering kisses over her hands, whilst they called from their hearts, 'Melek!' (angel). If she suspected that a family was hungry she would take something to them, presenting it in such a way that offence could not be taken. She was generally the first to be found at the bedside of the sick or dying and received many last-minute instructions or confessions. She poured out whatever tenderness she had on the poor and many died with her name on their lips. The halt and maimed who returned from the front aroused her especial pity and she was never too tired to answer their appeals to her. I suppose that against the general social standards prevailing in our street we were comparatively wealthy. The women automatically called her 'hanim efendi'—a title, in old Turkey, used only for the better classes. They would ask her opinion on everything to do with their family life, feeling no embarrassment in acquainting her with the more intimate details.

As that year drew to a close she worried incessantly over my schooling, for I was almost seven and entirely ignorant. She had taught me the alphabet and kept my Turkish pure but she knew only the barest rudiments of arithmetic and a little polite French, which could not equip me for the battle of life. Most of the district schools were closed through lack of teaching staff and were being used by the Red Crescent as military hospitals for the emergency treatment of casualties. So when my mother had taught me the little she knew herself, I languished both mentally and physically, and learned instead how to peel potatoes and rock my sister to sleep.

Winter began early and coal was scarce, of poor quality and very dear. My grandmother provided us with a winter's supply which we supplemented with logs of firewood and huddled over the little stove in the salon—cold because of the lack of proper food and because of the poor quality of the wool with which our jerseys had been knitted.

There was much sickness in the street and death weeded out the old and the infirm and the very young. My mother was kept busy going from one house to another giving advice or consolation or merely holding the hand of the one who was left. Then came a time when she herself fell sick and the fever came back to her and she cried out in her delirium, but this time there was no fashionable physician to visit her many times in a day, for almost all the doctors had gone to the War and the few who remained were too busy to visit badly paying patients in poor districts.

But the street surged in to help her. Thin old women looking like crows in their black clothes, black çarşafs tightly binding their foreheads, would sit beside her bed and give her sips of water or rub her forehead with eau-de-Cologne to cool the surface blood and so help reduce the fever. Loving and dirty hands washed and dressed and fed us children and laid us in our beds at night then went back to the more serious business of tending my mother. Curious groping fingers sought for lice in our heads and drew back disappointed because none were to be found. They rocked Muazzez all day long and sang 'Nini' to her when they wanted her to sleep, and she would lie regarding them with alert, bright eyes and was never known to cry in their presence. Other thin black crows would do the washing on the gloomy landing, silently and grimly, and I was so afraid of them that I used to creep past them and sit perched in my corner seat, longing for my mother to be well again. When my grandmother called they would try to ingratiate themselves into her favour—reporting the progress or lack of progress, as the case might be, of the patient, recite a long, interminable list of what they had done, bow deeply and wait for further instructions. She was terribly, embarrassingly autocratic with them, treating them as her servants, but it was not she who kept them loyal to our house. They loved my mother and this was their only way of repaying her kindnesses to themselves.

Day and night the house was filled with them and they were roughly kind to Mehmet and me and spent the money my grandmother gave them as honestly as she would have spent it herself. Their own children were blissfully permitted to go about the day long in dirt but poor Mehmet and I were unmercifully scrubbed twenty times or more in a day for they felt that super cleanliness must be one of the peculiar attributes of the upper classes. They expended more time and energy over us than Inci had ever done. They would remove their shoes before entering the bedrooms or the sitting-room, exclaiming over the softness of the carpets against their bare feet. They would examine all my mother's table- and bed-linen with rough red hands—gloat over the silver and polish it until the old treasures were in danger of snapping under their hurrying fingers. Inquisitive hands pried everywhere. Nothing was safe from them. Curtains were touched joyously and held against the cheek, china examined to see how fine and delicate it was, and then in the midst of their wanderings through the three rooms in search of more treasures to gloat over they would espy Mehmet and me and they would sweep delightedly down on us, gathering us against their withered bosoms and proceed to take the skin off us once more with yet another washing.

The relief when at last my mother was able to get up again!
Her illness had seemed like years and years to us and when she
saw our faces and hands and bodies shining from all the soap
that had been used on us she commenced to cry, saying we
looked too clean. We hastened to assure her it was all a mistake
and that left to ourselves it would never have occurred to us
to be so clean and she commenced to laugh, the tears still
shining in her eyes, and she said that anyway the neighbours
had been very kind. We could not answer this—feeling that
there were limits to kindness.

One morning a few months later, when my mother was
thoroughly well again, a servant called from my grandmother's
house to say that the old man was dead. This was a great
shock for my mother had not heard he was ill. The servant
explained that it was a heart attack and that my grandmother
was overcome with shock for it was she who had discovered him.
My mother was asked to return with the servant but this she
refused to do. It was a strange thing for she never spared herself for other people and this reluctance to go to my grandmother's home was a new thing for her. But perhaps she knew
that genuine grief calls for every effort whereas the grief manifest by my grandmother was a purely synthetic thing to impress
outsiders.

Whatever the true refusal of my mother she did not speak
about it to us, and later that day, when the curtains were already
drawn and the lamps lit, my grandmother arrived. She looked
tired and a little frightened, disposed to be short-tempered
with my mother. For a long time she ignored her, taking to
Mehmet and me, and my mother lay back in her long chair and
refused to ask any questions. This attitude piqued my grandmother and when at length she could no longer bear it, she
burst out that my mother grew more and more callous and that
she had expected her to at least have asked after the state of
my grandmother's nerves—which were, she declared, simply
shocking. She conventionally squeezed a few tears from her
eyes and lamented her husband but with so little enthusiasm
that at last she gave up even trying to deceive herself. She was
attempting to whip up a decorous picture of herself, the new
widow, weeping for her husband as if her marriage had been
a normal friendly, happy one. She said that she intended
to spend the night with us for she could not bear to go

back to that dreaded house. My mother said nothing. Then my grandmother, all decorousness swept away, said with animation that now she was a very rich woman and that we would all go to live in her house. She said we would never have to worry again about money or anything else and waited for my mother's comments. She became more and more spry and my mother began to laugh at her but very soon she herself became infected with enthusiasm. There was only one small, rather insignificant fly in the ointment but it was large enough to occasionally dampen happiness. Apparently after the old man's death the Notary who held his will had been summoned, also the nephew who controlled his various business concerns. The nephew had said to her:

'Well, Fatma hanim, what are we going to do with you, I wonder?'

And had added that anyway, this was not the time to discuss these things and that they would inform her later of the terms of the will.

'What do you think he meant by that?' my grandmother kept asking my mother, but the latter replied that everything would be all right since she had been the old man's wife and had first rights of the property.

'Are you sure?' my grandmother wanted to know doubtfully and sunk her chin on her hands and went into a reverie. She got quite peevish because my mother suggested we wait a few months before we moved to her house, so that the neighbours would not be given any opportunity to talk unkindly behind us.

'Neighbours!' snapped my grandmother and with that one word withered us all.

After Mehmet and I were sent to bed we heard their argumentative voices rolling back and forth in battle for a long time until finally we went to sleep.

A few days later my mother accompanied my grandmother to see the Notary and the nephew and we were left in the charge of the widow. I watched them walking down the street, my mother pulling black gloves over her hands, her step firm and confident and my grandmother beside her, very upright and looking anything but a bereaved widow.

Later that day they returned looking no different perhaps to the uninitiated eye but to Mehmet and me there was a certain grimness to be noted about the mouth and eyes, sufficient reason to keep us angelically quiet and not to ask questions. We heard no mention of going to live in my grandmother's house and the next day a porter arrived with her remaining furniture from her old home. I was very curious and wondered where it was going to be put. An outsize in china cabinets ousted me from the door and when a console table followed it I retreated into the farthest corner of the salon and thought that if any more furniture came in I should be buried under it. A covered ottoman was carried into my mother's room, Muazzez's cradle having to be moved to make room for it. Tin chests arrived and the porters were told to leave them on the landing since there was no room anywhere else. Every available inch of space seemed crowded and our rooms looked terrible, all the spacious gaiety so carefully arranged by my mother fled. Amidst all the confusion she moved tight-lipped and uncompromising yet with a contradictory air of serenity which I had not seen for a long time. I was aching to ask questions but was cowed into silence by my grandmother's attitude.

Soon after that the widow moved from the downstairs rooms and went to live farther down the street and my grandmother moved in to take her place. Furniture was re-arranged but there was still far too much of it and everywhere looked ugly and overcrowded and the tin chests remained filled and carpets were hung on the walls because there was no room for them on the floors and the rooms took on a dull, darkened look.

For many days my grandmother was very subdued and quarrelled with my mother on the slightest provocation, reminding her frequently whose money was buying our food and the clothes we were wearing. This was so out of character that we could not but deduce that something very seriously was amiss. And indeed it was!

Her late husband had exacted his revenge on her. He had cut her completely from his will, leaving her penniless. All his property and ready monies had gone to his nephew—to-day to be found in America, the old house in Bayazit closed and shuttered. The house where we were living was left to my mother, for her life-time or for as long as she cared to live there —afterwards reverting to his nephew. He had not even stipulated the use of one room for my grandmother, ignoring her existence as completely as if she had never been his wife.

All of this I learned from my mother when I was older, when we had lived in that house for many years. My grandmother always remained with us, but never docilely. She never mentioned the old man's name but took to talking about my grandfather, as if the past year of marriage was only a dream. She became suddenly very religious but remained autocratic to the end of her days, for that trait in her would never die until she did.

CHAPTER XIII

NINETY-NINE KURUŞ IN EXCHANGE FOR A HERO

WITH MY GRANDMOTHER'S arrival at our house, life became easier for me, since she began to look after Muazzez whenever my mother was out. But the cramped, communal life of a small house did not suit her temper however, and she was more than ever uncertain and hard to please these days. She objected to Mehmet and me playing in the salon, regardless of the fact that there was no other place for us. So we took to accompanying my mother to the market-place, in order to let my grandmother have the house to herself. We depended upon her too to get any food, for my mother had long since exhausted her own meagre supply of money.

My grandmother kept all her money and valuables in a large tin chest in her bedroom, the keys of which she always carried with her. This habit annoyed my mother and she ached to be independent. My grandmother continuously grumbled about expenses but would not forego her wine for dinner. In her especially bad times she would tell us that my father still owed her money from the sale of the business—which was totally untrue, since she had never been left any ready money by my grandfather. We ate poor-quality food and this, she complained, upset her stomach. She insisted on snowy table-linen, despite the fact that soap was expensive and hard to obtain, and would not countenance the same table-cloth on two occasions. She sometimes bought little luxury foods and then said that we ate too much. She never forgot she had been a lady and would sit idle in the salon, whilst my mother toiled in the kitchen, cooking the choice dishes she still demanded. Muazzez was the only one of us she seemed to like and she spent a great deal of her time petting and spoiling her, and then complained to my mother that the child was unmanageable. News reached us that Orhan Bey, the husband of Madame Müjğan, had been killed, and the names of other men and boys they had known also died from the lips, for one did not like to talk too much about the peaceful dead.

One morning my mother excitedly returned from the market with news that a Unit had returned from the Dardanelles to Yeşilköy and that perhaps my father was with them.

This caused a great deal of speculation amongst us but finally my grandmother declared it to be nonsense, since if my father had got as near to home as Yeşilköy, he would somehow or other have sent a message to us. But my mother was not to be so easily turned from the scent. The sons and husbands of other old neighbours had come back to Yeşilköy—why not my father? So one early morning she set off for Yeşilköy, taking me with her for company. We took the train from Sirkeci station and I was very thrilled, for it was the first time I had ever been on a train. Despite my mother's warnings, I could not sit still but had to thoroughly inspect knobs and handles and the tattered upholstery of the seats and, a dozen times or more, poked my head out of the window to watch the exciting country flying past us. I was in a seventh heaven of delight, for riding in this train was far more fun even than it had been to ride behind Murat in the old days. I suppose I was not especially curious about meeting my father, being too thrilled with the noise the train was making and the shrill, almost continuous sound of the whistle. I was very disappointed when we at last reached our destination, and as my mother hurried me along the platform I kept looking regretfully back to the great, dark monster which had transported us here.

My mother enquired from the station-master how far it was to the Military Camp and he looked doubtfully at her thin, lady-like shoes and replied that it was a long walk. His tone implied doubt that she would ever make it but he directed her the road to follow. We set out along the bare winter road, but that day there seemed to be just the littlest hint of Spring in the air, but long before we reached the Camp our pace slackened. Many times we halted to get our breaths back and to ease our aching feet, for the road was bad and our footwear light. At length we came to the top of the last hill and there, at our feet, lay the Camp with its camouflaged tents.

Excitement lent new wings to my mother and in any case it was far easier to descend the hill than it had been to ascend it. We met only a peasant, with his mule, on the way down and everywhere was very still with that stillness especial to the country, only the caw-cawing of the crows to now and then disturb it. When at last we reached the camp we were breathless, and when an officer, in a very ragged uniform, came forward to ask our business, my mother had considerable difficulty in answering him at all. She explained however why she had come and he looked vague for a moment or two, as though the name of my father perhaps struck a chord somewhere in his memory. With very great courtesy he begged my mother to wait a little whilst he made enquiries. He walked away from us and when I turned to say something to my mother, I was amazed to see that her eyes were filled with tears. A few spilled down her face and she said:

'Poor man! He looks so tired and shabby and did you notice that he had his arm and his shoulder bandaged? That means he has been wounded and should be in hospital and not walking about this camp——'

And I had a horrible moment of remembering the first words of the song they had sung when they took my father to the War.

'Ey, gaziler . . .', they had sung ('oh, wounded ones . . .'), and my heart began to beat unevenly, for fear my mother should remember too, or read the words in my eyes.

Presently two soldiers came towards us and I held my breath expectantly as my mother gave a little gasp.

'Can it be your father?' she said in an unsteady sort of voice and I started to run towards the soldiers, but she called me back.

'Don't go,' she said. 'They are neither of them your father.'

And she sat down again to wait until they came up to us and there was a dull, flat expression on her face that heightened the cheekbones and broadened the nostrils.

As the soldiers came abreast of us we saw that they were officers although their uniforms too were so shabby that, but for the insignia of rank on their shoulders, we could not have distinguished them from the soldiers.

'Ali Bey!' she cried to one of the officers and he saluted her, going red with some sort of emotion that I should never know, and I looked at him curiously, wondering who he might be and how my mother knew him.

She asked eagerly for news of my father and he looked uncertainly at her as though perhaps weighing up her capabilities for shock, then he said slowly:

'We left him to his God a long time ago——' and paused wondering what else there was to say to her.

Although her face was whiter than I had ever seen it in my life, she said with swift impatience:

'Yes? Go on! I want to know whatever it is you have to tell me.'

Then the man called Ali, who was a captain, plunged into conversation to tell her this story.

On the march to the Dardanelles my father had suffered badly from foot trouble. He had to march day and night, night and day, and his feet began to swell and in the end they had had to cut his torn boots off him. The two feet were found to be badly infected right up to the ankles and soaked in fresh, bright blood. He had been left by the roadside, as was the custom, and they had called back down the lines that a wounded man lay under a tree. And eventually this message would reach the end of the marching lines where a horse-drawn cart lumbered for the express purpose of picking up the sick and wounded. But if the cart was already full to overflowing with all the other sick soldiers who had dropped out on the way? Ah well—in that case a man just lay by the side of the road under the blazing sun and waited for the next lot of marching soldiers to take up the same old cry, that a man lay wounded under the trees by the side of an alien road. Down, down the weary lines the cry would go, but perhaps by the time the sick-cart reached the spot a man would be dead and there was not much point in carrying a dead man—when there were so many living who still might be saved. But of course, Captain Ali hastened to assure my mother my father was picked up and taken to a Base hospital—where he died.

As he told her all these unsavoury things, his pale face flickered and his eyes were loth to meet hers—for how could he tell this white, courageous woman that neither he nor anyone else knew where her husband had died? But she persisted in subjecting herself to this useless agony, demanding the name of the hospital—as if the young Captain could have told her, even supposing he knew. He was infinitely patient, holding himself stiffly to attention, assuring her that everything that could have been done had been done. And in the end she had to be contented, for there was nothing else he could tell her. So she thanked him and he saluted her, as one brave soldier to another, and she took my hand and we began the long trudge back to the station.

She did not speak to me at all but walked as if mechanically propelled, never slackening or altering her pace, although my small legs were breaking under me. I begged her to sit down, to let me rest, crying in my tiredness and with cold, for the day had become overcast and all signs of Spring had left the air. I tottered beside her and plucked at her skirt and she looked at me, as if she did not recognise me, as if I had brought her back from some far place, and I cried all the more bitterly in this new loneliness. Then I saw expression creep into her dead eyes and she caught me to her and sat down with me in a ditch.

'Poor tired boy!' she said over and over again, as though she knew no other words or as though this repetition would still remembrance of something else, something that lurked in the foreground of the mind and would not be pushed back, back with all those other memories that could not be looked upon because they were still too new.

She put her arms around me and repeated her meaningless refrain and frightened me unendurably, for her arms held no security and her voice no comfort and I did not know if she were speaking to me or to some image of my father, whom she held in her empty, rocking arms.

Back home, the wind of discontent blew coldly through the house. My mother became almost unapproachable and hard as we had never known her before. My grandmother forgot her grumblings and walked silently before such coldness and insensibility. Back to those days flies memory to feel again the soft breath of fear on the cheeks, to feel the slow ice around the heart and the feathery, barely perceptible insecurity that crept up on a child. I would catch sight of my mother, sitting idly at her work in the kitchen, or looking steadily at some half-finished piece of sewing in her hands, her face expressing surprise that she should be holding anything, for she could not remember having picked it up. In her eyes would wander a gentle vagueness, its harsh shadow flitting now and then across her face, darkening sanity—although a child's mind did not put it like that. A child was conscious only of strangeness, and she would not emerge from her dreams of the past, even though her children pulled at her arms and their cries beat on her brain.

She shut herself away from them all and sat silent for long stretches and became strange and odd and absent-minded. And fear flourished in the little house, in the unreasoning, illogical way fear will. Whatever she did, she did with the heartless precision of the automatic and was never heard to mention my father or wonder about the future. My grandmother would try to rouse her out of this lethargic state, suggesting with intentional brutality that she should go to the War Office and find out what she could about my father. At these times my mother would look with her vague look at my grandmother, and one could feel the difficulties she was having in focusing her attention on what had been said to her. Then she would turn her head away and say fretfully that she did not want to discuss the matter and my grandmother would retire, defeated, helpless in the face of such implacability.

It was about this time too that my grandmother became almost totally deaf and her thick, dark hair showed more and more grey and began to fall out. Decay and rot were setting in everywhere.

The day eventually came of course when my mother seemed to grow out of her morbidity, when her eyes showed alert awareness again and she took an interest in those about her. Just as she had been listless before, now she was teeming with energy as though long sojourn with grief had revitalised her. She spoke of going to the War Office, and when she had made the decision, was impatient to be off at once. We were left to my grandmother, who nowadays seemed bowed and old, mumbling into the Koran most of the day, doling out money from her tin-chest without murmur or protest. The day my mother went to the War Office, she sat in the salon, reading from the Koran, talking to herself in a loud, grumbling voice for she was so deaf that she did not realise she spoke aloud. By the time my mother returned we were starving, for my grandmother could not be weaned from her prayers to prepare a meal for us.

My mother looked tired herself and clicked her teeth exasperatedly when she saw that nothing had been prepared for her. She went to the kitchen, Mehmet and I excitedly running around her, the good smell of cooking that she was creating causing our mouths to water and our empty stomachs to ache. She was unusually patient with us, ignoring it when we snatched eagerly at the fresh, crusty outside of the bread she had brought home with her. When all was ready, we were told to call my grandmother and we bellowed loudly from the foot of the stairs and, reluctantly, she put away her Koran and came down to eat.

My mother told us of her day. The War Office had been crowded with other black-clad, anxious women, demanding news of their husbands. Harassed officials had bleated that no information could be given and had attempted to restore law and order and dignity to the War Office. But to have restored these that day would have required a Herculean effort, more than the few officials between them could manage, and one of them had retired to get more help. My mother had stood for hours in that smelling, angry queue of humanity, eventually learning that what she had been told by Captain Ali, at Yeşilköy, had been true. The records showed that my father had been dead for many months. Timidly, my mother had asked where he died, and the official, dealing with her, had snapped that he could not be expected to know everything. Surely it was enough for her to know that her husband was dead?

'But are you sure?' my mother had pleaded, impotent against such open, uncaring cruelty. 'I have received no confirmation from you. Why did you not let me know before this, without my having to come here?'

The official had broken into her words brutally, saying:

'Hanim, your husband is dead, and with so many dead and dying we *cannot* be expected to notify everyone!'

My mother, remembering, said that he had spoken with great petulance, as though she and all the other unhappy women waiting here were in some way responsible for the deaths of their menfolk, thereby causing this gallant young man a great deal of unnecessary trouble.

She had wanted to ask him something else but he had forestalled her, slamming the wooden window-shutter in her face, so that she had been forced to retire. She said that all about her the women were being treated in the same way. Crying, wailing, beseeching for information, old ones and young ones with babies, being unceremoniously pushed back from the enquiry windows. Then one woman, driven beyond endurance, commenced to shout insults whilst she held her startled baby above her head.

'Dogs!' she had shouted passionately. 'My husband left five

children behind him, and a mother to support. Are *you* going to support them, you miserable sons of bitches? Did my husband ask to be taken from his work and his family to fight for people like you? Will you give us food to put in our hungry stomachs? Do you care if we go hungry and naked, if strange men insult us in the streets or if our children die of disease and starvation? Our husbands died to save their country and then bastards like you shut the windows in our faces, because we ask for news——'

She had been roughly handled by the police and dragged, screaming further abuse, from the building. My mother, re-telling her story, became heated for the injustice done to that woman and to all the women of Turkey.

'She was right, right!' she insisted passionately to my grandmother's disdainful face. 'And she was no street-woman either and she would never have said what she did say without provocation. We didn't ask for this war. My poor, wise Hüsnü was right when he once said that the conceit of a few men could ruin our country.'

She commenced to cry bitterly, my grandmother stirring uneasily in her chair. She was so deaf that she had heard only part of my mother's speech and she did not know what to do to give comfort.

My mother raised her head to look at my grandmother.

'If we had not had your money,' she said to her listening, straining face, 'we could not have survived. There are thousands who have nothing; still the Government ignores them and leaves them to die in the streets. Is this what our men went to fight for? Did my husband leave me for this? If there is a God above He must show mercy to the widows and orphans who are left! *If* there is a God above!'

My grandmother's half-silent ears had caught some of the last words and her lined face puckered with distress.

'No!' she protested gently. 'Do not call upon God in that way. You will be punished, my child. It is not right for us to question His ways.'

'Ach!' said my mother in disgust. 'Will He feed us, mother? Will He come down from His heaven and put food in my children's hungry stomachs?'

My grandmother strained pitifully to catch the angry words and shook her head protestingly.

'No, no!' she repeated. 'It is not right to talk like this. Have you not had enough punishment? Do you want to see your children struck dead or blinded before your eyes?'

Her direful words made us shiver with horror. My mother said to her:

'You are old, mother. You will never understand what it is to lose your husband when you are young, to know that never again will you be able to lie beside him at the end of the day or to feel his warm body close along the line of your back. Your day is finished and you lost your husbands when all passion had gone from you long ago. But I lost mine before my body had time to wither. All the young and the brave are dying and only the women and the helpless children are left. And our good Sultan keeps to his Palace and assesses the worth of a man in terms of money and will give me ninety-nine kuruş a month, to compensate me for the loss of my husband. My husband who was young and strong and who rots in some grave we do not know where. Ninety-nine kuruş!'

'*What* is the ninety-nine kuruş?' asked my grandmother, bellowing in her anxiety so that Mehmet and I trembled.

'The pension I shall receive for myself and my three children,' replied my mother.

'Pension?' queried my grandmother, not fully understanding anything, I think, but anxious to appear intelligent to the passionate young woman who faced her across the table.

My mother carefully kept her patience to explain.

'A pension is money you receive from the Government if you have lost your husband in the war. They have decided to give me ninety-nine kuruş because that is all Hüsnü was worth to them. I have lost my home because we are at war. Ahmet is dead and Ayşe—and Sariyer will soon be less than a memory. My children grow and must be fed and you and I cling to life because sometimes it is easier to live than to die. Bread is fifty kuruş a kilo and lasts us one day, two if we go hungry, and a man at the Treasury to-day congratulated me because I gave a man to the war. "God has blessed you," he said, "your husband died şehit (for his country) and his place is in heaven— and now, if you will just sign here please——" and he gave me the paper which said I was willing to accept ninety-nine kuruş for my husband.'

Her passionate voice broke and she sat staring into space, her

eyes full of the saddest dreams and curiously but not frighten-
ingly so, oblivious of her family about her. My grandmother
noisily sipped her soup but spoke no word for her deafness gave
her a remoteness from life and she could not always follow my
mother's tripping tongue.

The first time my mother went to collect her pension, I went
with her, to the building that is to-day the Istanbul College.
Everywhere was crowded with pushing, shouting women and
the queues reached far down the street. But they were not the
orderly, disciplined queues that I came to know so well in
war-time England during the Second World War. No indeed!
These queues could scarcely be called queues at all, since they
consisted for the most part of women shrieking insults and
imprecations at each other, pushing each other out of the way
and arguing spiritedly with the police who, for a time, tried to
instil some sense of decorum into the crowds. But the women,
en masse, were too much for the police, so they left them to
fight out their battles.

My mother and I awaited our turn, she with considerable
asperity, and if anyone attempted to take her place, she
rounded on them so venomously that the attacker was forced to
retire. Her sharp, uncompromising attitude brooked no interference and I admired her for being able to defend herself
against these rough women.

When it was our turn at the pay-window, she took the money
offered, handed it to me and told me to buy sultanas for
myself.

The official said sharply:

'The Government gives you that money for food, sister, not
to give it as pocket money to your children. Or are you too
rich to need this money?'

My mother turned to him viciously, returning to where he
stood at the little window, lightly pushing aside the woman who
was awaiting her money.

'Your job,' said my mother, with remarkable self-control,
'is to attend to the people who come here, not to give them
advice for we none of us need your advice'—a cheer went up
from the other women—'I wonder how much your munificent
Sultan pays you in a month? Enough to feed your family
well? I do not think so, for your suit, God help you, is a disgrace to you and your thin body looks so weak that it is no

wonder they did not send you to fight the English. If I give
the money I receive here to my son, for sweetmeats, it is all I
consider it to be worth. I came here to collect a pension, not to
listen to your uncalled-for advice.'

'I'll have you arrested——' spluttered the young man, very
red in the face, and I shook with terror for I thought perhaps
he could really do this.

And my mother's clear voice rang out challengingly:

'Try to have me arrested!'

And the voices of the other women rose threateningly,
against the arrival of two policemen, who remained however
at the edge of the crowd, not yet brave enough to wade through
that angry, milling crowd, to lay hands on my mother.

The women shouted hoarsely:

'Well spoken, sister!'

And they moved protectingly about her, ready to defend her
if the police came too near. She stood staring at the hesitant
police, her head thrown back proudly, but they made no move
towards her. She moved through the ranks of women, her head
still high. Some of the women caught her sleeve as she passed
and cried:

'God bless you, hanim efendi!'

And the police made no attempt to touch her, even though
the words she had spoken that morning were treacherous in old
Turkey.

After that episode she did not ever again go to collect the
meagre pension but would let me go, for I used to buy nuts or
sultanas for myself and Mehmet. But one morning I too had a
never-to-be-forgotten experience and after that the pension lay
forgotten for none of us bothered to claim it.

That last day I went, the crowds were as thick as ever and I
patiently awaited my turn. Although many people left the
pay-windows, still so many more were entering the hall that I
never seemed to get any nearer to receiving money. I swallowed
my fear of the fierce women and pushed my way between them,
sometimes crawling under them, ignoring the threats of the
angry men and succeeded in almost reaching one of the
windows. There was a tall man behind me and, seeing that I
was not tall enough to reach up to the ledge with the pay-book,
he lifted me up. Then, to my intense embarrassment, he
quickly inserted his fingers into the crutch of my short pants and

I wriggled and shouted like a mad thing. My threshing legs hit a young woman on the side of the head and she angrily beat me. The man who held me continued with his investigations and I screamed wildly and tried to hit out at him. There was an ominous muttering from the crowd and I struggled to free myself, easy now, for the man had partially released me. I almost fell to the floor, hurt and bewildered that anyone should want to do such things, and I fled through the crowds, the pension-book forgotten.

I ran home as fast as my legs could carry me, although they were trembling so much that I do not suppose I really made very much progress. When I got home I sobbed out the whole story to my astonished mother and I saw her mouth tighten, then she bade me wash myself and to say nothing of this to Mehmet.

Afterwards she explained:

'When you are older I shall tell you all these things, for now I am your father and your mother. But always remember that, to certain men, boys are more valuable than girls, especially a nice-looking boy like you.'

She said no more, beyond adding that I must try to put this day out of my head.

But it was hard to put this memory behind me. The shock had been so intense that for many a long day afterwards I flew like the wind from every man I met. And right through childhood and youth the suspicion remained, and all men were potential enemies.

CHAPTER XIV

POVERTY MAKES A BARGAIN

MY GRANDMOTHER WAS ageing fast. She still read from the Koran each day and latterly had taken to accusing my mother of trying to get another husband. She would mumble that nobody wanted her any more, that her money would soon be finished and that once my mother had married again she would never be allowed to see her grandchildren. She wallowed in self-pity, refusing to listen when my mother explained that she had not the slightest intention of re-marrying. She shouted everything out in her loud voice for the whole neighbourhood to hear. One day she bellowed to the widow, who was passing the door, to come up and drink coffee with her whilst she told all her troubles to her. The widow being a kindly soul forgot the many times my grandmother had snubbed her almost out of existence and declared herself willing to drink coffee. She entered the house saying that she never drank good coffee unless she drank it in our house.

'Where you get the sugar——' she sighed but my grandmother did not enlighten her and probably heard only part of the conversation in any case.

Although it was the widow who had been invited to partake of refreshment it was she who made it, my grandmother roaring instructions at her, scarcely pausing for breath, insisting on the best cups being used. In a very short time the whole street knew that coffee was being brewed in our house and very soon too they were going to hear that the family was practically destitute.

Wood was added to the great white stove and armchairs drawn forward for the two women. I hovered uncertainly in the background and, no notice being taken of me, finally sat down on the soft, warm carpet. The widow was delighted with her good luck and showed no inclination to leave this cosy room. My grandmother started to tell her that we had no money left but the widow paid little attention to this, since she herself had never known anything else but a lack of money. When she finally got a chance to talk, she said cheerfully:

'But you have a sewing-machine, hanim efendi, and with a sewing-machine you can never be hungry. Why, I have eaten my bread from one for the last fifteen years!'

'Nonsense,' said my grandmother. 'How can I learn to use a sewing-machine at my time of life?'

'What about your daughter-in-law?' yelled the widow, drawing closer to the crackling fire.

'Şevkiye?' said my grandmother, in great surprise. 'Why, she is as useless as I am!'

'No, she isn't,' contradicted the widow. 'Look how quickly she learned how to make the children's clothes?'

'Yes,' said my grandmother, thoughtfully. 'Of course she does the most exquisite embroidery——'

'Embroidery!' snorted the widow, with great disdain. 'That's no use to-day in the world, hanim efendi. But machining—now that's quite another thing. Perhaps my patron in the kapali çarşi would give her some work to do. I shall ask him to-morrow and if he is agreeable I shall help her and show her how to do the things he wants.'

'You are unusually kind,' said my grandmother wonderingly, and the widow looked pleased.

In the midst of their talking, my mother came in, looking so odd, so dishevelled, that my heart gave a lurch of fear.

'What is wrong?' cried the widow in dismay, and my mother replied in the new, hard voice that she always seemed to use nowadays:

'I am past wondering what is right and what is wrong. To live nowadays is to bear insults from everyone. At the Government departments they treat us like vermin or tell us how fortunate we are that we have given a man to the war. I hunt bread each day, running from one baker's shop to another, and in the end, what do I get? A piece of hard, black bread that I would be ashamed to feed to the animals. The crowds push and kick and snarl with rage and all decency seems to be gone from humanity——'

Her voice broke and I thought she was going to cry but she controlled herself, a faint furrow appearing between her delicate brows, almost as though she was wondering what she was talking about. She put out a hand to steady herself and her face became very white, deadly white so that the cheekbones were thrown into high relief, and the nose appeared more pinched and sharper.

'Did anything unusual happen this morning?' roared my grandmother.

'Plenty!' retorted my mother. 'When you are a woman and alone in the world, you have to grow used to insults. This morning I tried several shops for bread and in the end I found one open and joined the queue to take my chance with the rest. Just as I had handed my money and taken the bread offered to me, a woman beside me snatched it from my hand, saying that it was hers and that she had given her money first. I snatched it back again and so the battle started. She was like a wild animal. She fought and kicked and screamed and pulled my veil from my face, saying only the rich wore veils and that I had no right to queue for bread, when the poor needed it worse than I did. My veil!' my mother repeated, horrified. 'Before all those people she pulled aside my veil, as if I was a prostitute, and then she called me one! Me! In front of all those people! I thought the world would fall on top of me. I tried to get away from her but she had hold of my skirt and I was afraid she would tear that from me too. Two men interfered and gave me back the bread and I ran away from that dreadful place—with my veil all torn and the people shouting after me in the streets. They thought I was a bad woman and that I had been fighting with another bad woman! Oh, such disgrace! To think I should live to see this day, that I should fight for such a thing——'

And she held up the piece of dry, black bread. Then she swayed forward and before I had time to properly realise what was happening, she was lying across the sofa, lifted there by the strong, kindly arms of the widow. My grandmother, more agile than I ever remember seeing her, was chafing her wrists, her own face almost as white as my mother's.

My mother commenced to grind her teeth and I was terrified she was going to break them but the widow jammed a spoon between her lips, raising her head to settle cushions more firmly behind it. After a while the awful grinding stopped and my mother opened her eyes.

'Cognac!' shouted my grandmother, busying herself making strong coffee.

She was almost crying to herself, calling upon the names of

her dead sons to come back and defend their women. Her weak, long-pent-up tears rolled down her cheeks and fell into the hot ash of the mangal, making strange little sizzling sounds.

My mother opened her eyes and sat up, the colour fast returning to her face. She stretched herself languidly, as though she were very tired and had come back from a long way away, then she accepted coffee and presently seemed perfectly normal again.

The widow remained with us for the rest of the day; if she had work to do she gave no hint. Good soul that she was, she only wished to stay here with my mother, to serve her as best she could.

Dusk came early and Ezzin was read from the little Mosque, the signal for my grandmother to start praying. Every evening she waited for Muezzin to climb into the minaret, for since her deafness this was the only way she could know the right time to pray. That evening she prayed in her loud, rumbling voice for her sons who were dead, for my grandfather, for my mother and for us children. She put in a special little bit for herself at the end. Her voice filled the room, the old, liquid words falling softly on the ear. The widow had prepared the evening meal and, because my mother was still not really well enough to go downstairs, we had it in the salon. The fire blazed merrily and all the lamps, oh, rash extravagance! were brightly lit.

After dinner was over, my grandmother illogically wished to visit the little Mosque to pray and said she wanted me with her. We started out into the black night, I pleasantly fearful and excited. My grandmother carried a lighted candle in a sort of storm-lantern and I could clearly see another candle glowing on the tomb of the holy-man. We walked swiftly for the night was bitterly cold, and, when we came abreast of the window in which rested the tomb, my grandmother sternly bade me pray for the soul of the holy-man. She opened her hands to the sky, palms upwards in the Muslim fashion, and I did the same thing. I do not think I said much of a prayer, for my teeth were chattering with the cold and the wind had chosen just that moment to come whistling icily around the corner, cutting through my thin coat.

When we went into the Mosque, we sat down on the women's side and I was immediately acutely embarrassed, for my grandmother insisted on saying her prayers aloud. There were only a few other people there but no peace was given to them for, whether they wished it or not, they had to listen to my grandmother. Again and again she exhorted her God to be merciful to her dead ones and to make my mother well and strong again. I wriggled with impatience, trying to quieten her but she refused to be quiet until she had finished what she had come here to say.

One day my mother and I went to Beşiktaş, some distance from our home. I have forgotten the reason we went but remember the occasion, for it was the first time I had ever seen the Sultan, Mehmet Reşat. In the main street of Beşiktaş soldiers were marching and a band played military music, whilst the police were roughly keeping back the curious crowds from the royal route. We waited to see the Sultan, and the Cavalry came first, mounted on their high-stepping Arab horses. As far as I can remember, they wore blue jackets with brightly shining brass buttons, scarlet trousers and great tall kalpaks on their heads, with flowing white plumes. They pranced towards us, their uniforms making a splash of welcome colour in all that drab humanity and their spurs clinked and jingled and gleamed in the watery sun. A carriage came after the Cavalry, drawn by elegant, aristocratic horses and, dimly, from the windows we caught a glimpse of an old small man with a little white beard. He was in uniform, many medals marching across his breast. A great, loyal cry went up from the people, half of them in rags, a deep-throated, rumbling roar of welcome: 'Padişahim çok yaşa!' they roared and then he was past us and other voices took up the refrain. Even when the carriage had finally disappeared from sight the echoes of the cheering crowds came back to us. Then the quiet streets grew quieter for the people had dispersed and my mother and I continued on our journey.

She had found work to do in these days. The widow, true to her word, had obtained sewing for her from her patron in kapali çarşi. The money was pitifully small and nowadays the salon was eternally littered with made and unmade work and the never-ceasing whirr of the sewing-machine dominated all else. So the winter of 1915 passed to the sound of my mother's machine and the merry, comforting crackling sound of the logs in the china stove. Somehow or other life was readjusting itself and we had become used to bad food and not enough of it and my grandmother did the marketing and I now hunted for bread. But the soft, early days of Spring changed all that again. One had already learned that security was a fragile thing, sensitive to the first cold breath, yet one could not learn to accept this with finality. That Spring of 1916 over-rides all other memories and carries its scars to this day.

Sewing, for my mother, came to a sudden, abrupt end for the patron of the kapali çarşi explained that there was no more work for anyone, that the Government had bought all the available materials for the Army. He said that an Army Sewing Depôt had been opened behind the Gülhane Parki and that anyone applying there would be given work to do. He had stretched his large, hairy hands to them, begging them to understand his position, and the women had looked at each other and wondered what to do. The widow said immediately that she, for one, would go to the Army Depôt, declaring that it was all the same to her where she worked as long as she got money for it. My mother and many of the new poor were uncertain. They felt that to work in the privacy of their own homes was one thing but to expose themselves in a Government factory, quite another. When my mother came home, my grandmother looked with surprise at her empty hands and asked what was wrong.

'No more work,' declared my mother. 'The Army have bought all materials and have opened a factory behind the Gülhane Parki. The widow has gone there to-day to look for work.'

'Well, you will not!' roared my grandmother, so loudly that a pile of plates on the kitchen table vibrated slightly.

'What is the use of talking like that?' demanded my mother wearily. 'We have so little money and the children must be fed. Can we see them going hungry, because of our pride?'

My grandmother stood up and called to us to come with her. She led the way into the bedroom, produced a key from somewhere about her middle and unlocked the tin chest where her valuables were stored.

'We have these five gold coins left to us,' she said to my mother. 'Take them. They will keep us for a little longer. And when they have gone I have still my jewellery—my rings and my emerald pendant. I was keeping them for Muazzez.'

She drew them out of their silk-lined box and they glittered palely in her hands.

'No!' said my mother. 'These rings will never be sold. The dealers will rob you nowadays because they know that people like us are selling our valuables because we want money so desperately. Why, only last week I heard from one of the women at the kapali çarşi that she had sold a diamond-and-ruby chain, far finer than these, mother, and all she got for them was a little gold. She did not know their value and she was so hungry that she let them go to the first Jew dealer who offered to take them. No!' she said more softly, so softly that my grandmother could not catch her words, 'these shall belong to Muazzez,' and she touched the pretty trinkets, taking them from my grandmother and locking them up again. She put her hands on my grandmother's shoulders, lightly brushing her forehead with her lips. 'All our pretty things are gone,' she said into the straining ears. 'So let us keep Muazzez's pretty things. They will look very well one day on my daughter's neck!'

So the first crisis was averted and the little house grew silent again, without the weight of the machine's noise to disturb it. And gold in the pocket gave a temporary, transient gaiety, for would it not buy good meals again—even for a brief while—and wine for my grandmother? Feckless and improvident and wildly extravagant were they, ignorant of the long years still to be lived. All through childhood their beauty and tears and gallantry pierced my heart to torment. Their blood ran fiercely through my veins and I have been as wildly improvident, but without their courage and wit and graciousness to face the sort of heartaches they faced.

Now and then the widow would come to visit us, amusing yet terrifying us with her coarse humour of what life was like in a factory. She had to stay there day and night, sleeping and eating with the others, doing different turns of duty and only allowed off one day in a week.

The pay, she said, was poor but sufficient for her, for the Army provided her food.

'Me,' she said proudly. 'I'm as strong as a lion, thank God! Only the strong can survive in a place like that.'

She no longer pressed my mother to join her there, realizing my grandmother's fierce distaste for such work, but, since they talked openly to her, she could not help knowing that money was low again and perhaps she knew too that it was only a matter of time before my mother joined her of her own free will. When has money not been low in my dear, idiotic family? They were excellent for spending but terrible for saving and even life at its most cruel could not teach them anything else. One morning my grandmother went round all the rooms, ticking off on her fingers all the largest, and to my mind the ugliest, pieces of furniture we had. Several times she wondered aloud how much they would fetch if she sold them.

'It's good walnut furniture,' she would mutter. 'Not to be bought anywhere to-day. And Şevkiye was quite right when she said that these rooms are very overcrowded.'

Brave soul that she was, she was trying to convince herself that the sale of her furniture was a matter of no importance. She was hoping to defer the day when my mother would have to go to the factory.

She sent for a Jewish dealer and it was I who ushered him into the transformed presence of my grandmother. She had dressed herself up for the occasion and wore all her rings and her emerald pendant, defying the dealer to guess she was desperate for money.

The Jew looked over the furniture with a cautious, jaundiced eye. Perhaps he did not know what to make of the situation, for though the house was small and in a bad district, the old lady wore diamonds that he could see were real enough. She was dressed in silk too, the hall-mark of respectability, and the furniture and carpets were the best that money could buy. He can be forgiven if he did not quite know how he stood in this place, before this indomitable, proud-faced old woman.

He ran his fingers over the smooth, polished wood, 'hemming' and 'hawing', and I trailed after him, a curious figure no doubt in my assortment of colours. I had been put into the best clothes that could be found to fit me and I was afraid to sit down, for everything was uncomfortably tight, the seams in danger of giving way. The Jew rapped out a figure and my grandmother's knuckles whitened over her ebony stick.

'Are you mad?' she demanded imperiously, her loud, self-conscious voice booming reverberatingly through the room.

The Jew looked doubtful again and ran his fingers over the wood for a second time, and opened a few drawers as well.

'My offer stands,' he said, and my grandmother drew herself up with great haughtiness.

'Then I think we have nothing further to discuss,' she said, with an edge to her voice and made a movement towards the door.

'Wait a moment,' said the Jew, adding 'efendim' uncertainly for he was still unsure of her status or—more importantly —her financial position.

There was a long pause, each eyeing the other suspiciously, each trying to assess the obstinacy of the other. The Jew shifted his eyes first and slightly raised his figure, very slightly, mind you, but that was where he made his first mistake. My grandmother remained immovable, not a flicker of emotion crossing her poker face. I was entranced for I had never seen her like this since my grandfather's day. I had almost forgotten she could look like this. She leaned on her stick and waited, the Jew slightly raising the figure, for he knew a good bargain when he saw one and was prepared to give way a little. But she just stood there like a statue and refused to give in. When at last he could bear it no longer, he burst out:

'I'm offering you the best price you will get anywhere. If you're in need of the money I advise you to take it.'

And that was his second mistake for it made my grandmother arrogant and when she was arrogant she was at her most dangerous, and better people than the Jew had been known to grow reckless under this danger.

'When I am in need of money,' she said, 'I shall no doubt be willing to let you cheat me. At the moment I am merely trying to get rid of the large furniture for, as you can see, this house is far too small to house it. If, however, you do not wish to buy then that is quite a different matter and I can only regret that we have both wasted our time. Good morning.'

And she walked determinedly towards the door, holding it open for the Jew to pass through. We heard him going down the stairs and I wanted to cry with desperation, for perhaps my grandmother would never again get such an offer. I looked at her mutely, longing to cry but I heard the Jew's returning step on the stairs and I looked at my grandmother, who had not heard. I was afraid she would make some false remark he would overhear and which would send him bounding out of the house, or to return with a lower offer. But she said nothing and showed no trace of surprise when he came back into the salon. He sketched a gesture on the air, of desperation, of resignation— who shall know? And he took a deep breath, saying:

'You're ruining me, efendi, and I shall never be able to get rid of such heavy, old-fashioned stuff as this, but here's my final figure, take it or leave it——' and he named a sum and my grandmother's mouth relaxed.

'Add twenty liras more,' she said grandly, 'and the furniture's yours.'

'Five!' said the dealer.

'Fifteen!' said my grandmother.

'Seven and a half!' shouted the dealer, perspiring by now and looking as if he would like to discontinue but could not, because he loved a good bargain too.

'Twelve and a half!' retorted my grandmother, indomitable to the last.

'Ten!' said the dealer, passing his hand over his brow.

'Very well,' conceded my grandmother and the Jew handed over a greasy bundle of liras and went to the window to call up his porters, who had been waiting in case business was done.

He walked back to my grandmother.

'You drive a hard bargain,' he said. 'But if ever you want to sell those diamonds and things of yours, I can put you on to a man who will give you a good price for them.'

'Thank you,' said my grandmother, with distaste, anxious to be rid of him now that the business was concluded. 'But my jewellery is never likely to be for sale.'

And she sat down on the sofa and waited for the porters to clear the rooms. She called out constant instructions to them and warnings to be careful of her carpets and made them remove their footwear before they entered the rooms. When at last they and the furniture had gone, I saw that she was trembling violently.

'What is wrong, grandmother?' I asked, going over to her.

'Nothing,' she said. 'Only happiness—that I, an old woman, have been able to get the price I wanted out of a Jew!'

And she pulled me down beside her and there was a great ripping, tearing sound from under me. We looked at each other in dismay, then suddenly burst out laughing, for the trousers, unable to bear the strain, had finally given way.

'Never mind!' comforted my grandmother. 'We shall buy

you some more. See! We have plenty of money again!' And she held up the greasy liras triumphantly, then carelessly threw them on a little inlaid table. 'After handling those,' she shouted happily, 'my hands need washing!'

And she stumped downstairs to the kitchen, from where, presently, came the merry, splashing sound of water running. When she came up to the salon again she took the eau-de-Cologne to fastidiously sprinkle over her palms and she said to me:

'Always remember! Never let anyone know when you are desperate. Put your best clothes on and pride on your face and you can get anything in this world.'

'Why?' I wanted to know.

'Because otherwise you will get nothing but kicks,' she roared. 'If that Jew had known how desperate I was, he would have succeeded in beating me down to his own price. As it was, I succeeded in beating him. Why,' she continued complacently, 'he even complimented me on my jewellery,' and she patted the emerald pendant affectionately. 'Your grandfather always had very good taste and only bought the best.'

She took off the flashing lovely pendant and all the rings from her fingers and they lay gleaming in the palm of her hand with their lively, separate life.

'Now I shall lock them away again,' she said to me. 'And the next person to wear them will be your sister, who is going to be a great beauty one day.'

My mother came in from market with Mehmet clinging to her.

'What are you dressed up for?' she asked my grandmother suspiciously.

'Look!' commanded my grandmother, pointing to the half-empty salon.

My mother's eyes flickered a little then she turned back to my grandmother and said in an ordinary, normal conversational sort of voice:

'A great improvement. It was time to clear the room of all that heavy old furniture.'

And her eyes met my grandmother's and held for a moment and they both smiled and my mother pushed a chair to a different position, standing back to see the effect.

'Oh decidedly better!' she said merrily.

And I was immeasurably touched by her gallantry and by my grandmother's too for neither of them broke down to weep that half their home had gone. Instead they stood in the salon and tried different arrangements with the furniture that was left and pretended that they had sold because the room was not big enough to house everything. And young as I was my heart swelled with pride.

Then my mother caught sight of my burst trousers and the bare skin showing through and she said, laughing at me, that she hoped that this had not happened whilst the Jew was here.

'No indeed!' said my grandmother energetically. 'If it had I would have slapped his backside hard for that bit of bare skin might have cost me fifty liras or so!'

And everyone laughed together; even Mehmet—that solemn little boy who rarely smiled—puckered his mouth into a grin and clasped my grandmother about the legs, deducing rightly that she was the cause of our happiness.

Life flew back to the little house again and there was much gaiety and good food, and my mother even sang for us and my grandmother bellowed advice like the old autocrat she was. And the neighbours marvelled at her cleverness with the Jew dealer and shook their heads in pity over the poor man, saying that if there were a few more of my grandmother's calibre— why, the Jews of Istanbul would soon be bankrupt!

CHAPTER XV

CHARITY SCHOOL IN KADIKÖY

No matter how the women of my family tried to stave off poverty, it came eventually—this time the real, unadulterated thing. There was nothing left to be sold or, more correctly, what was left was unsaleable, for though the carpets and furniture were very fine the price they would have brought would have only been sufficient to keep us a matter of months. And all prices had dropped considerably—that is, excepting the price of food. And this still continued to soar. Even had she been so disposed to sell them, my grandmother's jewels were useless. The people wanted food—not jewellery, as the dealers took pains to point out when they offered a few liras for genuine stones, worth hundreds. There seemed to be no way out of this impasse and eventually my mother had to leave us and go to the Army Depôt behind the Gülhane Parki. It was the first time we had ever been separated from her and we were overcome with a sense of loss. My grandmother did the marketing, leaving us three children to look after ourselves and returning with the shopping-bag pitifully empty, for the money she had bought only the most meagre supplies. It seemed to us that we had lived forever on lentils and cabbage soup and the dry, black apology for bread. Yet although our stomachs recoiled against this diet, we were always so hungry that we would wolf down the tasteless, insipid mixtures almost with relish.

Up and down the length of the street continued to come the tragic news of the dead or dying or wounded relatives. And fresh sickness broke out, for the people were starving and likely to go on starving unless they bought from the Bourse Noir. And who in that poor street was capable of raising sufficient money to buy from the Bourse Noir?

One day my grandmother took us to see my mother. I remember it was a soft mild day, mild enough for us to dispense with our thin coats. We were very excited at the thought of seeing my mother, and when we reached the Depôt and a soldier halted us, enquiring our business there, we were afraid perhaps he would not let us pass. My grandmother could not hear a word he said, but I explained that we had come to visit our mother and he stood aside for us to pass. The building was old and dirty and we went up a long, tortuous flight of broken wooden stairs, making a great deal of noise, and another soldier, stationed at the head, again enquired our business. I stammered why we were here and he showed us into a large, gloomy room, where many women sat working at their machines.

There was a great silence in that room, as though the women were either far too occupied to gossip together, or as though the discipline was too severe. We stood uncertainly in the doorway, nobody taking any notice of us, and presently Mehmet espied my mother and broke away from us, flying on his thin, brown sticks of legs down the busy ranks of the women. He reached my mother and flung himself into her arms, sobbing as though his heart would break. We followed him but there was no place to sit, so we stood around her table, our shadows blocking the light from a few of the other women sitting near her. It was the first time we had ever visited her here, and I was shocked by the dirt and the meanness and the poverty-stricken air of the place. My mother looked tired, her eyes red-rimmed and her hands slightly soiled. All the fastidiousness in me was revolted and I felt impotent, childish rage that my mother should have to work in a place like this. Perhaps my face spoke volumes to her for she said to my grandmother:

'It would have been better not to have brought the children here.'

My grandmother shrugged indifferently, shifting the weight of Muazzez to the other arm, then, in answer to my mother's outstretched arms, gave her over to her.

'What else could I do?' she grumbled loudly, all the other women momentarily pausing to listen to what she said. 'There was nobody with whom I could leave them and I need money.'

My mother reached out for her purse, pushing the small contents across the table. My grandmother querulously asked if that was all. I saw that my mother flushed brilliantly and the widow, who was sitting next to her, said—perhaps to create a diversion:

'We get all our food here, you know. Not much, but better

than I could get at home. And they give me money and a place
to sleep and what more do I want?'

'Perhaps *you* are contented here,' roared my grandmother
pointedly. 'But you have no family to depend upon you. I
have these three children to try to feed and this money will not
buy very much for them.'

Her lips folded obstinately and she looked with disdain at
the few coins in her hand and I saw the shadow of distress in
my mother's eyes. She looked as though she wished to apologise
for us children and I ached to comfort her, to give some sort of
assurance, but I did not know how. Then I saw her lift her
hands in a little gesture of helplessness and she said:

'I wish I knew what to do! I wish something could be done
for the children.'

My grandmother's face was cold and obstinate.

'They will die with hunger if they stay much longer with me,'
she declared. 'I am old and I can do with little food if necessary,
but these are young and keep demanding, demanding——'

My mother could not answer. She sat looking down at her
roughened, soiled hands and a few of the women threw sympathetic glances at her but nobody said anything. There was
nothing that could be said.

After some minutes, my grandmother retrieved Muazzez
and prepared to depart. She looked anxious and mutinous and
grey-faced and was probably as hungry as I, but in that moment
I hated her with a passion that had nothing childish about it.
She had humiliated my mother and spoken roughly to her and
given her additional unhappiness.

'We are going now,' she said.

My mother offered her cheek to be kissed and there was no
way of clasping her and telling her that one loved her and that
she was not to worry. Her kiss was as distant and as cold as the
waves that break on the seashore, her eyes looking past us to
some torment we could not see but could perhaps dimly com-
prehend. In an effort to bring awareness of us back to her
remote face, I wriggled against her shoulder, insinuating my
warm face against her cold one.

'Yes, yes,' she said absently to me, not thinking of me, and I
withdrew rebuffed and helpless in my inarticulateness—feeling
unwanted.

We left her and passed back through the ranks of the disillusioned women and at the door we turned to wave to her but she was not looking at us. She had her face cupped in her hands and perhaps she was crying. We did not know. We trudged home with my grandmother to the silent, cold house in Bayazit, all the world seeming dark, for my mother had seemed to renounce us that day, and my grandmother said she did not want us. There was nothing we could do, for we were children and our voices would not be heard amidst the greater clamour of the world.

The next time my mother came home from the depôt it was earlier than usual and we wondered what had brought her at this hour. She said she was home for three days and my grandmother ladled the everlasting cabbage soup into her bowl silently, intimating perhaps that one more mouth to feed could make little difference to the food. My mother said she had received a letter from the Depôt commander, telling her that, if she wished, her children could be cared for at the school recently established in Kadiköy for the protection of children who had lost their fathers during the war. The idea appalled and frightened me and the more my mother elaborated the theme, the more frightened did I become. It appeared from her conversation that she had made up her mind to send Mehmet and me to this school, and I felt as if everything of the old life was ending and that my mother no longer wanted us with her.

My grandmother seemed relieved by the decision, saying she would keep Muazzez with her, and I ran to my mother, crying:

'No, anne, no! Don't leave us, don't send us away.'

And Mehmet took up the cry but there was no softening in my mother's eyes as she looked at us.

My grandmother snapped irritably, as if all life was not ending for us: 'Stop crying, both of you! There is nothing to cry for. You will enjoy being at school and you will get plenty of good food to eat.'

'I don't want good food,' I sobbed, longing for some relaxation of my mother's hard, disinterested mood, some softening of expression that would let me run to her to be comforted.

But there was none. Only separation and school for us, no love for there was nobody to give it to us. I wonder, did my mother make her decision with tears and misgivings or with relief that at last a place was found to house us, so that she need no longer feel responsibility for us? These are questions to which only she knew the answer, and she did not tell us these things. But it is not an idle thing to say that the heart and mind and spirit of a child can be broken, and the events of that melancholy day governed the whole of my future life. Love can die as easily in the childish heart, if more bitterly, as in the adult. Where the senses scream and beat helplessly against the ruthlessness of a decision, whether lightly made or not, and are forced to fall back, unrecognised, unheard, then love dies too, although a child would not call it that. Perhaps it is only fully realised afterwards, when the child himself becomes adult and feels an old enmity, looking back to that withered day.

So Mehmet and I went to bed that night knowing that rebellion was useless, that we were only children and would not be listened to, even if we had had the words to explain our agony of mind. My mother went to Kadiköy to register our names, and I asked my grandmother to explain why it was we must go. She gave me several very good, cold, material reasons but was farther from understanding my distress than I was from knowing how ruthless she could be. She could not see that the poor food of home meant nothing to us, as long as we could remain there, that home meant security if nothing else. So I gave up futile questioning, for even one's flesh and blood can be most cruelly unaware of sorrow.

The next day Mehmet and I were taken to Galata Bridge by my mother, to cross the Bosphor for Kadiköy on the Anatolian side. On the boat she told us so many times how we would like this school that we became quite silent, no longer answering her. And she misunderstood the silence for sulkiness and set her lips tightly.

From the Kadiköy boat-station we walked to the school— the building that is to-day the French Hospital. It was in a beauty spot, looking out across the sea, the school building so clean and fresh that it gleamed like gold in the mellow sun. We went up some wide, stone steps and still one of us hoped for some reprieve, some hitch in arrangements, for defeat is a difficult thing to accept. A uniformed porter in a cold, anti-septic-looking hall told us to sit down whilst he fetched someone to attend to us. I sat on the extreme edge of a rickety chair, my heart thumping so loudly that I expected everyone to hear it, and a big, white-faced clock on the wall ticked away the minutes in time with my heart. Tick-tock, tick-tock, tick-tock it said unceasingly, uncaringly, and the big hand moved inexorably, not to be stopped by my silent pleading to stand still forever. Several starched-aproned sisters passed through the hall, bending incurious eyes on us but there were no children to be seen or heard.

Presently a woman dressed in a blue dress with a stiff white apron about her—who we afterwards learned was the Matron —came across to my mother and they started to converse softly. She spoke appalling Turkish overlaid with a thick, guttural accent, for she was a German matron with fair braided hair and blonde skin.

After a little while she turned to Mehmet and me and said: 'Say good-bye to your mother.'

We began to cry and she said sharply:

'Your mother will come to see you sometimes. Do not cry.'

So we leaned towards our mother and brushed her hands with our lips. I longed for a kind word from her, for a look that held expression but her face remained closed, empty, with nothing in it for us. We watched her go through the big glass door then her shadow preceding her down the glittering steps, but she did not look back or give any sign of her feelings. Was she distressed at having to leave us here—or hard, as we had never known before? We could not know, we little insignificant two who stood beside the plump German matron, who told us to kiss each other good-bye—for Mehmet was to be taken to the Kindergarten, a separate building from the one we were in.

Mehmet clung to my arm and would not let me go, his brown eyes asking what was happening to us, and I whispered to him that everything would be all right, that I would soon be seeing him again. A red-haired Nurse led him away, a small, silent boy of three and a half who did not know what to make of this topsy-turvy world. Another nurse took me from the Matron's side and I was bathed and put into a drab, grey uniform—a Charity school's uniform. Next I was taken to the dormitory and shown my bed, a narrow iron bed with a white coverlet and a low stool beside it for my folded clothes each night. I was then shown the classroom and the place where I was to sit, the dining-room and the Sister to whom I was responsible, a gimlet-eyed woman with no understanding of children. Big-boned she was and sadistic, with enormous red hands capable of chastisement. Timidly I asked her if I could see my brother and she snapped that I could not and that, further-more, it would be as well for me to learn to speak only when spoken to. And during the whole of the time I remained in that school, some two years, I never saw Mehmet, even though once I heard my mother begging the Matron to let him see me occasionally, as he was fretting for me. But the uncaring Matron said that the rules of the school must be abided by. It was 'verboten' for the juniors to mix with the kindergarten and the Matron was not a German for nothing. Verboten was verboten and that was all there was to it.

The food was very good at first and everywhere very clean and always smelling of disinfectant. We had classes every day and there was no chance of dreaming over the lessons, for the teachers would pull one back to attention in their excruciatingly bad Turkish, and the punishments even included going without meals. Twice a week we had singing lessons. One of the Sisters would play the piano and we would sing old Turkish and German folk-songs, enjoying ourselves for it was one of the few times we could really let ourselves go and shout as loudly as we wished. In the evenings we used to gather in the garden, that lovely wilderness which looked out across the Marmora, and the busy sisters would form us into martial lines about the Turkish flag. Lustily we would chant 'Deutschland über Alles!' and, as an afterthought, 'Padişahim çok yaşa!' We were all too young to see the irony of this.

Every two weeks my mother used to visit me and for many days beforehand I looked forward to her coming.

Sometimes during the play-hour I used to go to a corner of the garden, away from the others, and sit on the broken, low stone wall and look over the Marmora and I would think about my mother and wonder if she were missing me, or was she glad to have handed over the responsibility to someone else, someone more impersonal? I would bury my face in the long grass and cry for her and for Mehmet, whom I never saw at all.

There was a small building to the left of the main school building and in it was our cinema, such as it was. There was a little window just inside here, with a high step leading up to the operator's room, and sometimes I used to climb on this step for

I could see the large main gates from here and I would wait there as many hours as I dared. I waited to see my mother's figure turn in at the gates, my heart pounding with excitement and always the fear that perhaps, after all, she would not come to-day. When I saw her, I would rush from the cinema and hurtle towards her like a small rocket, flinging myself into her arms which never warmed, eternally begging the one thing:

'Am I coming home to-day, anne?'

'Not to-day, my son. Perhaps soon——'

Always the same question, always the same answer. Soon. Soon. Soon.

She would bring nuts and sultanas for me and tell me about my grandmother and my sister but as the months flew by these things interested me less and less. They had all receded far into the background, even not seeing my brother had lost the first bitter poignancy. Only one thing remained real and bright and shining, my mother. Still I clung to my early image of her, trying to force her to show some love for me and would cry myself to sleep after she had gone, for her visits were never anything more than formal, duty visits. Time healed tears too, even dimmed love, and the months flew over my head and I grew taller and stronger, and good food filled out the hollows in my cheeks. New uniforms were given to me and I went up two classes and the habit of school grew strong within me and longings for my mother's love became fainter and fainter until eventually they died altogether. I still watched for her visits but without the excited heart and I no longer asked when it was I would see my home again.

But the Spring of 1918 saw the return for us to bad food and even worse conditions for my mother. The War was going badly for us and food was running short in the whole country. At the school we had now begun to leave the dining-room hungry after meals, and no more butter appeared on the tables. We went to sleep hungry, awoke hungry and went through the day hungry. When my mother nowadays brought me precious nuts or dried fruits, I ate them so quickly that I was almost always sick after them. The German Sisters disappeared, and old Turkish women replaced them, and the school began to smell less and less of disinfectant and one missed the stiff crackle of the white aprons in the corridors. Lessons were rare and singing had stopped altogether, for how could we sing if we were hungry? But there still hung in the music-room a large portrait of the Sultan, Mehmet Reşat, and we used to shout 'Padişahim çok yaşa!'—even on our empty stomachs.

When the summer of that year was upon us we did not even have dry bread in the school and the old women used to take us to a place called Fenerbahçe, where grew many big sakiz-ağaci (gum-trees), where the small red, resinous berries grew in thick clusters. We used to throw stones into the trees, some-times being lucky enough to knock down the berries into the long, wild grass. These we would scramble madly for, knocking each other down to find the berries to eat them avidly, like little animals. They had a sour taste but were curiously satis-fying and we used to fill our pockets, taking them back with us to the school to eat during the night. At other times we would go to Fikir Tepesi, where we would pull and eat kuzu-kulaği (sorrel), helping the younger amongst us to choose the right grasses. We would search at Kalamiş for bayir-trupu (small white radishes), which gave us a raking thirst. And many times I remember eating the almond-blossom from the trees, stuffing the blooms into my ever-hungry mouth. Once in a sea field, bounding one side of our gardens, soldiers were pulling broad beans and throwing the green stalks to the edge of the field, the edge nearest our palings. We put our fingers through and took the stalks, sucking them afterwards with great relish.

When my mother took to giving me a little pocket money, I, like the others, used to buy broad beans for myself, eating them raw, feverishly stuffing them down me until in the end I would vomit—then feel hungrier than ever. It became the custom amongst us to carry salt and red pepper in little bags concealed about our person and if we were ever lucky enough to find potato peelings or raw aubergine skins, we would wash them at the pump, expertly mix them with the contents of our little bags and eat them when we were desperate with hunger. Our food-starved eyes overlooked nothing in the way of sustenance. But one day in my hunger I ate something unknown, something I had thought was bayir-trupu (radishes), and which made me very sick so frequently that I was rushed into the school hospital. Here it was discovered I had poisoned myself and almost at the same time scabies developed. I had been suffering from itchiness for weeks but had thought nothing of it, and in any case the old women who had replaced the smart German

Sisters never paid any attention to things like that. Scabies spread over my body until I was almost crying with craziness, with the red-hot, prickling itch that would not let me rest. Every morning I was taken to the Turkish Bath, the scabby places scrubbed with a hard brush until my body was bleeding and agonizing. It was a torture and I would scream continuously but to no avail, for the scrubbing continued mercilessly.

The food in the hospital was a little better, not very much, but at least we were not driven to the fields with hunger. We were given a little lapa (watery rice) in the middle of the day and a thin vegetable soup at night—but no bread, for there simply was not any to be had. We were always hungry and half an hour before a meal was due we children allowed up would gather impatiently under the big clock over the door. We used to count the seconds until sixty, then say triumphantly, 'One minute!' and so on, thinking thereby to reduce the waiting time. And it became a habit with me, and my right leg would jerk in time to the counting so that automatically to-day when I am very tired or depressed my right leg commences to jerk to the ticking of a clock.

All the time I was in hospital my mother had not been to see me and I was worrying for news of her, for never before had she failed in her two weekly visits. The long weeks passed and still no sign of her. I was released from the hospital, weak as a cat and very thin, for the last few months of starvation had taken all the roundness from my body and cheeks. When I got out of the hospital I found that we were no longer allowed into the cinema to spy from the operator's window, but instead a blackboard had been erected in the garden, and as the visitors arrived, the children's names were inscribed on the blackboard. Like all the others, I took to waiting beside the blackboard on visiting days but my name never appeared. After a while alarm swept through me that I should never see my mother again, that she had at last deserted me for ever. I would have to remain in this frightful place for years, and vague, formless notions of escape began to take root in my mind. But then, unexpectedly as all miracles are, the lovely thing happened and one summer day of 1918 I saw my name being written on the blackboard. I walked slowly towards the reception hall, my heart ready to suffocate me and my right leg perilously inclined to jerk as I walked. When I reached the hall I saw my mother sitting on one of the chairs, though indeed she was so changed that only the eye of love could have singled her out from the rest of the drab humanity about her. I ran to her, crying, and she clasped me in her arms, holding me tightly with hands that trembled.

Then she said to me:

'But what is this, my son? You are so thin and white-looking! What have they been doing to you?'

So I cried again, in the unaccustomed luxury of sympathy, and told her that I had been in hospital, how they had scrubbed my body until the blood poured and that we had no food to eat. She looked horrified.

'Why,' she said, 'you would have been better off at home with me.'

I asked her why she had not been to visit me and she said that she too had been ill, a return of the fever which would not entirely leave her. And then I realised that she too had become pitifully thin and gaunt, like a faintly animated skeleton she was, with her white face and her large eyes that never smiled. She had kept her beauty, largely because it was a beauty of bone and would never die, but now it was a mournful, disillusioned beauty that met the eye, with fine lines beside the mouth and sorrow etching the broad forehead with gossamer threads.

She put her hand over my cropped head and said that I looked like a charity boy. I asked eagerly after my brother and a troubled look ran across her face and she said no, for he too was ill and they had not let her visit him at all. Presently she stood up to go and this time I did not ask when I would be coming home, for one had learned not to ask embarrassing questions and home seemed remote as a dream nowadays, only a word with no meaning.

She took my hand and said we were going to the Matron's room—not the same Matron of two years ago, but a Turkish woman, more formidable, more unapproachable. We saw her without difficulty and I could not believe that I was hearing aright when my mother said she was taking me home with her and that she would come for my brother in two weeks time. The Matron coldly commenced to argue but my mother was in no mood to be browbeaten. She said she would not move from this place without me and that my uniform would be returned when she came for Mehmet. She pressed for information regarding him but the Matron was vague, disposed to be distant, either because she knew nothing or because she chose not to tell.

All the time they talked, I stood by the door, my heart beating in a strange fashion. This day had come at last, this day I had longed for for over two years, but it had come too late and now it did not matter whether my mother took me or not. It was true that I wished to be out of this place but where I wanted to go I did not know. Home held no promise of heaven and it was so remote it was difficult to remember, and it held in my mind an even lesser security than did this mean, charity school.

So we went home, to the same sort of conditions I had left two years ago, and bitterness brooded because one had left this meanness for another kind of meanness and one had returned no better off. My mother was brave in 1918 to make such a decision but childhood asked—perhaps unreasonably—why she had not been brave in 1916, when she banished two small boys to a German-influenced school, killing all trust and love, then trying to win it back when it was too late. For that is how it seemed to us, and does to-day, even though she is long since dead and past all criticism.

Home was a strange and alien place, with my grandmother still serving the eternal vegetable soup, and the rooms appearing smaller and darker after the large, bare rooms of school. Muazzez was now three, a thin little creature with blue eyes and hair that had lightened to brown. She was fretful and listless, for she was hungry too—like all of us. I would try to play with her but she seemed uninterested, as if playing was something strange for her. She could not talk plainly either, stammering and flushing and running away from me, preferring to be alone for she had never known anything else. An odd, nervy, sensitive child, always hungry and always inclined to tears. I could not feel closeness to her, as I had once felt for Mehmet, that little, brown-eyed, silent brother who had known my father and shared my toys.

My mother was still at the Army Sewing Depôt and my grandmother looked after the little house. One day I went with her to market but we could not buy anything. The shops were shuttered and closed, the few that remained open having only a little Indian corn and rotten vegetables for sale. Flour was treble its normal price, black and sour-looking, giving off an acrid smell. My grandmother looked at what she had bought and at the few remaining coins in her hands, then said in amazement:

'This is the first time I have ever come back from market with money still left in my hand!'

And that day we ate sour bread and soup which tasted like salt water. Then came a succession of days when only olive oil, much adulterated, could be poured over our ration of bread and I became so weak I was even unable to walk. I remember lying most of the day in the salon, faint with hunger and unable to as much as move a limb. Muazzez was with me, sitting on the carpet and whimpering that she was hungry, but I was far too light-headed to pay much attention to her. My grandmother did not return until dusk, from some long trek she had made into the hills to God knows where. She gave us bread, fresh, almost white bread and quartered raw onions and butter which was rank but made no difference to our appetite. We ate until we could eat no more and Muazzez went to sleep where she was, stretched out on the carpet and no one cared because she was not in bed.

My grandmother sat by the window crying and talking to herself as was her habit nowadays.

'There is no food anywhere,' she said. 'For the first time in years I have money in my pocket and there is nothing to buy with it!'

Where she had got the money I do not know. Perhaps she had sold some small thing for less than half its worth in order to buy food from the hoarding, greedy peasants who would never be too hungry.

I think she sat by the window all the night through for when I awoke the next morning she was still there, her old eyes rimmed and strained from tiredness, and Muazzez still lay sleeping on the hard floor.

CHAPTER XVI

ENDING WITH THE BARBER'S APPRENTICE

I SHALL NOT easily forget the day we went to Bebek, to the hospital where Mehmet lay dying.

It was a fine, warm, summer day and from Galata Bridge the green hills of Anatolia shone fair and peaceful under the light-filled sky. Seagulls cried in the wake of the boats, the big and little boats that rode the Bosphor, so divinely blue this day that the heart expanded with happiness in the human breast. Hunger was momentarily forgotten in this translucent illusion of peacefulness, and when we arrived at Eminönü, to board the tram, I was giddy and slightly light-headed from the shine and sparkle of the new day and the crisp, salt tang blown from the sea. The tram hurtled through the streets in the heart-lurching way of all Istanbul trams. Up hills we flew and down again, faster and ever more furious and with a constant clang-clang-clang-clang, as though the driver and the tram together were impatient of these mean, secretive streets and were wistful to reach the clean, breath-taking sweep of Bebek as soon as might be.

So deserted was Beşiktaş that day, that we might have been alone there. On, on we flew exhilaratingly, past Ortaköy, catching a glimpse of its white, shining Mosque with the two tall minarets piercing the heavens, the Mosque itself looking over the Bosphor. Down to Kuru Çeşme, with its tumble-down wooden houses over which lay the black film of coal dust from the innumerable depôts. Still down until we reached Arnavutköy—the word spelling romance in itself, since it means 'Albanian Village'. All along the low sea wall we ran now, looking across to Anatolia, Çengelköy like a jewel in its wooded hills, the long white Military School of Kuleli skirting the Bosphor, until finally the tall granite walls of the Summer Palace of the Khedive of Egypt hid the view and we spun furiously down the single-track line which led to Bebek and the glorious sweep of the bay.

Bebek catches the heart with its fragile, fadeless beauty—a

beauty which is made up chiefly, I think, of the blue waters that lap the shores and the tall, white-masted ships that seem to lie there eternally at anchor. And the old narrow houses that rise high behind the town; on up the steep hills they march, up to the forests that brood greenly all the year long. That summer morning in 1918 I had my first glimpse of Bebek and I was transported with joy that such subtle, pictorial beauty should meet my starved eyes at last.

From the tram terminus my mother enquired the way to the Children's Hospital and when we found it we had to wait in the cold, tiled hall until a Sister was free to see us. She came at last, efficient and rustling in her starched skirts, the traditional white veil bound low over her forehead, hiding all trace of hair so that to-day she would resemble, were she still in existence, a surgeon ready for the operating theatre. There was difficulty in locating Mehmet. In those days in Turkey there were no surnames, consequently there was quite often the greatest confusion in identifying people. The formula went something like this: Mehmet, the son of Hüsnü and Şevkiye of Bayazit. Clumsy as this method was people could usually be safely identified in the end as there were rarely two or more parents with exactly the same set of names or a child with the same name.

When the Sister had finally sorted out who Mehmet was, she informed my mother that she could not see him as he was too ill. But my mother was obstinate and pressed hard for details. The Sister hinted at malnutrition and my mother thought about this for a moment or two and then said she wished to take him home with her. The Sister raised horrified eyebrows and said that Mehmet would certainly die if he were moved from the hospital. My mother insisted and the Sister doubtfully went to find a doctor. Whilst she was gone, my mother opened the package of clothes she had brought for Mehmet and fretted that they would be too small for him but that there had been nothing else to bring.

A doctor, old and untidy-looking, came back with the Sister and proceeded to bully my mother but she replied in kind and said that she only wished to remove her son from this place.

'I want my child,' she insisted stubbornly. 'If he is to die, he can die at home as easily as here. I am prepared to take all the responsibility.'

The doctor shrugged with total indifference and turned to the Sister and told her to have Mehmet got ready. My mother handed over the bundle of clothing and signed a paper which the doctor gave to her. We sat back to wait for Mehmet.

When the Sister returned she was carrying across her arm a small, lifeless-looking child. She handed the child to my mother, who only however gave a very brief glance, saying:

'This is not my son. This is a baby and my child is five years old. There is some mistake——'

But her voice trailed away uncertainly for now she was looking more closely at the child across her arms. And, indeed, it was Mehmet. Even I could see the likeness.

'He is light like a bird!' said my mother wonderingly.

'He is very ill,' said the Sister severely. 'It is wrong of you to take him home.'

I peeped at Mehmet in awe, at the little brown closed face with the jawbones sticking pitifully out from the fleshless cheeks, the faint, dark line of eyebrow, so delicately traced like my mother's, the skeleton arms and wrists and the poor, wasted body that was dying with hunger. I saw swift tears prick my mother's eyes, but she thanked the Sister and we came away.

Back to Istanbul again, in the hurtling tram, Mehmet held close against my mother so that the jolting would be minimised for him. I, nose pressed against the windows, conscious of my mother's sorrow and the shadow that surrounded my brother and the bright day was dimmed for me; the Bosphor had lost most of its blueness.

For several days Mehmet lay in a sort of stupor, with my grandmother constantly reading the Koran over him, and Muazzez and I, now and then, going to look at him, silenced in the face of such tremendous silence. After a while they tried to spoon-feed him with condensed milk obtained by my mother through the Sewing Depôt, and sometimes he would sip a little boiled water, moving his head plaintively from side to side as though in pain. If he did not seem to get any better at home, he certainly became no worse. And then a day came when I remember two important things happened to me. The first concerned Mehmet, for he opened his eyes and looked at me. He looked first at me unrecognisingly but, after a bit, awareness crept back to him and he smiled and held out his small hand.

'Brother!' he said to me in a weak, wondering voice, a voice that was not a voice but a thin thread of sound on the air.

I flew over to him, holding tightly to his hand and I asked him if he wanted anything. He said that he was hungry and I went to the kitchen for a spoon and the half-empty tin of condensed milk. I spooned it into his avid, greedy mouth until the tin was shining and empty and he begged for a glass of water. Muazzez staggered to him with the carafe, spilling a few drops over his sheet and we laughed uproariously, as though it was a great joke, and presently Mehmet turned on his side and went to sleep. I stayed by his bed until my grandmother returned from the market, and as she came into the house, I could hear Muazzez's excited, high-pitched voice telling her the joyful news. Upstairs rushed my grandmother like the wind and in a loud roar, which she thought was a whisper, asked me what had happened. When I told her, she threw up her hands in delight and began to recite a prayer of thanksgiving from the Koran. She crept across to Mehmet and listened for a few moments to his still, even breathing, then she said simply and with great faith that he would get better now and took us with her from the room, leaving him to his good sleep.

She had brought back a few uninspiring things with her from the market, and presently she told me to go to the Sewing Depôt, from where my mother would be returning to-day. She instructed me to tell my mother about Mehmet and to ask her to come home via Sirkeci, where the shops might have something other than the eternal Indian corn which my grandmother always bought in Bayazit.

She could not get me out of the house quickly enough, so great was her desire to prepare something appetising for my brother, and she grumbled that her legs would not carry her as far as Sirkeci these days.

So we come to the second thing of importance that happened to me that day.

I went to meet my mother, delivered my message and we walked towards Sirkeci, she very excited that her son had chosen to live.

I remember we managed to get some haricot beans and dried peas and a little sugar, rare luxury nowadays. We were on our way home, just behind the station at the time and making slow progress along the narrow, cobbled street, for this was one of the busiest spots in the city. We sidestepped out of the path of horses and of men pushing barrows and presently, above all the street cries, there came another sound, a sound more insistent on the ear, and my mother paused and looked to the sky and I followed her eyes and there, coming in across the Golden Horn, were three aeroplanes.

'English 'planes!' a man shouted, dashing past us into a shop doorway.

My mother and I stood looking at them, both of us unaware of the load of destruction they carried. People were hurrying by us into shops, into Sirkeci station, into doorways but I think my mother was too paralysed to move very swiftly. I remember she eventually pulled me under a shop awning and we cowered there, and it was only in after years I learned that she had been convinced that day that the awning would have saved us, that if the pilots could not see us then nothing could hurt us!

The aeroplane flew into Istanbul with a roar and then came a dull explosion which shook the earth.

I thought the noises would never cease. Clouds of dust billowed towards us and I discovered that my legs were in danger of giving way.

They bombed Mahmut Paşa Street that day, Istanbul's busiest market-place, and scarcely a gun to defend the city. And soon the aeroplane had gone, and the scream of ambulances hurtled piercingly on the ears from all directions. We began to go home, having to pass Mahmut Paşa Street on the way and already flames licked the little shops and the mean houses. A horse lay on its side, neighing horribly, its cart overturned across its broken body and the driver perched high above the débris with his face blown in. There were not enough ambulances, so lorries were commandeered and they passed us with their load of wounded, some unconscious, some crying out in agony and their flapping stumps of arms flaying the air sickeningly. Carts piled with the dead came nearby and one even passed us, and I was almost sick with horror when I saw its gory, exposed contents—heads lolling fearfully without their bodies, hands and legs jumbled together indecently, all bundled in together—for these were the dead and were no longer important when there were still the living to be saved.

'They meant to bomb the War Office,' someone was saying; 'but the bombs went wide and fell here——'

And the people who heard him commenced to boo him and he was suddenly in danger of his life, for the rest of the people were convinced that Mahmut Paşa Street had been deliberately bombed, because it was a crowded district. Still I remember that day and the murmurings of the people and the crying of the bereaved and none of us will ever know, or care to know, for it is ancient history now, whether the pilots went wide of their target or not. And all the way home my mother's eyes were blinded by the tears she shed for the innocent ones who had suffered and even for the unaware, surprised ones who had died. And that bombing lived in my mind for many years. Even recently when I had occasion to pass through Mahmut Paşa Street, still with its ugly, unbuilt-over scars, I saw that day again and I wondered if anyone else in that still overcrowded street remembered its tragic history.

Mehmet continued to thrive, albeit slowly. I would take him out each day as far as the wall that bounded for us the sea of Marmora, and his brown face became browner under the friendly sun. He had become more than ever a quiet, thoughtful little boy, not talking overmuch and flinching if one made a too sudden gesture. To this day he is the same, preferring to listen rather than contribute, rarely expressing an opinion—as if the two years in the school at Kadiköy had taken all initiative from him.

Summer passed and the first leaves began to fall, choking the dirty gutters and scurrying along the pavements like prim, frightened old ladies, and as the weather grew chillier, we went less to the sea wall. My tenth birthday loomed but birthdays were no longer important, and then suddenly the war was over for Turkey.

One night we went to bed still at war and the next day we heard that our country had had enough and was quitting. But for us who were left it mattered little. We had lost everything; but then there were many families like us, so we had no right to complain either.

My mother left the Sewing Depôt and we wondered what would become of us now. Gold, we heard, was fetching fabulous prices but we had long since spent all our gold—those gleaming, chinking coins that had rattled merrily in my grand-mother's trunk, many years ago now it seemed. But wait! Had we not an old salver that my great-grandfather had given to my grandmother on her wedding day? A golden salver that shone like the sun and was never used because it was such a clumsy size? We had indeed! And my grandmother took little time in remembering where she had last seen it, lying at the bottom of the ottoman in my mother's room, amongst all the china and glass which was never used nowadays. Out it came to be polished, for it was black and tarnished, and to be talked about, for whoever would have thought that such a useless thing might now fetch us money? My grandmother was given the job of getting rid of it, for we none of us could ever forget how she had once bested a Jew.

When she was ready to go to the Gold Market she was dressed with great care, and once again her jewels sparkled on her hands and her bosom, and the whole street turned out to see her and admire the giant salver that bloomed by itself in a corner, a little self-consciously, for it had always been a despised thing, even in my grandfather's day.

'Now you know the market price, per gramme,' reminded my mother sternly. 'And do not sell it at all if you do not get the right price!'

'Certainly not!' snapped my grandmother importantly, just as though the house was filled with money and we had no further need of any more.

Off she went, the tray hastily and shamefully wrapped in brown paper but so eager to show itself off that bits of it peeped through and winked and sparkled at us all down the street. And all the neighbours gasped with admiration and said what a beautiful tray it was and were we not blessed by God to have such a thing to sell in these hard times? All the morning we and the neighbours waited for my grandmother to return—they speculating on the price the tray would fetch and I was almost dizzy with disbelief as I heard the liras mounting by the hundred for, in those days, one hundred liras by itself was worth a thousand or more to-day. The old men and the young women and even the children counted up how much she would get and once I ran into my mother, gasping and choking with the piles of undigested liras ringing in my ears.

'I know *exactly* how much she will get,' said my mother

severely; 'or nearly——' she amended. 'We had it weighed on bakkal's scales yesterday, so run off now and do not listen to the neighbours' nonsense!'

And off I went, disappointed by my mother's matter-of-fact tone of voice.

When my grandmother was sighted, slowly ascending the hilly street, the crowd surged forward to meet her, but I was fleetest of all and reached her first. I knew the moment I saw her that she had been successful for she carried her head proudly again— a sure sign of triumph in my family. There were many packages in her hands, and tucked under her arm of all things a bottle of wine! She handed some of the packages to me but refused to surrender the wine and home we marched with the excited, talkative neighbours, who were much too polite to ask how much she had got, yet who knew her well enough by now to recognise victory in her step.

'Well!' said my mother's voice at the door, 'well, you are a disgrace, mother! How did you ever carry a bottle of wine through the streets—like a drunkard?'

'I missed my wine with dinner,' roared my grandmother, for all the world as though dinner was still a habit in our house. 'And what is more,' she added, 'I have fresh coffee here and sugar from the Bourse Noir so let us invite our good neighbours to drink to our good fortune.'

In surged the ready neighbours, up the stairs and into the salon, all of them politely removing their shoes before they trod the precious Sparta carpets. They were as happy as if the good luck of this day had been theirs and helped my mother dispense coffee and cognac and lifted their cups and glasses to shout:

'Güle-Güle! Mahṣallah, hanim efendi!' (Good luck! God bless you!)

And we were all overcome with emotion and the easy tears of old age started to the eyes of some of the older ones.

'Now we can buy plenty of good food,' shouted my grandmother, waving her coffee cup in the air excitedly. 'And clothes for the children——' she added, her eye catching mine.

And I dreamed of bright picture-books and scrap-books and a box of paints to carry me through the autumn days. I do not know how much my grandmother got for that old salver but I think it was more than she and my mother had anticipated, mathematics not being their strong point. And it is a funny thing too but when we had enough money in the house again, so that we need not worry for a long time to come, more came in unexpectedly—as is sometimes the way in life. So that from appalling poverty we jumped to comparative affluence in the space of a few weeks.

It came about because my mother started to embroider again, supplying orders to the bigger shops in Beyoğlu. Tray-cloths, table-cloths, pillow-cases, babies' dresses, all passed through her nimble fingers. She used to design and trace her own patterns which gave a touch of uniqueness to her work, an individuality that was liked by the discriminating foreign customers of the big shops. So the machine lay idle again, relegated to the kitchen, where it was forgotten for months on end until my grandmother suddenly had a passion for making new clothes for us. Muazzez began to look like a little doll, usually dressed all in white with exquisite embroidery done by my mother and two white bows atop her brown hair. She was developing into a winning and imperious little girl, very like my grandmother in temperament, ruthlessly bullying Mehmet and me into performing small duties for her. My grandmother was very proud of her and spent hours each day on her clustering curls.

'She is really going to be a great beauty,' she would say to a bored Mehmet and me, 'and one day she will marry a very rich man. You will see!'

And Muazzez, already vain, became vainer.

I had become very restless at home and was often insubordinate. My mother worried incessantly about my education, but all the schools were still disorganised and many teachers had never come back from the war. I used to haunt the streets, playing a corrupted version of football near the gardens of the Mosque, for I had nothing to keep my mind constantly occupied. My mother and I used to have fierce and bitter quarrels and, because I could not bear being confined to the house, I took to roaming farther and farther away from home. No doubt had I had a father to discipline me I should never have dared to do these things, but I would not listen to my mother or grandmother, flying into a passion if they attempted to interfere with me.

My mother was rebelling against life too—but for a different reason. Her rebellion was, unexpectedly enough, against wearing the veil, for she had noticed that none of the foreign women wore them and that even a few of the more daring Turkish women from good families had ceased the practice also. She used to complain about it to my grandmother, declaring she was sick and tired of keeping her face covered, and I would interrupt, with lordly ten-year oldness, saying I would not have her going about the streets with her face open. I would chastise her too for her many goings-out.

'You are never at home,' I would declare and although usually I was told to mind my own affairs, one day I was very surprised when my grandmother actually agreed with me.

'It is quite true,' she said heatedly. 'You are always out these days. And it is not right for you to complain that you have to wear the veil. Why, many women are still behind the kafes and they never see the colour of the sky, excepting from behind their veils. But at least you cannot complain of that for you tore the kafes from here and it is a wonder to me that you were ever accepted in this street, for you behaved exactly like a fast woman looking for another husband or like a prostitute. Yes, you did!' she assured my mother's astonished face. 'And now you talk of leaving aside your veil. Why, I lived for thirty years with my husband and I never went out without his permission and I had to keep my face covered all the time. If I went out in the carriage with Murat, immediately all the windows were closed and sometimes the blinds were drawn too. I say it is a scandal that women are to-day revealing their faces. God will punish them! Do not let me hear another word from you, my daughter, for surely the sky will open on you for such impiety.'

Never had I heard my grandmother talk at such length or with such obvious passion. My mother replied:

'You are talking a great deal of old-fashioned nonsense, mother! My place is not in the home these days. If I were to sit at home all day, or you either for that matter, who would go to market for us? Do you expect me to stay here all day, reading the Koran and wearing my veil for fear the passers-by should see me from the street? I tell you again, from now on I shall go without my veil!'

And she angrily tore the pretty veil from her face and threw it petulantly on the floor.

My grandmother lifted her hands to heaven.

'I never thought I should live to see this day,' she said.

'Times are changing,' said my mother.

'They will say you are a prostitute!' wailed my grandmother, genuinely distressed, totally incapable of accepting such a fierce gesture as the 'opening' of the face.

'If they do, it will not worry me,' retorted my mother. 'Their words will not bring bread to me. And from now on, you will throw aside your veil too, mother.'

'Oh no, no, no!' said my grandmother in superstitious horror. 'God forbid I should invite punishment upon me!'

But the next morning when my mother went into Beyoğlu, with a box of embroidered articles under her arm and her lovely face naked to the world, she was stoned by some children near Bayazit and received a nasty cut on the side of her head. After that she was cautious about going anywhere alone, but was adamant about not re-veiling herself; Mehmet or I would go with her to Beyoğlu, my grandmother steadfastly refusing to be seen with her. The reaction to her in the street was mixed. The older ones were stricken with horror, more especially since they had always recognised my mother as a good woman, and now their faith in her was sadly battered. She was still young and attractive—she was twenty-five—and despite the shadows that lingered now and then in her eyes, was so unusually beautiful that people could not help but stare at her, and certain sections of the street wondered if she were trying to catch a husband. They came in their droves, the old men as well, to remonstrate with my grandmother, urging her to put a stop to this terrible thing, and my grandmother, thoroughly enjoying herself, would groan to them that she had no authority left in this wayward family of hers. But the younger women sided with my mother, and some of them even began to follow her example. Their fathers, however, in the absence of dead husbands, took a stick to them muttering piously that no woman in their family would so disgrace themselves. So they put on their veils again in a hurry.

Not a few wished to apply the chastening stick to my mother also. They gave my grandmother sympathy until she was sick of it and prophesied gloomily—but with a little bit of anticipatory relish too, I think—that my mother would come to a bad end.

And indeed she very nearly did!

For one day in Bayazit, when she was alone, an impressionable Frenchman attempted to flirt with her. She tried walking hurriedly on but this had no effect at all, or if anything a worse effect, for the gallant Frenchman became more than ever aware of the swing of her silk skirts and the little dark curls that twined so coquettishly at the nape of her neck. Naturally he followed her. And all the little boys of the district became aware, as is the way of all little boys, of the one-sided flirtation which was in progress. And naturally enough they followed the tall Frenchman, so there was that day in Bayazit the very, very unusual sight of a young Turkish woman, with open face, followed by a foreigner and an innumerable number of small, dirty-nosed boys. When my mother made the mistake of stopping, trying to explain in her totally inadequate French that the gentleman was making a great mistake, he took off his hat, bowed elegantly and declared with obvious feeling:

'Vous êtes ravissante!'

And all the small boys who could not understand a word of what he said, cheered or jeered, according to their several temperaments, and my mother—very properly—hurried on, blushing and breathless and perhaps wishing a little bit for the security of her veil.

So it was that when she came down our street, with her procession behind her, the neighbours were more than ever scandalised and ran into their houses to tell the ones inside. But when my mother called out to them in Turkish that she was being followed, and very much against her will, they set to with a vengeance and brought out sticks and brooms and shooed off the gallant representative of Gallicism in no uncertain manner. Mehmet and I, who were watching the whole proceedings from the window, were bursting with laughter but my poor grandmother was quite ready to die with shame.

'Such a disgrace!' she kept saying. 'We shall never be able to live in this street again.'

But in this she was wrong for when the street had finally disposed of the amorous Frenchman, and a few old men had in fact chased him half-way to Bayazit with tin buckets in their hands, to break his head, the street settled down again to lethargy, exonerating my mother from all blame. All excepting the old women, that is.

Still the problem of my schooling was unsettled. It was eventually decided that I should be sent to a private school, but when my mother enquired about these, she found that Turkish was excluded from the curriculum and this made her so cross that she said she would rather keep me at home. Whilst she continued the search, I roamed the streets, usually with boys older than myself, defiant to all discipline, impatient of the slightest restraint. A few of the old men attempted to advise me, but their outworn, futile shibboleths so infuriated me that I threatened to run away somewhere if my grandmother did not stop enlisting the aid of these doddering, antiquated people.

Then my mother had a talk with the local Imam, and the decision they reached was very unpleasant for me, although I did not know that at the time.

They decided that as schooling was, for the moment, impossible, the next best thing to keep me out of mischief was to put me somewhere as an apprentice. Although really, apprentice sounds far too grand a word to apply in the circumstances, since I was only to remain 'apprenticed' until such times as a school could be found for me.

They chose a barber's shop.

I was practically incoherent with ten-year-old rage when they told me, and point blank refused to go. But the Imam, with indescribable cunning, painted such a rosy picture of my independence, of the 'tips' I would get, of the fascination of perhaps one day owning my *own* barber's saloon. What with one thing and another, he talked me into enthusiasm, my mother and grandmother for once having the wisdom to remain silent. Though I suspect their silence had something to do with previous warnings from the Imam, a capable man who liked to take matters into his own hands. By whatever hypnotism was employed I found myself the next day being taken to the barber's shop, only a few streets from our house.

The barber greeted me with an oily effusiveness which I instantly mistrusted. He said in a hissing whisper to my mother that he would train me well and see that I did not get into any mischief.

'You do understand,' said my mother insistently. 'He is not here to earn money but to keep him occupied until a suitable school can be found for him.'

'Of course!' said the barber in a perfectly indescribable voice. He bowed to my mother, hiding his eyes from her open face, and his enormous shoulders shrugged under his soiled, patched shirt.

'I shall look after him like a father,' he added. 'Like a father!' he repeated, flicking his eyes over me rapidly as though wondering just what sort of father he ought to be to me.

My mother looked terribly doubtful now that we were here, but nevertheless she left me in his care and went home, perhaps feeling thankful that at any rate I was not roaming the streets that day. I had terrible doubts too. Looking about me I could not recognise the glowing picture which had painted itself on my mind. The shop was very small, with only two customers' chairs and primitive in the extreme. A copper mangal stood in one corner, used for heating and at the same time for brewing coffee. The window was draped with some sort of muslin, much in need of washing, and the glasses were all fly-blown and bluish with the haze of dirt and smoke and dust. I no longer believed in the romantic aspect of such a job, but the thought of the tips still lured me on.

After my mother had departed, the barber lost all of his oily civility and said to me:

'This is a good job, my boy. If you are clever and keep your eyes open you will learn much and then you will pray for me all your life, yes?'

His little eyes snapped at me and, as he bent his face closer, to me I could smell dirt and perspiration, and the blue tassel of his greasy fez waggled with a separate life of its own.

'Over here,' he said, waving his hand, 'is the box where you will put all the tips. When I shave a customer or cut his hair, you will stand beside me and you will watch what I am doing. At the same time you will watch in my eyes and when I want soap or a towel you will get them immediately. You will make coffee and take it to the neighbouring shops and they will pay you for it. You will *not* come back without the money, you understand—yes?'

'Yes,' I muttered sulkily, already in a mild state of rebellion against this dirty saloon and the dirtier old barber.

'Smile when you say "yes",' he snarled, pulling back his upper lip from his broken teeth and giving an imitation of a smile.

'You gotta learn to smile in this job,' he continued, 'and if you break any coffee-cups I take the money from your tips, and if you haven't any tips I break your god-damned head, yes?'

'No,' I said and fled from his upraised hand.

All the morning I spent beside him whilst he shaved and cut hair and passed rough jokes with the customers, all of them street-sellers or small shop-keepers, curious about me and inclined to jeer at my accent. My eyes became tired with the strain of watching what the barber did and at the same time trying to watch his eyes for signals, although I never brought the right things for him. My head was constantly twisting and turning until finally I thought it would twist itself off my neck altogether.

At midday I was sent across to a delicatessen store and ordered to bring back one and a half portions of haricot beans, already cooked in oil and onions. I got bread too, great hunks cut by unclean fingers. The half portion was for me and we ate in the customers' chairs, washing down the meal with water from smeared glasses.

The afternoon passed quietly enough until suddenly an order came from a shop across the way for five coffees. I was set to make it but the fire had died in the mangal, so I tried to light it again with charcoal. This is not nearly so simple as it sounds. The barber swore at me and threatened to break my bones, but I had learned to ignore him and placed pieces of wood on the mangal, afterwards building up with charcoal. Then I poured oil generously over the whole lot, to the consternation of the barber, who said that I would set the place on fire. A match was applied and 'wouf!' went the contents of the mangal and a yellow sheet of flame almost enveloped me and dust flew everywhere. The barber chattered with rage, and just at that awkward moment a customer came in and the dirty remains of the haricot beans had to be removed from the chairs before he could sit down. The barber was forced to fetch water and towels for himself and alternated between bright, pleasant conversation with his customer and brief, pithy asides to me. I lay stretched full length along the stone floor, going 'pouf-pouf' at intervals at the reluctant mangal, red in the face with my labours and oblivious to the fumes and dust I was creating. Finally the barber lost his patience, left the customer half shaved and lay down beside me on the floor and blew with tremendous energy. His fat, pendulous belly wobbled under him, I watching it with fascination, and the customer came over to us, one side of his face still white with lather. He gave encouraging advice to the barber, who did not want it.

When the charcoal was eventually persuaded to burn, the barber was tired from all the puffing and blowing he had done, and black streaks ran down his face, charcoal dust and perspiration mingled. The customer started to lose his patience and within a very short time they had nearly come to blows. I quickly brewed coffee, preferring to keep out of their way until their tempers were cooler. When the five coffees were ready, I placed them on a brass tray with a suspended chain to carry it, and went over to the shop that had called for them. I gave the coffees and asked for the money, and they all laughed at me and said between the spasms of laughter, 'Tell Ali Bey he has our compliments.'

Ali Bey was the name of the barber.

When I got back to the saloon and delivered this message, the barber tore at his sparse grey hair, pulled me by the ear to the box for 'tips' and emptied the meagre contents into the palm of his hand.

'This is for me,' he said grimly and I was sad, reflecting that it was not easy to earn money—even 'tips'. 'You will learn the job like this,' said the sadistic old barber grimly. 'If you are such a fool that you let them drink coffee without paying for it, then you must pay for it. You see?'

I commenced to argue with him and called him a son of a donkey and many other choice expressions I had picked up in the streets.

'Pezevenk!' I yelled indignantly, which even to this day in Turkey is a deadly insult, and he danced around me, threatening to break my bloody head if he got at me. I continued to dance with him, but in the opposite direction, feeling that closer acquaintance would not be beneficial while I searched my vocabulary for more insults.

Were it not for the fact that a customer walked in, he would probably have half killed me. As it was, he collected himself sufficiently to attend to the customer. But his temper had suffered so badly that he nicked a piece out of the customer's cheek and heated words flared up immediately, and I crouched sulkily in a corner and refused to hand towels or anything else.

Another order came in for coffees and I made them, anxious to be out of the saloon for as long as possible before some harm befell me. Unfortunately, in my haste to get out I collided with two more customers in the doorway. The tray with the coffees lurched dangerously and deposited all the contents over the legs of the prospective customers. I yelped with dismay, dropped the wet tray with a clatter and streaked through their coffee-stained legs. Their threats and curses filled the air after me. One man even gave chase, but I was fleeter than he and continued to run like the wind until I arrived home. Even there all I could do was to choke and gurgle with aching laughter, for the brief glance I had had of the barber's face— after I had upset the tray—was excruciatingly funny.

Thus, ignominiously, ended my first and last day as a barber's apprentice.

CHAPTER XVII

KULELI

NINETEEN HUNDRED AND nineteen, the War over and Istanbul filled with Allied Commissioners and officers in their dull khaki uniforms. The sibilant twittering of the English language filled the air, and the English with the French and the Italians supervised the police and the ports. They were everywhere—advising and ordering and suggesting.

One day my mother came home from Beyoğlu with two items of exciting news. The one concerned herself, for her designs in needlework were attracting attention and she had taken so many orders that morning that she wanted my grandmother to help her to complete them. This my grandmother was perfectly willing to do for although she perhaps lacked true creative skill, she was an expert needlewoman—quite frequently paying more attention to detail than my mother. My mother had great sensibility and during the times when she was working out her patterns she could lose herself to the exclusion of her family and the world.

Her designs were most vivid and appealing. They lived in bold colourings and outline as though painted on the materials. A number of foreign women had asked for repetitions of her work but she refused to repeat, even if the money offered was high. Instead she would work out some new design for them, intricate or simple according to her mood of the moment, offering it casually as though it did not matter whether they accepted or not. I often wonder what they thought of her, so slim and haughty with the flaring wing of nose and the delicate eyebrows that seemed painted on, her unveiled face and her halting French. To-day all women in Istanbul and the other cities and towns go unveiled but in 1919 she must have been a rare sight. Many of the shops in Beyoğlu suggested that she should open an atelier but she would laugh at them, saying she had no head for business. My grandmother, excited by the fuss created by my mother's designs, also nagged that an atelier was becoming essential. She even wanted to turn her bedroom into one, declaring that she would sleep somewhere else, but my mother held out against this for a long time.

The year 1919 saw my family on its feet again, my mother being the bread-winner.

The second item of news that Spring day concerned Mehmet and me. She had met in Beyoğlu the wife of the Colonel in whose house I had been circumcised but he was a General now and an important person in the War Office. His wife had been so delighted to see my mother after the lapse of years that she had insisted upon her returning home with her to partake of coffee and gossip about all that had happened in the years they had not met. She had hustled my unveiled mother into her husband's motor-car, driven by his batman, and my mother never having been in a motor-car before was too terrified to speak during the journey to Bayazit. She told us that the sense of speed was terrible, that her heart had been perpetually in her mouth and that every time another motor-car had whizzed past in the opposite direction she had closed her eyes and left herself entirely to God's mercy. This feminine attitude annoyed Mehmet and me who would have given much to have been in her place.

'But you are not afraid of trams,' Mehmet said in great contempt and she replied that trams ran on lines and were, in consequence, perfectly safe, and did not go so fast as a motorcar. During coffee the General's wife had asked about us children and when she heard of the difficulties of having us suitably schooled came out with the suggestion that we should be sent to the Military School.

'The what?' roared my grandmother, perhaps feeling like us that she had not heard aright, and a queer little excited feeling began to pull at my heart.

'The Military School,' repeated my mother with some impatience. 'She told me that a very close friend of her husband's is in the War Office and can use his influence to enter the boys. Apparently the Government intend to establish a junior school, which will be attached to the Academy, and they will only accept pure Turkish children so that eventually only Turkish officers will be in the Army.'

'I shall be a General,' I said boastfully and Mehmet said gently:

'I shall be a doctor and then I can help the wounded soldiers to get better——'

And if I may digress a little, of the two of us he got his wish.

'But what sort of education will they get in a Military School?' demanded my grandmother, who knew nothing about schools but who always liked to put in her opinion.

'How can I know?' demanded my mother, displeased that her startling news had not had a better reception. 'And I do not suppose it matters very much,' she added, 'for if they are going to be officers they need to know very little, excepting how to kill each other of course.'

'I shall not kill anyone,' interposed Mehmet in his soft voice and taking her words with literal seven-years oldness.

'Do you really think the General can do anything?' I asked, thrilled by the idea of life in a Military School, picturing it to be anything but what it turned out to be.

'Let us see,' returned my mother. 'Anyway, the General's wife is going to see her husband's friend this afternoon to discuss it for me.'

'Shameless woman!' interjected my grandmother in horror, still firmly entrenched in the past, and we began to laugh at the bewilderment on her face for she was half inclined to believe that the General's wife was conducting a clandestine affaire with her husband's friend.

That evening the General's batman arrived with a letter from the great man himself which said that he had talked over matters with the General in charge of the scheme, that he was willing to see us at the War Office the following afternoon, that he himself had given some information about the family and its present difficulties, that he hoped my mother would take advantage of the good life offered to her sons, etc.

My mother thoughtfully folded the letter, and the widow, who was spending the evening with us, declared that good luck was returning to the family.

'Perhaps you are right,' said my mother. 'But of course I was told this afternoon that everything at the school is still very disorganised after the War, that it will take a long time before it settles back to normal. Still, it is a great opportunity.'

I began to laugh, remembering the barber's shop and my mother with remarkable intuition looked across at me, saying:

'Well, at least there will be no more coffee-cups to break!'

The following afternoon Mehmet and I were taken to the War Office, excitement and fear gnawing at our vitals, hunger too, for we had been unable to eat any luncheon. My mother seemed nervous also but tried to put this behind her when we arrived at the War Office. A soldier showed us into the office of a very beautiful young officer, the General's adjutant, and he blushed when he spoke to my mother, asking her name and her business. She gave him this information and he asked her to be seated for a moment and dashed gracefully into an adjoining room where presumably lurked the General. Mehmet and I stood awkwardly whilst my mother sat stiff as a ramrod on a hard chair, a bright spot of colour in either cheek. The adjutant returned, saying that the General would see us at once. He held the door open, keeping his eyes respectfully on the ground as my mother passed him. I passed through the door last of all and looked back to see the beautiful young adjutant staring at my mother's back, an unreadable expression in his eyes. Maybe he thought it strange for a Turkish woman to go with open face.

The General was tall and lean with silvery hair and a kind intelligent face, or did it only seem kind as it looked at my mother with that especial look that even old men reserve for lovely women?

He pushed forward an armchair for her, hard ones for Mehmet and me and said with an affectation of joviality:

'What! Are these young lions yours?'

My mother replied that this was so.

'Well, well!' said the General, as though this was a great surprise. 'Our old friend, General X, has told me all about you. I once knew your father-in-law, in my youth you know. A very fine man. I was sorry to hear that you lost your husband during the War. I am afraid things cannot have been easy for you.'

'I lost my brother-in-law too,' said my mother.

'Very sad,' said the General, painting sympathy on his face, and he fiddled with papers on his desk and for a few more moments they talked family gossip.

Then the General turned to me and said:

'So you are Irfan! How old are you, my boy?'

'Ten, Sir,' I replied in a weak voice.

'This War! This War!' He sighed to my mother. 'This child should have been at school three years ago. However he looks intelligent; let us see what we can make of him. So you would like to be an officer?' he demanded, turning suddenly to me.

'Yes, Sir,' I said, adding boldly, 'I should like to be a General like you!'

He laughed.

'And perhaps you will,' he retorted. 'It is something at least to know what one wants from life. And what about the little one?' he asked, chucking Mehmet under the chin then saying thoughtfully to my mother, 'Yes, he is like his grandfather. I can see the resemblance quite plainly.'

He mused over Mehmet's small, shut-away face, then asked: 'What is your name?'

'Mehmet, Sir,' stammered my brother, very red in the face with such close, unwelcome scrutiny.

'And what do you want to be, Mehmet? A General too?'

'No, Sir,' said Mehmet. 'I want to be a doctor.'

'Two young gentlemen who know their minds!' declared the General. 'I remember when I was their age I wanted to be a street-seller for they seemed to be the only people who ever had horses. But the only way I ever got a horse was by becoming a Cavalry officer, so perhaps to all of us Fate gives our desires in a roundabout way. Well,' he declared, turning his attention back to my mother, 'you appear to be a fortunate mother for here you have, in embryo, a future General and a future doctor.'

He patted our heads and rang for his adjutant.

'I shall leave you in my adjutant's hands,' he said to my mother, adding in a conspiratorial whisper, 'He knows far more about this business than I do!'

We went out to the adjutant's office, who said:

'You understand, hanim efendi, that you have to sign a contract for the Military education of these two boys?'

'No,' said my mother.

The adjutant grew red and could hardly bear to look at her.

'But did not the General explain?' he said in astonishment.

'No,' replied my mother.

'Dear, dear!' said the adjutant fussily, then he cleared his throat and tapped a piece of parchment with a finger. 'This contract,' he began, 'states that your two sons shall be educated at the Military School in Kuleli and afterwards at the Military College—providing they pass their examinations—entirely at the expense of the Government. In return for this they will serve in the Turkish Army for fifteen years but if they fail in their final examinations they will serve as Sergeants for the same number of years, without any chances of promotion. There is no promotion from the ranks.'

'That seems very hard,' murmured my mother doubtfully. 'If I sign this contract I sign my sons' lives away for twenty-five years and how can I tell if they will be able to pass their examinations or not? How can I tell?' she said again, looking up at the young officer, and he smiled a little, remembering his own years in the Military institutions.

'It is generally found, hanim efendi, that if a boy wants to become an officer he passes his examinations.'

My mother smiled too.

'I think perhaps you are right,' she said. 'Nevertheless, I should like a little time to think this over before, with a stroke of the pen, I take their freedom from them. How long will it be before these contracts are ready for my signature?'

'There are many formalities to complete first,' replied the adjutant. 'Perhaps in fifteen days' time?'

'That surely gives me time enough to decide,' answered my mother, and I was in an agony that she, with her feminine prejudices, was going to take this chance from my hands. I dared not interrupt their conversation but I felt sick with apprehension that my bright and shining dream of becoming an officer, a General, would end in nothing.

The adjutant explained that he required certain documents from the local police, from the Muhtar, a certificate of good health from the proper authorities and twelve photographs of each of us.

'References are not needed,' said he with some embarrassment. 'For General X has already given them.'

'Thank you,' said my mother with a faint ironical inflection in her cool voice, and the adjutant bowed us out of his office, his eyes once more on the floor, his attitude beautifully restrained.

For the next few days there was a great deal of argument at home for my mother was extremely obstinate, refusing to be advised or guided by anyone. My grandmother said she could not understand why so much fuss was being made since nothing very serious could go amiss with our lives whilst we were in the hands of the Military authorities.

'But can you not see that other schools can be soon found again? Civil schools with as sound an education but without the tie of signing away their lives for twenty-five years?'

'I do not want to go to any other school!' I wept, impotent and unable to stand up against my mother's reasoning. 'I want to be an officer! Please!' I begged, as a last sop to politeness.

The battle rolled back and forth, now in favour, now against the Military School. The neighbours animatedly joined in the discussion, my mother not listening to what they said, mistrusting everybody's opinion. In the meantime however she took us to the Bayazit Police for the necessary papers. We went to the Muhtar's office, to the hospital for examination, and having obtained all the relevant documents, we went to be photographed and still no final decision was forthcoming from my mother.

I took to going to the Mosque, praying fervently in that cool, quiet place. I prayed no prescribed prayers for I was unable to concentrate on anything but:

'Please God let me go to the Military School. Please God let me go the Military School!' saying the same thing over and over again in feverish intensity.

And perhaps a benevolent God heard my anxious prayers for the evening the finished photographs arrived my mother announced that she had carefully thought everything over and that she was convinced she was doing the right thing in allowing us to go to Kuleli.

Once again we visited the War Office, my mother leaving us in the adjutant's room whilst she went to speak to the General in private. As she was departing, he said:

'Personally, I think you have made a wise decision and good luck to you and your sons.'

The contracts were signed at last and only then did I feel able to breathe properly. It was done now and could not be undone! Oh, proud and lovely moment! We had been given to Kuleli Military School, that long, white, rambling building that I was to know so well.

The adjutant solemnly shook our hands.

'Report to Kuleli on the 15th of May,' he said crisply in a man-to-man tone of voice and I grew scarlet with pleasure.

May 15th, 1919, is a date in Turkish history for on that day Kemal Atatürk sailed towards Samsun. It was the date the Admiral of the British Mediterranean Fleet declared that the Greeks would occupy Izmir—and that was the date too that I entered Kuleli. Young and insignificant and as yet untried by life, yet could I also claim a share in the date that was making Turkish history.

The morning dawned fair and promising and Mehmet and I were taken by my grandmother to the Mosque to pray. We prayed for different things, we three. My grandmother prayed for our health and our success in school-life. I know for I heard her, her loud rumbling voice intoning, intoning. . . . Maybe Mehmet prayed to become a doctor, but who can say? for Mehmet could be as secretive as the grave. And I prayed one little prayer only. I gave thanks because I was going to Kuleli at last. Over and over again I prayed: 'Thank you, God. Thank you, God,' and felt His invisible presence all around me.

Good-byes were said to the street for we did not know when we would be returning again and the old women cried over us and the old men sighed and wished they were young again. And eventually we got away for Galata Bridge and the boat that would take us down the Bosphor, to the beginning of our youthful dreams.

Were we nervous, I wonder, that May morning, just the littlest bit reluctant to leave home and familiar faces so far behind us? I do not think so, although looking back from this distance it is no longer possible to judge that with any accuracy. We went to the boat dressed stiffly in our best, our faces and hands so clean and shining that all who saw us must have realised that this was a great occasion. And in my case whenever we passed a French or British officer—and the way to Galata Bridge was thick with them—I felt proud of the future my mother had chosen for me and told myself that I too should one day walk like this, in uniform, the badges of rank on my collar.

My mother allowed me to buy the boat tickets and I felt very important, as though the humble clerk who attended to me should know that I was bound for Kuleli and adventure. When I requested three tickets for Çengelköy he paid no attention to me at all, as if I was the merest passenger and not a potential General. But my inflated ego was not jolted and I talked loudly to my mother and Mehmet about Kuleli and what I would do there. Once my mother said:

'Hush!' but not sharply. 'It is very vulgar to boast, you know.'

But thoughts of vulgarity would never be able to dampen enthusiasm.

We bought simit on the boat and I dimly remembered Sariyer and my father came back fleetingly, for less than a second, to tantalise with his shut-away face, and Aunt Ayşe smiled welcome but Uncle Ahmet stayed maddeningly just outside the line of mental vision, refusing to show his face.

But Sariyer was more than just an hour down the Bosphor; Sariyer was four years away and deader for us than its dead owners. I asked Mehmet if he remembered Sariyer and Uncle Ahmet and he looked vague and said he did not. And I tried to paint a picture for him, there on the boat, of that old red-roofed house we had visited before the War. The pictures poured through my brain like pictures shaken up in a kaleidoscope and I talked of the magnolia-trees that had stood on the lawn, of the shine on the grass when the sun came out to dry the rain, of the dogs, Fidéle and Joly, of the grapes on the house-vine of which my aunt had been so proud. And as I talked I was in Sariyer again.

'I used to fish in the Bosphor with Uncle Ahmet,' I told Mehmet's listening face. 'We never used to catch very much but it was fun rowing home under the moon and sometimes hearing the voices coming across the water from Istanbul side.'

'I did not know you would remember so much,' said my mother. 'And you have a gift for words, my son. You have brought Sariyer back to me again too. I hope I have not done the wrong thing in entering you for a Military School. Perhaps you would have been better somewhere else.'

'Of course not, mother,' I said indignantly. 'I wanted to come to Kuleli and I should have hated any other school. I am going to be an officer and one day I shall be a General, you will see! And I shall carry you everywhere on my arm and all the people will say that you look young enough to be my wife and the women will be jealous of you.'

My mother laughed merrily.

'Your imagination is too vivid,' she said. 'And misplaced at that!'

We reached the boat-station of Çengelköy and disembarked, feeling less important now that we were so near our goal.

'Kuleli?' my mother asked the ticket-collector. 'The Military School?'

'Turn to the left,' replied the ticket-collector briefly, only barely glancing at Mehmet and me. 'It is only a few minutes' walk from here and the school is so big you cannot miss it.'

So out to the quiet dusty roads of Çengelköy and along the sea-road, tree-lined and white in the noonday sun. The school loomed up on our right, like a Palace, I thought, so white it was against the cloudless summer sky that fifteenth day of May in 1919, the day Atatürk's little boat rode the waters to Samsun.

We mounted the stone steps to the main door and my heart had commenced to thump furiously. A porter on sentry duty asked my mother's business and she said she had come to leave us at the school, as arranged with the War Office.

'This is the Military College,' he informed her coldly. 'The school is on the hill, along this road and up. It is a big grey building and you will find it quite easily.'

Up the hill road we toiled, hot and uncomfortable, disappointed that the white shining palace was not for us after all. We arrived at the school panting and out of breath and a great iron-barred gate prevented us from entering. There was the sound of boys' voices and a few of them came near to the gate to look at us. There was a sentry-box near the gate and a soldier on guard there shouted, 'Hüseyin Aga! Hüseyin Aga!'

And down towards the gate came an old, old man with a flowing white beard and a bent back and he grumblingly withdrew the bolts of the gates and asked our business.

My mother told him but this time impatience made her imperious and she tossed her piled-up curls and the old man grew civil and eyed her unveiled face with open curiosity. He allowed us to enter the garden, motioned to my mother to take a seat under the cool shade of the trees and said he was going to look for the 'Captain', and muttered a bit to himself as though uncertain where to find the Captain.

My mother sat down gratefully for the heat had tired her and whilst she was resting I strolled away to explore. I went near to the gate and I saw two men unloading lamb carcasses from a cart and another man was carrying a sack of something that from the partially opened top tooked like spinach. An old man who might have been a cook or a kitchen servant was haggling over the lamb and several mangy curs snarled under the horse's legs and were kicked away by the men. I heard Mehmet's voice calling for me and I ran back to where I had left him with my mother and saw that Hüseyin Aga was back again and waiting to lead us to the Captain.

We came near to the main school building and to our left there was a long, one-storied hut which, judging from the noise of cutlery, was the dining-room. The din coming from there was appalling and several big boys were entering. Most of them had very dark skins and one was, to my horror, quite black. They were shabbily dressed and looked jeeringly at Mehmet and me and talked amongst themselves. One of them said something aloud to us and I could not understand what language he was speaking. He is not Turkish, I said to myself, and wondered how many different nationalities might be housed in this place.

The Captain met us at the door of his office with a big stick in his hands! He looked a very nervous type of man and was very pale. He clutched his stick fiercely, as though he was accustomed to quite frequently defend himself from the hordes of young savages in the school! He took us into his room and gave us rickety chairs to sit on. The room was indescribably dirty and untidy and the Captain stuttered so badly every time he spoke that I felt a sort of hysteria beginning to bubble inside me. He thumbed through a pile of papers on his desk and finally extracted two which evidently related to us.

'Irfan and Mehmet?' he asked and my mother replied that this was so.

'Turkish and Muslim,' he said and sighed, leaning back in his chair.

'Thank God for that!' he said, stuttering very badly.   'Two more Turks in the school!'

He looked at my mother.

'We are, unfortunately, not yet organised here,' he said. 'There is still a great deal to do and we have been saddled with many Kurds and Armenians from Eastern Anatolia and there are, as yet, only a few Turks. No doubt one day the authorities will make up their minds which are to remain and which are to be sent elsewhere. Our intention, hanim efendi, is to bring up a new generation of purely Turkish officers.'

It was odd but when he commenced to speak in sentences, he forgot his stutter and poured out a lot of irrelevant detail to my mother as if now that at last he had begun to unburden himself he could not cease.

When he had tired himself with talking he stood up and said, with the stutter back again, his mouth twitching nervously:

'Well, hanim efendi, you may safely leave the boys in my hands. You may visit them once in a week if you wish but they will not be permitted to go home until they have had several months' training.'

My mother thanked him and we kissed her hands and Hüseyin Aga shuffled out into the garden, to escort her to the main gates.

Mehmet and I were left alone with the Captain and he looked at us quizzically and we solemnly stared back at him and I remembered all the things he had told my mother. And suddenly twenty-five years seemed an awful long time, a lifetime surely, and I looked through the unclean windows into the rank, untidy gardens where the hordes of boys were streaming from the dining-room and my heart began to beat nervously.

The gilt had worn a bit off the gingerbread. It was still true that this was the Military School, to which I had passionately wanted to come but where was the glamour I had expected, the pomp and the military splendour?

CHAPTER XVIII

MORE ABOUT KULELI

WHEN I THINK back to that day in Kuleli, in that grey, dilapidated building on the hill, I cannot but be glad that it has been abolished, that the present generation of cadet-officers are better housed and study under better conditions than obtained when we were there.

Sometimes when I see them in the Istanbul streets with their smart, dark-blue uniform, the dashing red line running down the trouser legs to show that they belong to the military caste, I cannot but remember my generation's early years as cadets.

That morning in May 1919 when my mother had left us and we stood there in the Captain's forbidding room awaiting his instructions, all the romance of soldiering left me.

Mehmet and I stood there uncertainly whilst the Captain rustled papers on his desk and ignored us.

I suppose I cried myself to sleep that night. A bugle commenced to play from the garden, low and mournful and full of sadness in its isolated loneliness. It was the one thing needed to make me feel conscious of being far away from home and I buried my head in the pillow and started to cry.

I awoke some time in the middle of the night yet no noise had disturbed me for the dark dormitory was full of gently breathing boys.

Something was pricking my body like a thousand red-hot needles and I scratched tentatively and as I moved my arm something ran down it and my flesh crawled with loathing for my bunk was alive with bed-bugs.

One dropped on my face from the bunk above me and I wanted to shout out with horror for the dark things that walked by night. But eventually I let them have their way with me and slept again—for exhaustion was stronger than fear.

I awoke to a bugle playing Reveille and a Duty Student stripping the blanket from me.

'Open your eyes!' he bawled and I looked around me dazedly, having forgotten for the moment where I was.

I moved and was conscious of stiffness for the bunk was hard and my ribs ached. To a lesser degree I was conscious of the swollen lumps on my legs and arms where the bugs had feasted all night.

The boy in the bunk next to me told me to remove my vest and at that moment I heard the voice of the Sergeant yelling 'Lice examination!'

We all divested ourselves of our vests and I discovered that my body was a mass of itching sore red places. I carefully examined my vest for lice but could discover none. Plenty of bed-bugs lurked in the seams though and I picked them off with repugnance, throwing them into the bowls of water which stood beside the lower bunks. Here they furiously exerted their fat swollen bodies trying to escape from the water.

The boy beside me proudly showed me two lice he had caught and I tried not to feel sick as he killed them, declaring to me that if one did not immediately kill the beasts they would eat one.

The lively bugs still kicked in the water-bowls and when the lice examination had been concluded we were permitted to wash ourselves. Everyone made a great clatter entering and leaving the wash-houses for we all wore takunya on our feet.

After dressing, with a great deal of fussiness on my part for fear vermin had embedded themselves in the seams of my jacket or trousers, we assembled in the corridor for morning Roll Call. The Sergeant read out our names in a brusque voice and meekly we all answered to our names. We filed to the dining-room for breakfast, which consisted of the black bread from the night before, a handful of black olives and the minutest possible portion of cream cheese and thick, strong tea—milkless and not sweet enough.

Afterwards we walked in the gardens for there was nothing else to do, but soon a bell clanged and we had to assemble at the main gates where the Sergeant awaited us. He took us to a hill at the back of the school, told us to sit down on the grass, then ordered us to undress. It was another lice examination and I wondered how many times in a day this would continue. We all sat there in the morning sunlight, diligently searching our clothes and I thought of my mother and how shocked she would be were she to see her eldest son sitting naked on a hill—searching himself for lice.

There were no lessons. The days slipped by and we continued to be ignored by the War Office and the outside world alike. They were lazy, sun-filled days and all of us had far too little to occupy our minds or our bodies, so physical exercise was mostly in the form of fighting.

I was told one day that I was to be that evening's Duty Student and I did not relish the idea. We were all filled with the wildest superstitious dread of the dead, believing that they had the power to come back to haunt us. That night when the retiring student had gone to bed and I was all alone now in the dark, all the old fears returned to me and it availed me nothing to tell myself that it was stupid to be afraid of the dark. It was uncannily quiet, in the way a place full of unaware sleepers always is, and I shivered a bit. The even rise and fall of their breathing was the only sound to be heard but after a bit I heard a clock striking far away, down in the well of the hall, chiming the hour. The little oil lamp flickered and seemed about to go out but it revived again.

Nothing happened that night but I was glad beyond measure when the first pale streaks of dawn crept up from the East and finally the new day broke over the peaceful, dewy garden.

But the new day heralded nothing for us but half-cooked food, lice examinations and fights. Our colossal boredom led us into troubles. There was no discipline anywhere, the Captain was practically always invisible and the War Office seemed to have forgotten us.

I learned that the Kurds and the Armenians were all orphans from the East of Turkey and that General Kazim Karabekir had collected them all and sent them to Kuleli. He was a popular General in the East but when his wild young protégés from Anatolia arrived in Istanbul, everyone had immediately disclaimed all responsibility for them, so they rotted in Kuleli until some day someone would remember them. The same sort of thing applied to the Arabs and the Albanians, who were originally brought to Istanbul by Enver Paşa, but when he escaped from Turkey after the War was over, they too were sent to Kuleli and promptly forgotten.

In the meantime the Sultan decided that he wanted Turks from good families or the sons of officers to be schooled at

Kuleli, so the War Office drew up a very magnificent but unworkable plan and ignored the fact that the school was already overrun with the hordes from the East.

The Turkish Army was demobilised—those who were left—the War Office did nothing and famous officers were reduced to selling lemons in the Istanbul streets. It was hardly surprising that nobody worried about us.

My mother visited us every few weeks and when she first saw us in our baggy uniforms she looked as if she did not know whether to laugh or cry. She asked many questions about our lessons, the sort of food we were being given and was disposed to lump all Kurds and Armenians as murderers. Impetuously she wanted to take us home again. She complained to the Captain that the place was dirty and that she did not wish to leave us here any longer. The Captain, it appeared, spread his hands expressively and repeated the same old refrain that everything was of course still very disorganised. He then gently reminded her that she had signed contracts for us and that if we were taken home he would be most regretfully compelled to send the Military Police after us. This really frightened her for it had never occurred to her that the contracts would be used against her in this fashion. Not to be entirely thwarted however she furiously told the Captain with more spirit than accuracy that she would use her influence at the War Office to have us removed. The Captain, no doubt having heard this before, remained unimpressed.

My mother would come to the school unveiled and several of the older boys said she was a 'tango' (tart) and I became involved in many fights.

I begged my mother to cover her face and although she indignantly refused at first, nevertheless she soon gave in. One day she complained that Mehmet and I smelled, and the next time she visited us brought perfumed soap with her. This we refused in horror, declaring that life was already sufficiently difficult for us without adding to the burden with scented soaps.

Kuleli Military School proper, the big white palace fronting the Bosphor, was occupied by older boys—boys who would eventually graduate from there to the snobbish Military College in Harbiye.

News circulated one day that the American occupying forces were going to take over the school for the Armenians. Rumours also spread that our turn would come too but what was to happen to all of us nobody knew and presumably nobody cared. About this time we heard too the first faint magic of the name of Kemal Atatürk, who was gathering together an Army in far-off Anatolia, who had already established a Nationalist government in Ankara.

The news about the Americans and the Armenians proved to be true enough and one day we saw from our gardens the older boys of Kuleli bringing beds and mattresses and desks into the school gardens. Their evacuation was commencing.

The hatred between Turk and Armenian is notorious, but that day in our grey school on the hill the hatred was intense. The Armenians could not be held, so proud were they to receive the recognition of the Americans. They swaggered and strutted and fights became more frequent than ever. When the American flag one morning waved over Kuleli, the Armenians went mad with joy and the Kurds berserk with fury. A number of broken heads resulted and the Captain's stick did overtime.

Our turn came afterwards. One morning we had to assemble in the main hall, the old Monitors attempting to keep law and order and refusing to answer all our questions. We must have looked a rough lot standing there, in our ill-fitting uniforms, our heads cropped and our faces pasty through bad feeding. Some American officers came in through the main gates, an Armenian priest with them and a tall American woman with a flat bosom and severe horn-rimmed spectacles.

She intimidated me far more than the officers did. A very dragon of a woman she was who would always know what was good for one. We watched them expectantly.

First they busied themselves with the older boys and some were separated from the lines and we uncomfortably wondered what this separatedness might portend.

Soon they came to us and an interpreter called out:

'All Armenians step this side!'

Many boys stepped forward, including our Sergeant. The priest—who looked quite terrifying with his black spade beard— began to ask us questions and the woman took matters into her own hands, apparently deciding that no harm would be done were she also to do a bit of separating. She glanced at us coldly as though all of us were so stupid that we did not know what nationality we were. Earnestly she peered into our faces then pulled a few more boys over to the Armenian side.

They were Kurds she selected and I could not but be curious to know by what means she wished Armenian nationality on them. She peered closely at me too but left me in the lines.

Soon the selections were completed and the Armenians were put into a large room off the hall. We were dismissed—no one having any further use for us.

We eagerly ran to the garden to look through the windows of the room where lurked the Armenians. They waved happily to us, jeering and shouting rude remarks. We, not to be out-done, replied in kind. We threatened to push in their faces and the old Monitors implored us over and over again to make less noise.

Suddenly above all the shouting I heard my name called and I recognised my brother's voice but although I looked everywhere for him I could not find him. His plaintive voice called and called to me and fear broke over me and I thrust my way to the front of the crowd, sobbingly telling him I was coming.

I saw him at one of the windows where all the Armenians were and I flew to him, stretching up and grasping his small hand.

He said with hysteria in his voice:

'They are taking me with the Armenians!'

I did not know what to do but I clung to his cold hands until a big Armenian thrust his body between us, forcing our hands apart. I ran to a Monitor, telling him what had happened but his slowness, his indecision maddened me. I dragged him over to the American officers to explain. The interpreter pushed us aside, demanding to know how we dared disturb the lordly American ones.

He would not listen to me and I noticed that the Armenians had been formed into long lines and were being marched out of the school. I left the old Monitor and the puzzled American officers and ran to the marching, jubilant lines searching for Mehmet. Feverishly I searched, my heart almost choking me, and when I found him I threw myself on him, holding him tightly. Someone tried to separate us and I said:

'Leave us alone. This is my brother. We are Turks and his name is Mehmet!'

An Armenian jeered.

'My name is Mehmet too but what does that prove?'

I pulled Mehmet out of the line but the interpreter who had come to see what all the commotion was about pushed him back again. I kicked him fiercely on the shin.

'Dirty Armenian!' I said. 'You are taking my brother with you. He is a Turk!'

The American officers with the woman and the priest had come up to us by this time and the woman asked what was the matter. The interpreter apparently said that nothing was wrong, bowing himself almost double in his efforts to please her. I kicked him again and one of the officers caught hold of me. Weakly I pummelled his chest, sobbing out the story in Turkish which he could not understand. As a last desperate attempt to make him understand, I jerked my head towards my terrified little brother and said:

'Turk! Turk!' and then as he still did not appear to understand, I searched back through the years to the fragments of French I had once known. 'Il est mon frère,' I said, and then he understood and he allowed Mehmet to come to me.

The woman interfered, saying something I could not understand. I was in an agony to kill her, this stupid, righteous woman with the hard, cold face.

'Cochon Américaine!' I said in desperation and she boxed my ears but more in sorrow than in anger, her face implying that only a Muslim, an outsider from Christianity, could say such a thing. Only a Turk, her face implied, could have used this expression.

With the Armenians gone from the school we were quieter, only the Kurds still on the look-out for fight.

We were still the merest handful of Turkish students but the Kurds soon tired of baiting such unresponsive elements and took to escaping to the far end of the gardens, where they could sling stones down the hill into the Kuleli gardens where walked the Armenians.

We would see them in their smart, well-fitting American uniforms and hear the bell which called them to lessons. Still we roamed, unlessoned, undisciplined and more warlike than ever.

One day though the stuttering Captain was replaced by a new Commanding Officer, and soon other officers came to the school and lawlessness became a thing of the past.

The Kurds and the Albanians and the excitable Arabs were marched out of Kuleli and there were many of us who wondered where they went. Perhaps they flooded the streets of Istanbul in warlike waves to sleep hungry under Galata's impersonal bridge. We none of us ever knew.

CHAPTER XIX

GROWING UP THE HARD WAY

ONCE AGAIN THE Occupation Forces stepped in to disrupt our lives for one day they ordered us out of our school on the hill within forty-eight hours.

The Commanding Officer announced the news with a grim, disillusioned face and instructed us to assist the young teaching officers to remove all the furniture into the gardens, then he stumped away from us for he was going to Istanbul to thresh the matter out with the authorities.

We worked all through that long summer day. The heat was intense as we staggered beneath tables and chairs and bunks and mattresses. Towards early evening we broke off to eat a hurried meal then continued working well into the night by the light of oil-lamps strung from the trees at intervals. Once an officer stopped me as I stumbled beneath the weight of a bed. He ordered me to find somewhere to rest and I dragged out a mattress from beneath a pile and searched for my brother. I found him under a tree, already half asleep on the hard ground. When I called to him he obediently rolled himself on to the mattresses and slept on the instant. The next morning my back was painful and I asked Mehmet to examine it.

He found a great red weal running across it and my vest had stuck to the dried blood for I had probably injured myself when I was hauling beds across the garden.

Mehmet bathed the wound for me in one of the wash-houses but it was so painful that I had the greatest difficulty in walking upright.

There was nothing for us to do that day for the school was now stripped and all the furniture lay out in the garden. Mehmet and I went and sat on a low wall which overlooked the Bosphor. Down here in this part of the garden it was very quiet. My back still ached so I pulled off my jacket and vest and lay face downwards on the grass, facing the sea with my back exposed to the healing rays of the brilliant sun. I lay and watched the blue Bosphor and the little passing boats, and my thoughts travelled with the boats and ran on ahead of the big ships that were sailing to some unknown place. I forgot the discomfort of my back or that I lay here in the school gardens, and I thought instead of the many pictures I had seen of foreign lands, of brown-skinned races speaking a language I did not know. In imagination I saw great, swarthy stevedores unloading ships in a port I would never see and smelled the soft, aromatic perfume of spices and the warm scent of bananas, and my stomach ached with hunger and my heart with nostalgia for I knew not what.

Mehmet looking drowsily out to sea said in a contented voice:

'When I grow up I shall be a sailor.'

'But I thought you wanted to be a doctor,' I replied, and he hesitated a moment or two, trying to reconcile the two things, then he said triumphantly:

'But I can be a doctor in a ship.'

Strangely enough he never faltered in his determination.

I stumbled through life never knowing what it was I really wanted, only conscious that it was always just out of reach around some corner.

I forget exactly how old I was when I discovered that I should never make a good officer but it was some time in childhood.

All that morning Mehmet and I lay on the sun-drenched grass, and when finally a bugle called us to the midday meal, we found our dining-room under the shady trees. Whilst we ate, wasps and bees buzzed about us and earwigs sometimes dropped into our plates. The officers looked tired and dispirited, their shoulders sagging under their ancient uniforms, and when we had all eaten there was nothing for anyone to do, except to wait. The school lay empty under the afternoon sky.

That evening the Commanding Officer returned from Istanbul with the good news that we were to stay in our school, after all, so all the things had to be moved back again.

Those summer days of 1920 were filled with the now familiar name of Mustapha Kemal. He had become our national hero and gained in lustre when we heard that the Sultan had put a price on his head.

Lessons were difficult for me. I could not concentrate when

I could watch instead the shimmering, blue haze on the grass
and how the shadows crept out from under the trees as the sun
moved along the sky. Suddenly a teacher would rap out my
name and I would return from my trance-like staring at the
garden, to stand up dazedly, wondering what it was I had
been asked.

We had readings from the Koran every morning and as this
was the first lesson of the day we usually all started off in good
humour. All we had to do was to listen but later on our teacher
decided to give us religious music and that startled us considerably, for the idea of standing up in public to sing solo was
more than we could contemplate.

The Imam who taught us Religion was very fat with a large
bushy beard, a green sarik, or turban, and a loose black robe
that almost touched the ground. We used to call him yeşil
sarikli (the man with the green turban) and although we profoundly disliked him were at the same time very proud of him
because any Imam permitted to wear a green sarik is supposed
to be directly descended from Mahomet. We disliked him
because he was sensual and carnal and would call one of us to
his desk on the dais, pinch our cheeks or our lips with his fore-
finger and thumb, then put his fingers to his long nose to
ecstatically smell whatever perfume we exuded. More often
than not it would be of pilaf or potatoes or fruit stains would
linger at the corners of our lips and he would roguishly wag his
beard, saying:

'Some naughty boy has *not* washed his mouth after eating!'
He had a high falsetto voice like a woman's and we did what
we liked with him for he was no disciplinarian and never
complained about us.

Mehmet and I used to go home every week. We enjoyed
these excursions into the outer world, feeling very important
on the boat in our precious green uniforms. We would tear
into the little house in Bayazit, disturbing the peace with our
ribald shouts and our never-failing habit of reducing Muazzez
to tears after the first five minutes.

My mother had at last been persuaded to turn the downstairs
room into a workroom—my grandmother now occupying the
room which had formerly belonged to Mehmet and me. In
consequence at week-ends Mehmet and I were given camp-

beds to sleep on and we were forever in danger of stabbing our-selves in vital places with the needles left so carelessly lying about. It was nothing to discover a needle in one's bed or to step on one with bare feet in the early mornings or last thing at night.

Friday morning, the Muslim Sunday of those days, would see us lazily out of bed rejoicing in the undisciplined atmosphere of home. Yet towards evening we would be glad enough to return to the more masculine atmosphere of Kuleli, meeting our friends on the boat and walking together along the dusty sea road to school.

I learned how to be a soldier. I and all of my generation learned the hard way, schooled severely by War-experienced, impatient, frequently cruel officers. We learned how to stand for a long time without moving a muscle of our faces or flickering an eyelid. We learned not to cry out, not to flinch when an officer slapped our cheeks with a sound like doom. We learned too, at ten and eleven years old, to keep our tears inside us for the fear of further punishment was usually greater than our immediate pain. At first our spurting tears were common-place until held up to public contempt.

'Are you not ashamed to cry like a woman?' an officer would sneer bitingly.

We learned to jump to attention on the word and not let our rigid hands restlessly wander from our sides. We learned how to open our palms to the sky and accept the sting of the cutting stick without betraying emotion. We learned how to be good soldiers, and if many of us later on meted out much the same sort of punishment to the soldiers in our command, who could altogether blame us for our lack of imagination? We were taught that a good soldier needs no imagination, no feelings of humanity.

During my fourteenth year I became imbued with the spirit of piety. I spent so much time praying in the Mosques that my lessons suffered and the craze I had developed for football receded into the background. I would relentlessly flog myself to daily prayers. I became so holy, so priggish that my mother viewed this with alarm and looked about for other things to distract my attention. She, who had never been holy in her life, regarded such excessive sanctity as unnatural, but my grandmother and the school's Imam encouraged my fever. My delighted grandmother even prophesied to the Bayazit neighbours that I would end my days as a holy man!

But too much religion began to affect my nerves and my health for I rose from my bed for prayers before dawn and slept late each night because of night praying. I became pale and thin as a rake but prayed fervently, no longer remaining in bed at the week-ends. I would visit the Bayazit Mosque and to-day when I see Bayazit Mosque standing in its tranquil gardens I see the fanatical child who had leaped indecorously through its portals, eager to fling himself down and commune with his God. Sometimes the Sultan Mecit would dazzle my eyes when he attended at Bayazit for prayers. I would watch him enthralled, his fine, good-looking old face, his bushy white beard, the red fez adding colour to the funereal black of his dress. The band would play loudly and the soldiers march and Sultan Mecit would bow from his coach—first to this side he would bow then to that, and the cheers would hoarsely rend the air. The old Sultan would stretch his lips into a wider smile of acknowledgement, putting his hand gracefully to his scarlet fez.

CHAPTER XX

THE NEW REPUBLIC

IT WAS A popular belief amongst the Muslims of Istanbul that if they prayed in the same Mosque as their Sultan and at the same hour, God would listen with greater intensity to their supplications. Consequently the Shadow of God—as the Sultan was called—was everywhere followed by admiring, Paradise-yearning crowds. I remember a morning in the Bayazit Mosque when I was in the middle of such a crush that it was not possible to do anything but remain in a cramped, semi-upright position with danger from the movement of arms or legs all about me. When the prayers began I was in an even greater quandary, for the person in front of me, who was a porter, had a pair of evilly smelling feet, and when I attempted to make my obeisance, impelled forward and downwards by the pressure from behind, I was almost drowned in the odour of dirt and perspiration so perilously close to my nose. It was an odour sufficient, I swear, to kill even the rats who sported in the Mosque's lavatories. But fear of the Lord held me in my place securely and I stifled my squeamishness and eventually escaped from the Mosque to wash my hands and face in the water-basins in the gardens. I gulped the clean, sweet air as avidly as a man newly rescued from a gaseous mine.

In those days during Ramazan there were no lessons in the schools and we were allowed home on leave. Twenty-seven years ago the streets at Ramazan time were crowded as they have not been since and perhaps never will again. Not only the Muslims who were keeping the fast were in the streets but the British, French and American soldiers were there too to watch the ceremonies. And on the last night of Ramazan, in the year of which I write, Bayazit Square and its Mosque were places not to be forgotten by those who saw them.

The tall, slender minarets of the Mosque were ringed with gleaming electric candles, and between the minarets, silhouetted brilliantly against the dark sky, stretched electric lettering —'Elveda, Ramazan!'—(good-bye, Ramazan). The nostalgia of the words and the effect of so much nocturnal beauty caught at the heart in a strange sadness, even though this was meant to be a happy occasion. On both minarets were the Muezzins, their chanting, lovely voices busily calling the people to prayer, and the Square itself and the gardens of the Mosque were thronged with silent, listening people—like an army of dead people. And high above them swayed the Muezzins, their voices the only sound in that vast silence.

I edged my way to the Mosque, but cautiously, for one felt oddly guilty to be moving in that dead sea of silence. The interior of the Mosque was ablaze with light. Light poured down from the great chandeliers in the arched dome and the dome itself was ringed with light that glittered as the glasses swayed. And on the walls branching gigantic candelabra threw a blinding glare over everything. Many Muezzins were here too, reading from the Koran, and the faithful bowed and moved in unison and beat their breasts. I remember I was aflame that night with the pomp and the splendour, the majesty, and all my senses reeled.

One day the Armenians left Kuleli and the American flag was hauled down and up ran the red of the Turkish flag.

We senior boys left the grey, ancient building on the hill and moved into the white palace fronting the Bosphor and great was our joy to be here at last.

Kuleli's rooms were large and bright and, as a welcome change from oil lamps, we had our own electrical plant. The classrooms were on the ground floor, facing the dusty, quiet road, and there was silence all the day long for none came to Kuleli save the students or the officers stationed there.

A Mosque was established in the basement and on our first evening in the school we were all herded there for prayers of thanksgiving. Whether we wished or no, religion was forced down our throats. I had lost some of my early adolescent fervour but I needed no forcing. Many of the older boys however resented the interference of the officers, especially when they used large sticks as a better means of persuasion. In those days in Turkey when the Muslim religion was a national institution, a fixed habit of the centuries, the Kuleli gardens would be full of sullen, protesting boys washing their hands and faces under the fountains, balancing against a tree whilst they pulled socks over newly cleaned feet, rushing at the last moment to the lavatories for more private ablutions, and everyone in a panic for fear of being late. Muezzin would start to read and groans rent the air for that surely meant that we were late already. Irate officers would be stationed at the Mosque door, their sticks ready in their hands to whack smartly the backsides of the late-comers.

When Kemal Atatürk formally declared on October 29th, 1923, that our country was now a Republic, everything slowly began to change its face. Orders were sent to Kuleli that it would no longer be necessary to force the students to go to the Mosque. Religion was to be free. So the sticks were temporarily abandoned and only the merest handful of boys now attended the Mosque. But this time the sticks were brought out for quite a different purpose, for we who still visited the Mosque were frequently late for lessons and whereas before the sticks had soundly whacked the backsides of reluctant devotees, now commenced a crazy period when they whacked the backsides of reluctant scholars.

Atatürk and his Government decided that religion and public affairs must be separated and the new Constitution read:

'The language of the Turkish Republic is Turkish and the capital, Ankara.'

Whereas formerly it had read:

'The religion of the Turkish Republic is Muslim, the language Turkish and the capital, Ankara.'

The change was far greater than perhaps it would appear to European eyes. Religion was practically abolished since, although the Mosques remained places of worship, the people had no longer time to pray the prescribed five times in a day—save the old and perhaps the infirm who had no public duties to perform. The majority of the Turks simply had no time. The work of the Government offices could no longer wait on the prayers of the officials. Religious teachings were abolished in all schools, Muslim or Christian, and religious sects were no longer permitted to appear in the streets in the clothes of their particular religious order.

Nowadays, when Muezzin called, there were few to listen and fewer still to respond. The week-end was changed also and we observed the Christian Saturday and Sunday in place of the old Muslim Thursday and Friday.

The Mosque at Kuleli was abandoned and given over to broken chairs and tables in need of repair.

Our uniform changed and became the familiar navy blue of to-day's students with the smart red line down the seams of the trousers, and a hat with the smallest suspicion of a peak was issued, for the fez had been abolished by law.

At week-ends Mehmet and I would go proudly home, my grandmother being convinced that there were not two better-looking boys in all Turkey.

Muazzez was nine now and attending a girls' day school in Bayazit. A pert, conceited little thing she was, with her long twinkling legs in their demure black silk stockings, her brief skirts flying out jauntily. She was incredibly pretty and her hair had still further lightened with the years so that by now it was almost blonde. My grandmother spoiled her as she had never spoiled Mehmet or me; perhaps she had softened with age. She was as autocratic as ever and quite frequently had long, bitter quarrels with my mother.

After a time week-ends spent at home were no longer a novelty and I spent more and more of my free time at Kuleli. We would swim together whole summer days in the Bosphor, afterwards lazing in the school gardens, pleasantly conscious that this was the week-end and that no lessons loomed before us for two whole days.

Just prior to Atatürk's abolition of the fez the Military were issued with a small round cap that had the suspicion of a peak on it. The peak, we were told, was to guard the eyes against the sun. It was so small however that the idea of it being able to guard against anything, let alone the sun, was laughable. We had always previously worn a fez with the Turkish moon and stars woven into the front and we were now very much ashamed to be seen with our new headgear, which was really, we thought, too much like the hat the Christians wore. So we carried the offensive hat in our hands as often as we dared and the few boys who were brave enough to keep it on were called 'Gavur'— an epithet relating to a Christian in an unsavoury way.

When I used to pass through Bayazit all the old men in the coffee-houses and those sitting at the tables in the streets would look at the cap with the apology of a peak and shake their grey heads.

'What is this?' they would mutter in dismay. 'Where is this country going to?'

One day the district barber—not the barber of an earlier episode in my childhood—came up to me in the street and solemnly advised me never to put this terrible, Christian thing on my head.

'It is a Christian hat,' he warned. 'If a Muslim puts such a shocking thing on his head the good God will surely punish him.'

When I laughed at him he grew angry and later complained to my grandmother about my lack of piety.

It was in 1925 that Atatürk ordered that from henceforth all men in Turkey must wear the Christian hat. What a consternation there was then and the state of the nation's nerves! Was Atatürk playing with them? Was he sitting in his chateau in Ankara devising new things to disturb and break their habits of centuries?

The men indignantly refused to throw away the fez and it became a usual sight to see fighting taking place between the supporters of the new order and the die-hards of the old. Government officials were the first to give way to Atatürk. They were forced into this position by reason of their work and the streets became full of bowler hats worn with a self-conscious air. The children used to throw stones after them and the police arrested men who still persisted in wearing the fez, and the street sellers in desperation put fancy paper hats on their heads and added a note of unusual gaiety to the market-places. And out in the country places and the villages the men even wore women's hats in order to evade arrest. The old men took to tying handkerchiefs on their heads, placing the offending Christian hat over this, but the police became wise to this ruse and promptly arrested them. Arrested men were hauled to the police stations in such great numbers that they could not be dealt with and the white handkerchiefs were pulled off the bald pates, the insulting head-gear being firmly clamped over the naked, uneasy heads.

1925 is also memorable for me because I met Suna. She was sixteen and we saw each other at week-ends, our meetings being a great secret from our families. When I had enough pocket money we would go to a cinema, where we could sit and hold hands in the dark, never bothering to watch the flickering, leaping shadows on the screen. At other times we would climb the hill to the Casino, where we would drink iced lemonades through straws. If I had no money we would walk in the Gülhane Park or join the crowds on Galata Bridge to watch the boats. I loved to do this but Suna was not interested in a remote future of travel and would complain that the boats were smelly and noisy and gave her a headache. Nevertheless I was sadly and tenderly in love with her.

Sometimes I and a few others would take our text-books into the country at week-ends, asking farmers on the way if we could buy cucumbers or tomatoes from them. Usually they permitted us to take as much as we wished and then would refuse to accept payment from us. Well laden we would go to the top of the hill above Kuleli, a quiet lovely spot where a little spring trickled icily, and we would put our vegetables or fruits here to wash them before finding a comfortable place to study. Time passed swiftly there in that tranquil place. When we were hungry we would feast royally off the collection of food, feeling at peace up there in the lonely, silent hills.

Sometimes tiring of study I would lean against my particular fir-tree and look down to the Bosphor shining coolly below me. There was a good view from that tree, I remember, right down the Bosphor to the Black Sea. Little Bebek was in front of me in all its shimmering morning beauty. If I turned my head a little to the right I could see the famous fortress walls on Asia side. Back again to Istanbul to that other fortress, that old crumbling fortress built in 1452, and the parts I could see from my tree are the narrowest parts of all—being a little over six hundred and forty-nine metres only—and there is a story about this which says that the Sultan Mehmet once approached the Emperor Constantine and asked to be granted a piece of land on Europe's side. Constantine, it appears, acceded to this request, stipulating that the land would only be the size of a cow's skin. So Sultan Mehmet took a cow's skin, had it cut into narrow strips. He then laid them end to end and built his fortress according to this measurement, and no matter how the Emperor protested he was always told the one thing—that the land only measured just so much as a cow's skin.

When I was a child how often I heard this story!

And all down the Bosphor, down, down to the Black Sea, ran the tall trees and the old wood houses that suit the skyline so well. If I turned my head to the left there on the hilltop, I could see the Dolmabahçe Saray white and artificial as a wedding cake in its peaceful setting. Miniature mosques front the water's edge and there at the end of all the shining palaces lay Istanbul—my Istanbul that will forever hold something of my heart. Grey it would look from this hill and the smoke from the boats would lie over it like a soft veil and tall and tapering are the minarets that enchant the skyline, and from my hill I would see, behind the Mosques, the Marmara like a faint line of thread.

Study would be suddenly hard and I would turn back to the books reluctantly, only half aware of the printed word.

Towards evening, when the sun grew kinder, we would put away our books and stroll down the hill to Anadolu Hissari, where we would play football—for we never forgot to bring the football whatever else we might forget.

Later in the soft green dusk, the hot day behind us only a memory, we would return to Kuleli and there was none to notice our coming—save perhaps the fishermen in their rowing-boats and to them we were no novelty.

CHAPTER XXI

A BAYRAM MORNING AND A JOURNEY INTO BLEAKNESS

A BAYRAM WAS approaching and Mehmet and I hurried into Istanbul for three days' holiday and money in our pockets with which to buy presents for the family, as was the custom at Bayram. When we got off the boat at Galata Bridge we automatically made for the Kapaliçarşi—a sort of covered market very famous in Istanbul. Most of the traders were Armenian or Greek with a sprinkling of Turks amongst them and I do not know which were the worst for cheating—the Greeks, the Armenians or the Turks. Mehmet insisted on separating from me, telling me fussily that we would meet at a certain place at a certain time. He then went off by himself, his hands thrust into his pockets, his shut-away face oddly like the image my mind still held of my father's face.

He never liked to shop with me. My methods bored him profoundly for I would pore over something for a very long time until I was finally persuaded into buying it by a weary trader. Mehmet bought everything with great care and never afterwards regretted a purchase as I frequently did.

I went to the antiques section where I immediately lost my heart to an old samovar—a shining, elegant thing—a reminder of lost days. I stood admiring it for so long that the owner became quite nervous as to my intentions and was too apprehensive to even cry out his wares in the usual wheedling tone.

In the end I bought a brass candlestick for my grandmother for she had a passion for old things and knew about them in a way I could never hope to imitate. When I had paid over the price demanded there was an absurdly small amount of money left in my pocket. I hastily tore myself from the lovely old treasures in search of something which would please my mother and at the same time cause no heart-burnings over the candlestick. I searched wildly for something to fill these requirements and finally, in sheer despair, I bought some sort of a sachet which looked absurdly small in relation to the price asked for it. However, I felt I could not bargain for a present for my mother, so bought it resignedly. A red hair ribbon was purchased for my sister, on which I saved ten kuruş for I had no qualms about bargaining for a present for my sister. A solid-looking comb was bought for Mehmet, which might be a useless present since he had no hair to comb, but nevertheless the price of it was just right for the amount of money I had left in my pocket.

Well pleased with myself I sauntered to the spot we had arranged for meeting, to find him already there. He accused me of tardiness and this had so put him out that he did not utter a word to me all the way home. Sulkily he stalked along beside me, his parcels under his arm, and at Bayazit Square he left me on some mysterious, highly secret errand. The square was crowded with late shoppers, men jauntily carrying diminutive parcels and big parcels of exciting shapes, and women stepping sedately on their high heels, hurrying past the moon-faced men almost as though they feared assault.

I stood at the corner of the square and looked at the crowds and the great old arch of the University that twinkled with electric lights. The twin minarets of the Bayazit Mosque shone with electric candles too, and now a few oldish people were going in to pray, for it was the hour for prayer. And I could not help remembering the old days and the crowds who had answered the call of the Muezzins.

From everywhere came their lost, mournful cry, half drowned under the roar of the traffic, the klaxons of the cars and the never-ceasing clanging of the busy trams. The guns boomed out to proclaim that now the fast could be broken and I, like the rest of the crowd, hurried homewards for feasting and merry-making.

I caught up with Mehmet again at the corner of the street. He was loitering there waiting for me, and Muazzez met us at the door of the little friendly house. She pulled us into the narrow hall that smelled of a garden—so full it was of flowers put there by my mother to welcome the Bayram. We went together to the kitchen, where my mother was heating soup, an apron protecting her silk dress.

We kissed her hands and handed her our presents. She looked very youthful and gay with her face heated from the fire and tendrils of hair falling across her forehead and then she opened my present to her and said that the sachet was really very pretty indeed.

Muazzez was less tactful. She resentfully examined her hair ribbon and remarked on the poor quality of the satin.

'Red does not suit me,' she said pettishly, throwing the gay ribbon on the ground, and Mehmet said in disgust, when he saw the comb:

'What am I expected to do with a comb?'

Altogether there was no pleasing them. I hoped to fare better with my grandmother. We judged it time for her to have finished with her praying, for no loud rumbling noises were coming from the salon so we went upstairs to find her. She was just rising stiffly and her first words were:

'Now my heart is comfortable for I have just prayed for all our dead.'

We kissed her hands and I noticed that for this Bayram all her rings sparkled and the great emerald lay glinting across her breast. We handed our presents and when she saw the candle-stick she said to me:

'You have a very rare genius for knowing how to please people.'

And we all burst out laughing. Mehmet showed his comb and my sister thrust forward the offensive hair-ribbon and my grandmother's eyes twinkled and she said that some were very hard to please, but that for herself she was happy only in being alive.

She set Muazzez to prepare the table, handing out snowy damask and silver which shone brighter than the lighted lamps. Crystal glasses were set on the damask and wine in a carafe and I teased my grandmother, telling her that no good Muslim would drink wine. She shook her head sadly and said she knew well enough she was not a good person but that nevertheless, surely the good God did not begrudge her a glass of wine with her dinner.

I looked about the room at the high gleam on old furniture, at the flowers massed droopingly in dark corners, at the silver bowl of early roses which hung their tender heads in the centre of the table and I was glad to be home for this Bayram, proud that the spirit of my family had not died.

The next morning Mehmet and I were sent to the Mosque to

pray. We went to the little Mosque my father and my grandfather had attended when we were children, the Mosque which
stood near the burned, blackened skeleton of our old house.
And, too, we went there from custom for that Mosque was
associated with my family and on a Bayram morning it was
unthinkable to go elsewhere.

After the prayers were over we stood on the steps of the
Mosque and the little garden was thick with wild flowers and
people and the tall trees shadowed the lush green grass. The
Imam issued the traditional bon-bons and Turkish Delight,
and Mehmet and I respectfully saluted the old men.

One of them came over to me and said:

'Are you Hüsnü's son?'

I replied that this was so and he looked at Mehmet and me
and I saw memory slipping a long way back.

'I remember your father,' he said. 'But you are not like him.
This one here'—touching Mehmet—'now he is very like him
indeed. Very like.'

He paused a moment, struggling with the memories that
crowded the old brain.

'Your father,' he said heavily, 'used to come to this Mosque
to pray. I remember him when he was quite a small boy. He
used to come here with your grandfather. Ah, well,' he sighed,
'that is a long time ago—you could not know of that.' He
patted my shoulder with a frail, gentle hand. 'You are a fine
boy,' he said. 'God bless you.'

He pottered away from us muttering to himself, and I saw
him young again and upstanding, with perhaps a child on
either hand and watching the approach of the small boy who
was to become my father with the young man who was to
become my grandfather. And I clearly heard their voices and
felt the tug of the impatient small boy. I thought how sad a
thing is age and I wondered if that old, old man and all other
old people felt this same sadness.

What did they think when they saw their withered cheeks
that were once smooth, their dimmed eyes that were once
bright? Did they sometimes wish for death to carry them
swiftly from the ancient bodies before they could see any further
cruel encroachment?

We went home to feasting and merry-making, but before the

feasting a certain ritual had to be observed. My grandmother had to seat herself, my mother going to her to kiss her hands as a sign of her respect for her greater age. My grandmother would respond by kissing my mother's cheeks, then motioning to her to sit beside her. Now it was my turn to pay my respects to the women of the family, next Mehmet, last of all Muazzez for she was the youngest.

Only at the conclusion of the little ceremony could the serious business of the day begin. Muazzez handed sweets on the tray that had never known any other duty, my mother served liqueurs to drink each other's health and everyone sat a little stiffly in their new clothes.

Later in the morning Bekci Baba came to the street. He was accompanied by the man who played the big drum and another who played the clarinet. The man with the drum had gaily coloured handkerchiefs tied all about the drum—the symbol of all the 'tips' Bekci Baba had received from the various houses in the district. My mother handed a small blue handkerchief to me with money tied in one corner and I handed this in turn to Bekci Baba in appreciation of how well he had looked after us throughout the year. It was tied on the drum with the other handkerchiefs and the little group then called at the house next door and a crowd of children flew after them, shouting ribaldly. Then it was the turn of the famous local firemen. The dustmen came too and money was given to all of them. Local children played near the house and we tossed exotically wrapped sweets to them, watching them eagerly scrambling for them.

After luncheon neighbours called, and Mehmet and I decided to take Muazzez to Yeşilköy, to the sea. Yeşilköy, green village, is a pretty suburb of Istanbul and very popular in the summer months.

The little local trains were packed to capacity and although Muazzez protested of discomfort, Mehmet and I were perfectly satisfied to stand in the corridor amongst the dribbling, crying babies and the hot, sticky children.

At Yeşilköy we hired a rowing-boat but the Marmora was rough and Muazzez inclined to look suddenly white about the nostrils so we took her on land again, where she soon recovered. We climbed the hilly, village street, quiet and cool with birds singing behind high garden walls. The old grey houses stood back coolly amidst their flower-beds and the striped sunblinds mocked the early heat of the Spring sunlight. Down a wide gravel road, tree-lined and tranquil, we walked and up the hill to the Casino, which was less than a hundred feet above sea level.

We chose a table overlooking the sweep of the Marmora, a table with a bare, hot top, partially shaded by acacia-trees and, because it was Bayram, Turkish music was played by the orchestra and a singer sang sadly of her love who was gone. When the waiter came I ordered pastries and sickly chocolate cakes and iced coffee topped with mouth-melting crème santé. I ordered recklessly for my mother had slipped money into my pocket before we left home.

Muazzez in her white, soft dress and the gay blue ribbons thrust through her hair was in a seventh heaven of delight, trying to pretend that she was older than her meagre eleven years. Still I see that day before my eyes and the moment I realised that my sister was beautiful. For her eyes that day were the mad, mad blue of the Marmora, catching and matching their mood to the gaiety about her and her young laughter tinkled joyously.

We returned late from the Casino, glad to rest weary young limbs in easy-chairs and there was a languor, a pallor about my sister which was half childish, half sensual and I realised with a little wondering shock that she was growing up.

Back to Kuleli again, the Bayram over, and the surging happiness of meeting old friends again, but on the 4th of May of that year certain of us were transferred to the Military School at Tokat, in the North of Anatolia, for a year and a half; and great was our regret to leave Kuleli for such a long time.

Mehmet was given permission to see me off and he waved madly, growing smaller and smaller as the boat pulled away from the shore. We slid past Kuleli and I looked nostalgically back to it. Soon we had reached Galata and this time it was Istanbul to which I looked back, mysterious under the evening haze, and I thought that it would be hard to say good-bye to Istanbul, my own city. Most fair it seemed against the sky, like a lovely jewel in the Bosphor.

Down the darkening Bosphor we sailed and still I looked back to the dim face of Istanbul. Presently a friend pulled me by the arm.

'Stop dreaming!' he laughed. 'Come and eat something. I packed extra things for you because I knew you would not remember.'

I laughed too for it was true that I had not remembered, and I gladly accepted the bread, black olives and hard-boiled eggs which he proffered.

Soon we slid into the long length of the Black Sea and the Bosphor with all its memories lay far behind and one bade it adieu—as regretful, as sentimental an adieu as though one would never again return to its blue waters.

That night we slept on deck, only our seniors being privileged to sleep in the comparative half comfort of below. We on deck huddled beneath our overcoats and tried to sleep to the roll and lurch of the uneasy boat, conscious of the keen winds that blew from Russia even though it was May and we had left summer behind in Kuleli.

The next day we arrived at Zonguldak, a dirty, dusty, coal-mining city, its outline drab and somehow depressing and everywhere covered with a fine thin pall of coal dust. The buildings beside the wharf looked infinitely dreary, all of them coal-begrimed, only a few yellow houses on the hill to add a note of relief. These houses looked oddly incongruous and out of place here amongst all the drabness, having an air of temporariness, insolently clinging to the side of the hill. There was something infinitely sorrowful in the grey roofs against the skyline and we were desolate to think we had to spend twelve hours here whilst the captain of the ship took on supplies of coal, water and other commodities.

Our next port of call was Inebolu. We stopped about a mile off shore for Inebolu has no harbour. It stood like a picture in its green frame of trees and the high mountain forests behind it. Many rowing-boats were coming out to us and the soft day was still and calm and a brilliant sun shone on the pink-and-white houses of the little town, perhaps giving it a false beauty that would nevertheless sparkle in the memory. The rowing-boats came up to us and we leaned over the rails and watched.

First came a fussy little Customs boat, flying the Turkish flag, and a man jumped out and ran with remarkable agility up the ladder of our boat. The other rowing-boats carried more passengers for us or had come to collect passengers wish-

ing to disembark. Many of the little boats sold bread and
olives and hard-boiled eggs and cream cheese. Their shouts
mingled with the talk and laughter of the passengers and struck
gaiety from that still summer sea that lay quiet like glass, and far
away on the shore we could hear the morning noises of Inebolu.

Some of the passengers let down large handkerchiefs on
strings and bought foodstuffs from the boats. The seller would
make a deft package of the handkerchief, the passenger hauling
it up and money would be flung down to the grinning boatman.
Sometimes arguments would arise, the hoarse, bellowing voice
of the boatman swearing by Allah that the price he asked was
below the price he himself had paid for whatever it was under
dispute.

We left Inebolu to the cries of the vendors, the ribald songs
of the boatmen and gradually the voices grew fainter and our
view of pretty Inebolu dimmer until after a while it was just a
green blur many miles behind us. Because we had not been
ashore we grew sentimental about the town and wondered
what had lain behind the pink-and-white façades of the houses,
the formal green pattern of trees had concealed what romantic
things?

Now the scenery was sheer beauty. For a long time after
Inebolu we hugged the shore-line and the big mountains of
Anatolia smiled and frowned upon us according to the changing
position of the sun. The mountains were covered with thick
foliage and are the natural fortresses of Anatolia against our
Black Sea neighbours.

Sometimes we saw a tiny shore village, a huddle of small
mud houses only, and we wondered how they lived there so
remote from civilisation of any kind. And sometimes a village
clung to the rocky slopes of the mountains and we tried to
imagine the rough, primitive life of the inhabitants. Presently
the shore-line curved away from us and the following crying
seagulls left us and we were out in the open sea again.

That night the sea was rough and cold and many of us were
sick and the journey became a nightmare through the dark,
with the hiss of the foaming water in our wake, and torrents of
rain drove those of us on deck to seek shelter.

When we arrived at Samsun the rain had ceased but the
weather was still cold, the grey, angry sea still choppy under a
leaden sky.

Samsun is a big city, the most important Turkish city on the Black Sea coast, and it reminded me in a vague sort of way of Kadiköy, on the Asia side of Istanbul. Again our boat stopped a mile or so off shore and motor-boats chugged and battled across the huge waves. But they could not reach us and our Captain roared through a megaphone, telling them to go back until the sea was calmer.

Five hours we waited, cold and sick and longing for this nightmare journey to end. Finally the motor-boats were able to reach us and they rocked like toys in the grip of the breakers which now and then threatened to entirely submerge them.

I was one of the first down the swaying, greasy ladder and I jumped dizzily into the motor-boat to await the others. The waves tossed us furiously up and down and the horizon reeled and wavered and was sometimes lost from sight altogether. I was sick continuously.

That night I slept like a log in the narrow bed in the Samsun military hospital and next morning we left there for Tokat, and the end of our journey.

Buses appeared for us and we piled in anyhow and off we started with a great roar and a cloud of dust. We rushed at a terrifying pace out of the city, the buses swaying and the drivers leaning over the wheels like fanatics in a team of racing cars.

In the early afternoon we came to a small village and we crowded around the village pump to wash the dust off our faces and to drink avidly from the bitter-tasting water. We sat down to eat the bread and cheese the hospital authorities had given us that morning and the mongrel curs of the village sniffed us curiously and the shy wild children came to stare, their fingers in their mouths, ready to fly at our slightest movement.

On again we started, refreshed after our food and the rest and once again ready to brave the perils of the eccentric bus. For hours we ran by the banks of a cool, brown river and the fir forests ran steeply up on either side of us. Occasionally we would meet a cowherd leading his cows to his village and always he would look curiously at us, dour and dark-skinned with sullen eyes. The cows would bellow fearfully at the frightful apparition of the snorting bus.

Evening fell tender and green and presently the moon rose behind the hills, climbing steadily up the sky, high and silver and remote, and shadows stole out on the silvered roads and the fir-forests were bathed in radiance. We arrived at Amasya, that old, historical city famous for its luscious apples that have a smell like no other apples in all the world and are red and shining and delicate to the taste. The apple-orchards began about an hour before we reached the city itself and the moon shone tenderly on the young curled fronds of the blossom. We might have been on an enchanted road, so fairy-like it was, so unreal with the never-ending foam of pink beauty. We reached the big rock fortress and the slender charm of minarets came into view. We halted by the wooden bridge on the Yeşil Irmak—a river which flows through the centre of the city. Once again we went to the military hospital, where we were fed and given beds for the night. Our number however very seriously disorganised their resources and very nearly their hospitality.

We left Amasya the following morning and still the apple-orchards continued with us for some time. When they abruptly ended we were in a wilderness of dusty road again, flat, uninteresting, desolate meadows on either side of us.

'Tokat soon,' shouted our driver encouragingly and I, who was nearest the apology of a door, leaned out and saw the grey stone of a fortress appearing over the tops of some trees.

Over a bridge that forded a shallow river we ran and now houses began to appear, little houses set in wild gardens. The road had narrowed and the dust rose from it like a cloud, invading the 'bus and covering us with a film of white. We turned into the main street, a few straggling houses marking its beginning, and small shops came into view. Children and dogs lurked in the street and our klaxon made a great noise as we tore past with no regard for life, human or otherwise, and the dogs yelped in terror. On to a newly built stone road we ran and we saw a big dark huddle of buildings on a hill. It was the military school, and we had reached our journey's end at last. We sighed at the unrelieved bleakness and thought of Kuleli fronting the Bosphor.

CHAPTER XXII

RETURN TO ISTANBUL

I HATED THE fifteen months I spent in Tokat. I had stifled under a sense of frustration and had missed the sight and sound of the sea from Kuleli's wide windows. I had fretted in the stony, bleak mountains of Tokat and many times longed for the bustle and splendour and the squalid romance of old Istanbul and the splash of shadow caused by a sudden, unexpected tree in a lonely corner of the city. I had hated the dust and bareness of Tokat, had missed the green of trees and the cool, sweet look of grass. I had starved for all these things, yet had never fully realised it until that morning we were told we were being sent back to Kuleli again, three months sooner than anticipated.

The same old weary buses came to take us to Samsun, where we would board the boat for home, but twenty miles or so before we reached Samsun they broke down, one after the other, and we had no alternative but to walk the distance to Samsun.

We started off well enough through the clear night and at first we walked swiftly, then slower and slower as the night wore by. Before many miles had been covered we were footsore and weary and our throats ached with thirst. We became almost stupid with tiredness and began to see before us the vague shapes of appartements or Mosques—rather like the sort of mirage a traveller may see in the desert. Always the vague, indistinct shapes were a little ahead of us and never could we catch up with them. Sometimes they disappeared altogether and we marched along, sleeping as we marched, and all our uneasy dreams were coloured by the sight of brown, tumbling rivers and we clearly heard the sound of their rushing, soft waters. All the time our parched mouths burned like fires and we leaned against each other dazedly, trying to snatch sleep, not knowing even whether we were walking in the right direction.

Sometimes one of us would shout: 'Samsun! Samsun!'

And our tired eyes would come apart and because of the

intensity of our desires for a moment, we would indeed see the morning silhouette of Samsun lying before us—even though it was still night. But the illusion would fade and the lights we had thought we had seen became the lights of the hot, glittering stars.

Once we passed the first of the derelict 'buses lying at the side of the road and we shouted to the sleeping driver, asking where were the rest of the students, and he told us drowsily that, like us, they were walking to Samsun. We envied them the start they had had in front of us.

'How much farther?' we asked.

And the driver replied:

'Another ten miles.'

Our spirits and our bodies groaned against this. We thought of the hard stretch of road that still lay before us and the boat that would take us to Istanbul and we wondered how we would ever have the strength to reach that waiting boat in time.

'Water,' we asked him. 'Do you know where we can find water?'

And the driver already half asleep again told us that a little stream ran down from the mountains, just a bit off the road in front of us. And the coolness and the freshness of his words made us mad to find that water. On we went, looking everywhere for the little stream that ran from the mountains, and we tortured ourselves with the sweet sound it would make in our ears, of the coldness of the water against our lips. But we never found that little stream and either the driver had lied or our stupid, sleep-laden bodies had missed it. And we wept on each other's shoulders for the little stream that we had lost and we said that if only we could get a drink of water we should be all right. We said we could walk to Istanbul—if only we had a drop of water.

By dawn we had reached the suburbs of Samsun and we went into the gardens of a cool, grey Mosque and water gushed from a fountain. We were gasping with thirst and our swollen tongues had made a little hillock in our mouths and we flung ourselves on the fountain and the icy water trickled into my mouth and over my face and hair and I felt faint with relief. We drank until we could drink no more, until the water ran down our chins and we were tired of it.

On we stumbled to Samsun, this time complaining that our

feet hurt for we had had no time to notice the aching of our feet whilst the greater need for water held us.

Kuleli lay coolly under the painted sky and many students stood on the steps but we were too far away to see them clearly for our boat swung a course in the middle of the Bosphor. Long-distance boats did not stop at so insignificant a boat-station as Çengelköy so that it was necessary for us to go to Galata docks in order to board another, smaller boat to take us back to Kuleli.

It was good to see old friends again, to see Mehmet waiting to greet me—a tall, brown Mehmet suddenly grown good-looking.

We went home together. I was very excited as we walked towards Bayazit and landmarks stood out all the more clearly because one had been absent for more than a year.

After the bare aridity of Tokat, the trees of Istanbul looked green as they had never done before. The colourful flowers in the quiet old gardens made a splash of cool beauty.

The little house behind whose crumbling walls my family sheltered looked smaller than ever and more dingy than I had remembered, but the windows stood wide to the summer air and the soft sound of singing floated out to us. We looked at each other, Mehmet and I, and smiled in that rare moment of understanding, for it was my mother's voice that sang for us that morning. And we peeped in through the downstairs window and saw her at her eternal tracing of designs, her figure bent over the sloping board, her face tranquil as though some intricate piece of work had come right for her. She was unaware of us for we peeped slyly, being wishful to surprise her, then Mehmet pulled the old-fashioned bell-rope and the creaking, heavy footsteps of my grandmother were heard on the stairs.

She opened the door a fraction, a milk-pot in her hands, not immediately comprehending that two tall grandsons awaited entry.

'I thought it was şütcü,' she grumbled to Mehmet, then took in me standing there beside him and awareness leaped into her old eyes and the milk-pot went rattling to the floor and she held out her arms to me.

She called my name in a happy shout that shook the street

and the foundations of the old house and it brought my mother from the workroom, joy and disbelief struggling for supremacy in her face.

They folded me to them, these two, and the familiar, childhood smell of eau-de-Cologne tickled my nostrils. It was then that I really knew I was home again.

All the while they extravagantly praised my looks and my height in the way of families, I was noticing little things I should never have noticed a year ago. I noticed that this day my mother's black hair no longer curled, that it hung lankly, heavily streaked with grey. I noticed the dull look in her eyes and that they now and then slid away disconcertingly from the person to whom she was talking. It was as though only part of her was aware of the things going on about her. Perhaps it was for the first time in my life I wondered what her life had been in all the years we had been away from her. I wondered if she had forgotten the quiet young man who had been my father and the gay, pretty young woman who had been herself in my childhood, with her fashionable silk dresses. I thought of the young wife who had sat in my grandmother's salon and sipped coffee with the neighbours, never raising her voice above a whisper, never putting forward an opinion for fear she should be frowned upon. I looked at the changed face and wondered about her. The fastidious young woman she had been would never have permitted her hair to lose its lustre, its springy curl, or her figure to thicken—albeit it was ever so faintly perceptible.

I suppose the years of grinding poverty had taken their toll and even though nowadays money appeared to be no longer a problem, yet she looked as if she dared not sit back, dared not relax lest poverty come leaping back through the window again.

She looked so tired and worn that summer morning despite the seeming tranquillity of her face, the smile which had momentarily lightened her eyes when first she saw us. Her smiles were so brief that I could not help wondering whether half the time she were aware of her children or not. I looked back down the years to the day she had heard of my father's death. I remembered the night our house burned, the fever that had held her captive for weeks, and I thought that had she not had my grandmother with her through those weary days she could not have kept her sanity. My grandmother was so essentially sane that her mere presence was a sort of ledge for my mother to rest upon.

Few of us know the dreams or the longings of our own, and that long-ago morning when Mehmet and I stood together in the little house that has now gone taking our secrets with it, I was unaware of the dark menace the future held.

Muazzez was on holiday too, her long-legged, thirteen-year-old self as delicious, as refreshing as iced water on a hot day. She brought a note of youthful innocence into the house and seemed very close to my grandmother.

I remember one day when the sunlight poured into the salon, when the piled-up flowers were touched to brief glory, when my mother, looking unexpectedly like a young girl again, confessed to her longing to possess a garden once more. I remember wishing that I could satisfy that longing, that I had finished with schooling and the indignity of having to accept pocket money from her.

One afternoon I planned to see Suna, who did not know that I was back again in Istanbul and who probably would not have cared had she known. I walked to the street where she lived and hesitated for a few moments at the corner. I looked down its empty, sun-drenched length and toyed with the unsubtle idea of passing her house, on the chance that she might be at the salon windows. They were big houses in that street, big and grey and ugly, and since the war had housed many families.

I changed my mind and turned back to walk to Galata Bridge. I mingled with the hurrying crowds, the pedlars and the noisy trams, and I thought that when I reached the bridge I would turn my back on all of them and watch the busy boats on the Bosphor, which I had missed for so long. But I did not get that far after all, for half-way there standing together on a quiet corner stood a young officer and a girl in a gay red dress. And something about the stand of that girl held my feet sentinel for it was Suna who stood there, looking so intimately into the white face of a new Lieutenant.

They were unaware of me and somehow or other I did not want to go to Galata to see the boats after all.

I retraced my steps towards home.

CHAPTER XXIII

THE NEW OFFICER

MY LAST YEAR in Kuleli came eventually, bringing with it the dreaded final examinations which would decide whether we became officers or not.

We studied as we had never studied in our lives before. Most of us even gave up going home for occasional week-ends and a few of us bought supplies of candles for use at nights in the dormitory—when the electricity was cut off. We sat up through the nights poring over our much-battered text-books and examining each other in whispers for fear of disturbing the fitful sleepers. We grew thin and white and even in our troubled dreams saw examination papers, written in a language we did not know. And too we saw ourselves as failures, condemned to be Sergeants for the rest of our lives at the mercy of our friends and enemies who had gone on to become Staff Officers, and would come awake sweating with horror, relieved to discover after all that it was only a dream.

Inexorably time crept on and one morning we took our usual places in the classroom that looked much as before, yet was vastly different for the examinations would begin to-day. The first paper, I well remember, was History and by the end of the morning we were all dropping with exhaustion. Through worry I had developed a stye on one of my eyes, and it was a very small stye when I commenced the examinations but at the end of the History paper the swelling was as big as a hazel nut and the pain intense. My brain was fluffy like cotton wool. The last paper that day was French and I had hoped to get through it reasonably quickly, yet at the end of two hours I was stupid with fatigue and pain. I found myself repeating over and over again: 'Je viens mon vieux, mais où est mon chapeau?' and wondering what in God's name the dancing, familiar yet unfamiliar crazy words meant. Were they French or Greek or Chinese or just plain gibberish and who had said them to whom and for what absurd reason?

The next day my throbbing eye gave me no rest at all, despite the quantities of aspirin the doctor gave me. I staggered into the classroom and took up my Maths paper. I sat looking at it for so long that the Invigilator got the impression I was cheating and came fussily over to my desk, examining my pockets and the inside and the outside of my desk and the floor beneath it in an effort to discover possible hidden notes. Not satisfied with this he practically undressed me and finding nothing had to return to his place. He continued to eye me doubtfully for the rest of the day, unwilling to abandon the idea that I was cheating.

The examinations went grindingly on for fourteen days, and we who had started reasonably fat and healthy looking ended up as if we were in the last stages of consumption.

We heard the results some ten days later. Three hundred and seven of us were assembled in the Hall together, all of us in the final class, though divided all our school lives into classes of forty or so.

One of our Captains read out the results and he looked stern-faced and forbidding as he reeled off the growing list of names, most of them with the word 'failed' after them. I felt less isolated. When he came to my name I felt my face stiffen. He paused a little, then said the word 'passed' and there was a wild, mad moment when all the sweetest music in the world played in my ears and my heart pounded crazily in my chest. I did not hear the number of marks I had received for each subject, so I shall never know whether they were good or not. The magic, unbelievable word 'passed' stood on the air in letters of fire and my eyes ached with the effort to control the silly, conquering tears. I could only think that ten years lay behind me, ten years that had held good and bad in about equal proportions. Harbiye Military College lay before me and soon I should be an officer.

I became vaguely aware that friends were signalling their congratulations to me and I smiled sheepishly, coming back to awareness.

The Captain looked down at all of us from the raised dais, his eyes steely that his class had produced such bad results. The palms of my hands were sticky and clammy and streaks of violently coloured lightning sizzled in my brain, telescoping at last into the one shining, vivid word 'passed'.

On May 29th, 1929, I said good-bye to Kuleli and the bits of my life that would live there forever. There was a rousing send-off from the boat-station for us lucky ones but I think we were all of us reluctant to say good-bye to Kuleli, regretful not to sleep again under its tall roof.

The boat we sailed in was gaily decorated with flags and as we sailed down the Bosphor I leaned over the rails, taking my last long look at Kuleli, that still seemed as beautiful to me as it had that first long-ago morning in 1919, when I had gone there for the first time and a cross old porter had directed my mother to the inferior grey school on the hill.

At Galata Bridge the Military College band was there to greet us and a unit of the College students and proudly we marched with them through the Istanbul streets.

The watching crowds cheered and cheered until they were hoarse and the stirring martial music of the band held triumph and victory as well as the heartache of all marching soldiers.

On, on with the band we marched, our shoulders squared in military fashion, our dark-blue-trousered legs one unbroken line. Past Beyoğlu we went and all the shopkeepers stood in their doors to watch us go. Up to Taksim Square and then the great yellow building of the Military College came into view, its back to the Bosphor and close, high trees shading the gardens with their stiff, pale flowers in formal patterns. And on the other side of the Bosphor lay Kuleli, but it could not be seen from Harbiye however hard one looked for it was too far down the Bosphor, hidden by an elbow of land. But we who had so recently left it knew that it was there, that it would always be there to shine bravely to the skies, to throw its white reflection to the blue waters.

Up the wide steps of Harbiye we marched, feeling raw and new in this alien atmosphere, and the paused crowds in the street sent up their cheers and their blessings to us. Soldiers guarded the doors but we passed through for we belonged here now, and we went into a marble hall with marble corridors running to right and to left and let into the walls were plaques to commemorate the dead officers of Harbiye who had died in the 1914–1918 War.

Before us stood a door that opened to wide green lawns and away at the bottom glimmered the eternal Bosphor.

Great intricacies of electric globes lined the high ceilings and

I was awed by the splendour and majesty of Harbiye, proud to belong to this ancient place. For here I walked hand in hand with history where many more famous than I had walked before me, where Kemal Atatürk had once walked long ago.

The band had ceased playing and there was silence in that cool, white hall and we newcomers stood awkwardly, ill at ease, longing for Time to have merged our separate identities into the one great identity that was Harbiye.

We were granted three days freedom and our new Commanding Officer pointed out that during these three days we were to make up our minds for what it was we wished to train. I had never given any serious thought to this problem, my main objective having been to have done with school life. I was astonished when I realised that my friends mostly had their plans ready. Some wanted to be doctors, some dentists, some Cavalry officers. I could not make up my mind at all. I turned over all the professions in my mind but was uninterested in them all. I made instead a discovery of the most appalling magnitude. I was a soldier. I was in the Military College and I knew nothing of life outside the military establishments, yet my heart was not in soldiering. That was a terrible discovery to make at the beginning of my career, when it was too late to rectify the mistake. I wore the uniform of an officer-cadet and had worn it with varying degrees of pride for ten years, and for many more years still to come I would wear an officer's uniform—whether it fitted my ambitions or not.

But what were my ambitions? In so far as I could discover I had none.

At the end of the three days I was depressed and uneasy, as far from a decision as ever.

When a very red-faced Major asked me what I wished to put my name down for and I replied that I did not know, he looked at me as if suspecting insolence.

Finally they put me down for an Infantry Regiment and I escaped from their presence, not caring.

In the garden a friend hailed me and announced with pride that he was going to the doctors' school, and I could not help but envy him for his clear-cut decision.

I was jealous of him at the same time yet could not help

wondering what it was we had ever appeared to have in common with each other.

He said to me:

'I suppose you will go to Infantry?'

I nodded, not wishing to discuss it, then I said without being able to help myself:

'I don't really mind. The truth is there is nothing I want to be badly enough.'

'I suppose there is no use in wishing you good luck?'

I shook my head to his doubtful face.

'Not the slightest,' I said.

When I was a child I had wanted to be a General, now that I was a young man I wanted to be nothing.

Sixteen cadets, myself included, were sent to train for six months in an Infantry Regiment.

We went to Mudanya, four hours journey down the Marmora from Istanbul. When we arrived there the Commanding Officer, quite a different type incidentally from any we had ever met in the military establishments, divided us into the Units.

The officers treated us like dogs and the soldiers treated us like dogs for this was the only opportunity the soldiers would ever get in their lives.

We used to sleep in a large tent the roof of which had hundreds of holes in it. On bright nights when we lay down we could see the stars peeping through the holes, and sometimes mulberries used to drop from the trees on our sleeping faces so that one would come awake with a tiny shock of surprise to find an over-ripe, succulent mulberry just rolling off one's nose.

Our uniforms soon lost their crisp, conceited look and I never remember coming back to the Garrison from training with a dry jacket. Mud and rain and perspiration all combined to give our uniforms a greenish, indeterminate hue so that we sixteen cadets soon began to look like well-seasoned soldiers.

There was a young Lieutenant who used to give us physical training. He would walk up and down, up and down the field, playing with a whistle in his hand, his face sharp with the tortures he was thinking up for us. Suddenly he would blow smartly on the whistle and we would jump to attention.

'Lie down,' he would say and obediently, like dogs, we would lie down.

'Get up!' he would snarl and we would scramble to our feet with more alacrity than dignity. We had no time for dignity.

'Again!' he would command. 'Get up quicker the next time, you lazy young swine.'

Thirty minutes of it—up, down, up, down. Fling yourself on the stony ground, drag yourself erect again. Pant for breath and feel your jacket dampening with perspiration, and pick the jagged stones from your bleeding, lily-white hands. Listen for the whistle that will reprieve you for less time than it takes to tell, pause for the breath that comes painfully, chokingly. Wait for a change of command. Run! Lie down! Get up! Run! Lie down! Get up! On, on, cowardly body! Shake off the betraying puppy fat and grow slim like the sardonic young Lieutenant who is enjoying your misery, who is taking it out of you all the more because he is young enough to remember his own despair.

Hours and hours of training every day for months until our abraded knees through our torn trousers became immune, until our lady-like hands were tough and brown and insensitive and our waists were clipped in to imitate the young Lieutenant, who had become our model.

Then we went to Bursa area for the biggest manœuvre the new Republic had ever staged, where the Reserve officers had already poured in and we would really see field action. March, march, march. On under the blinding sun and the hot roads to scorch your feet and never mind if your ill-fitting boots hurt· you. This is the Army. This is the life.

We marched those days until we were ready to drop and the forty-year-old reservists felt it worse than we did. Sometimes we slept in the fields and were not aware of the heavy rain that soaked us, that ran into the tents and turned the heavy ground to mud. We could wake in the mornings stiff and aching and our jackets wet through, but presently the sun would come up again to dry us and burn us and parch us with thirst and we marched all the time. Sometimes we walked through the long chilly nights, leaning against each other and sleeping, or against the necks of our mules and even the mules would plod wearily too. Many times we started to march before dawn, our clothes chill with dew, our limbs stiff and heavy, not belonging to us any more. We would march on through the new day into the torrid sun of afternoon and soldiers would start to fall out of the lines. Down the lines of weary men would come the passed-on, never-ending cry: 'Sick soldier fallen out. Sick soldier fallen out.'

And when we came up with the sick soldier, or maybe there would be more than one, he would be lying on his side, too exhausted to care if he never lived again. Perhaps some of them would have their boots off, their torn and bleeding feet looking frightful under the glare of the shadeless sun and the flies already gathering to feast. Then I would remember the stories I had heard of my father and imagine him in that soldier's uniform, waiting patiently for the wounded cart which might never have come, for that was war and this was only a manœuvre.

I marched automatically, hearing only the steady plodding of the mules' feet and the wearier, heavier tread of the marching lines. At the end of that manœuvre they put a red ribbon on my arm and said I was a Corporal and I felt I had nobly acquitted myself, even though my body and my feet would never know pain again.

May 1st, 1931, dawned quite differently from any other day, for that day I became an officer, school life lying forever behind me.

On that proud morning I was handed a smart new uniform, a clanking sword and white gloves and my shoes shone like mirrors. I tilted my cap to an angle and thought there was nobody like me in all the world.

After a ceremony at Taksim Square we went back to Harbiye and were handed our diplomas, the Commanding Officer wishing us the customary good luck and telling us we were on leave until our postings came through.

The rest of that day seemed to be filled with the dashing sight of the new officers strutting a trifle self-consciously through the corridors and out in the wide gardens of the college. We were all awaiting the arrival of our families to take us home, for as usual, we none of us had any money. Taxis constantly arrived to depart again with a very important-looking new Lieutenant seated in the centre of his admiring family like a precious jewel in a casket. As the afternoon wore on I became anxious that nobody would come for me. Awful visions of sudden deaths or taxi crashes began to obsess me.

I remember that I felt the one kuruş that lay in my pocket and started to laugh at myself, for here I was, a new young officer, with but one kuruş in my pocket.

I drew it out and looked at it then I placed it in my sword, where it still rests to this day—a souvenir of that time.

Up and down I walked impatiently and sometimes no doubt I stared at myself in the mirrors and thought what a very fine fellow I was, to be sure. I thrust out my chest and squared my shoulders under their new khaki jacket, then slowly, pompously, I strolled out to the garden, my head in the clouds, already a General, but my sword clanked rudely against the stone steps and I heard the one kuruş rattling and I came out of my daydream.

At last a taxi arrived for me with a giggling, excited Muazzez within and we set off for home with a great fanfare from the klaxon.

At home I was rushed into excitement and congratulations and half the street had crowded into the little rooms. Old friends had arrived and strange old women kept kissing me and senile men I had never seen in my life before kept crying over me, telling me they had known my father. Drinks were circulated and through all the merriment I noticed my mother's proud, cold face keeping its secrets, but I who knew her, knew that she was happy for a red rose was tucked into her hair and her eyes smiled each time she looked at me.

Pretty Muazzez was there in a brief blue dress, seeming to eternally hand bon-bons on a silver dish. My grandmother wore black, her diamonds flashing scintillatingly, brought from their resting-place for this occasion. Her high old voice talked arrogantly, praising, always praising. . . . I saw the widow, fatter now than the day I had first seen her as a child, and I caught her worn hand and held it tightly for she was shy of approaching me in all my splendour. My head grew giddy and light as air with all the liqueurs I had consumed so that I laughed without reason and flirted with all the pretty girls.

Mehmet arrived from Kuleli, with the news that he had passed the examinations into Harbiye, and the laughter and the excitement grew more intense, the kissing more indiscriminate, and all the time the tray of liqueurs circulated non-stop. My head grew dizzy but what of that? Float, stupid wooden head, and care nothing for tomorrow. It is not often an officer comes out of famous Harbiye.

Woozier and woozier grew my stupid head and I loosened my jacket and sought fresh air, turning my back on the chattering, merry crowd. I looked out to the stars in the sky and I remembered that Kuleli was lying under these stars and I heard the faint sigh of the Bosphor as it lapped the shores where none walked by night. But they broke into my dreaming and called me back to the merry throng, for the neighbours were departing and they wanted to wish me once more good luck.

'Long life to you, my friends,' I said and tossed off yet another fiery, sickly liqueur.

In December 1931 I transferred from an Infantry Regiment to the Air Force as volunteers had been asked for. And I left Istanbul on January 20th, 1932, for two years of training at the Eskişehir Air College. We left Haydarpaşa station on a cold, frosty evening, and when we arrived in Eskişehir in the early hours of the following day thick blankets of snow lay everywhere beneath a heavy, white sky. The cold was so intense that our breath froze on the air.

We newcomers had the customary three days freedom from lessons and after luncheon on the first day were given a bus to visit the city. For the first time in our lives we were being driven somewhere, not forced to march as always before. Air Force life, we told ourselves joyously, seemed to promise better things than an Infantry Regiment.

The road from the aerodrome was very bad, rutted and uneven beneath the deceptive snow, and now and then our heads hit the roof of the bus with frightful cracks, oddly reminiscent of the journey we had once made to Tokat. We came to the outskirts of the city, the old Eskişehir of 1932 which has long since disappeared in the onslaught of progress.

Little mud houses marked the beginning, so small that one wondered how anyone ever lived there at all. Narrow side roads gave us glimpses of more of these primitive houses and here, where the snow had melted into slush, would presently be great rivers of uncrossable mud. There were no pavements and now and then a stone would fly from beneath our wheels, hitting one of the mud houses with a sound like a rifle-shot and passers-by would press back to avoid the snow we flung up from our wheels. These queer little houses belonged to the Tartar families and sheltered innumerable members of the one family.

We arrived at the centre of the city and hitched up our trousers before descending from the bus, leaping ungracefully into a spot that looked reasonably dry. Large stones formed the main street, treacherous stones that gave beneath the feet and deposited the unwary up to the ankle in muddy slush. We strolled on, passing more and more of the Tartar houses, beginning to be depressed by this flat, dreary city with its unendurably drab brown houses. We crossed the River Porsuk by a bridge and on one bank stood the Porsuk Palas Hotel, a big hotel with an open-air café fronting the river.

Farther on we came to small, poor shops and houses and a Mosque where the geysers had been trapped in iron pipes and the boiling water gushed forth steamingly on the raw air. We were unimpressed by our sight of the city and decided to explore the station road to see what mysteries it might conceal. But the station road was new like ourselves and boasted cement-and-red-brick, flat-topped houses with bare gardens wrested from the reluctant earth. A few cinemas rose garishly under the leaden winter sky and they bored us with their resemblance to a new, bleak city struggling in the throes of growing up.

We retraced our steps to the Porsuk Palas Hotel and went into its plush interior, where hot coffee warmed us. We asked for a tric-trac set and played all the afternoon for there was nothing else to do.

CHAPTER XXIV

MY BATMAN AVERTS A CRISIS AND
MUAZZEZ FINDS A BEAU

I DECIDED TO bring my family to Eskişehir. The little, improvised Officers' Club on the banks of the river had begun to pall and was, anyway, too expensive for the junior officers to patronise.

My mother replied to my letter suggesting the move with such alacrity that I more than suspected she was worrying as to what I was up to all alone in Eskişehir.

My batman was sent to look for a house and after over a week of searching he told me he had discovered an empty house on the newly built station road. He said it was a 'good' house and by that he meant 'new', for to him the two things were synonymous.

'Is there water in the house?' I demanded and he replied enthusiastically that indeed there was water, lovely boiling water that spouted from a natural geyser in the back garden.

'And what about cold water, drinking-water?' I wanted to know.

He looked shocked that I did not know there was no drinking-water in Eskişehir and said pointedly that we should have to do the same as everyone else—that is, fill vessels with the boiling water and leave it to grow cold. I was very dubious as to my mother's reactions to such an arrangement, but since there was no alternative, I accordingly went with my batman to view this remarkable house which could not provide cold water but gave us as much hot water as we required. It turned out to be a newish villa, looking extremely small in the very large garden surrounding it. When we rang the door-bell a thin wispy little woman opened the door, wiping her hands hurriedly on her apron when she saw the magnificent sight of an Air Force uniform confronting her.

She looked at me with an air of surprise.

I explained that I understood that the house was to be let

and she said that this was so, offering to show me over. I was quite incapable of knowing what things my mother and grandmother would look for in a house, but manfully plunged through the small rooms, already foreseeing storms over the fitting of our cumbersome furniture. There seemed to be a great deal of unnecessary cupboards but, knowing the contrary ways of family, I could not be sure that even this would please my womenfolk. There was no bathroom at all: the woman looked surprised that I should want such a thing, and the toilet was so small that the customary fittings together with the bidet left barely room to close the door behind one.

In the garden spouted the famous geyser and I was just on the point of asking what happened in the sudden event of one requiring cold water, when my eye lit on what looked undoubtedly like a pump. I turned accusingly to my batman and he grinned sheepishly, saying he had not noticed this on his first visit. The wispy little woman explained proudly that from this pump came ice-cold water the year round, but it was not for drinking purposes and at this my batman's face lit up triumphantly, with a 'I-told-you-so' expression. But it fell again several centimetres when she continued that a man called once in a week with fresh water for drinking. This she said could be stored in an earthenware küp, a sort of barrel with a covered top and a tap.

I was delighted to hear that civilisation had not entirely by-passed this city and afterwards told my batman that he was a blockhead. I arranged to rent the house, and my batman was set to find people to re-decorate it for me and a few days later I discovered him lording it over two bearded, very wild-looking painters who slashed the paint on with a reckless disregard for where it might eventually land. My batman was directing them and instructing them in a very knowing way, lounging grandly beside them, but when he saw me he deflated like a pricked balloon. From then onwards I took care to keep out of his way, leaving the workmen entirely in his hands. Heaven knew, he had little enough chance in his military life to feel important.

The day came for the great move-in. The furniture had already arrived from Istanbul and a lorry from the aerodrome deposited it at the house.

Next arrived my mother, my grandmother and Muazzez carrying many hampers and parcels and already looking over-dressed for their new place of residence. My batman and I proudly showed them the house. Their faces remained unitedly detached as though they had already planned to make all the difficulties they could. In an effort to arouse their enthusiasm I eagerly pointed out the obvious advantages of our unique hot and cold-water system. It failed to impress them. Then when they saw the way we had haphazardly arranged their precious furniture they ran clucking around, like three dis-traught hens, examining everywhere for scratches or other damage.

When they had finished their perorations they firmly declared their intention of returning by the next train to Istanbul.

'But you can't!' I appealed frantically, darting the most furious glances at my open-mouthed, gaping batman, who had never bargained for three obstinate women with whom to deal.

Do something, you great dolt! I implored him silently and he correctly interpreted my distress signals and put himself forward to quieten the three disillusioned ladies. He told my grandmother he would arrange all her furniture wherever she wished, guessing that this would be the best line of approach with her. To my mother he explained that the house was beautifully clean, that he himself had seen to this.

He was completely carried away by the signs of mollification in the faces before him and recklessly promised to do every-thing they wished.

I could see he was fast getting my mother on his side—which in the circumstances was just as well, since he would be more often under her orders than he would under mine.

My grandmother planted herself firmly on a packing-case and remarked that she had never expected to one day find herself living in a hen-coop. This inspired my batman to say that we could keep hens in the back garden and he quite dazzled my town-bred mother with the number of eggs we should be able to produce. Enthusiastically he said he would build a chicken-run for her—not even looking in my direction for permission. It was painfully obvious that already he knew

which was the safest side to be on. He then told my grandmother he would find her the best washerwoman in all Eskişehir
and that he himself would guard her like a child.

My grandmother cheered up somewhat at this, her face
implying that she and the batman would get on very well
together after all. I left them to it and hurried back to the Air
College, breathing with relief that it looked as if they might
after all settle down.

Life was far pleasanter with my family in Eskişehir. My time
became regularised and sometimes I would invite friends to dine
with me or to play poker. And always on these occasions the
women would vacate the salon, leaving it for us, for my grandmother still felt it was not seemly for the ladies of the house to
remain in the same room as the gentlemen. This was especially
the case where Muazzez was concerned and my grandmother
would whip her off swiftly, for fear the eyes of the men should
alight on her. Poor Muazzez never dared to protest but years
later she told me that had it been left to us to acquire a husband
for her she would have remained single all her days—since we
all seemed to combine to shut her off from masculine company.

During the same year though she acquired a beau.

There was a young officer who lived practically next door to
us, and he had an elder brother who was in the Foreign Office in
Ankara. This brother was what is known as a smart young man
about town, invariably to be seen in striped trousers and
impeccable morning coat. He took to visiting his brother in
Eskişehir with great regularity so that even the not-always-
observant I became suspiciously aware of his pompous figure
walking the streets frequently. The mother of this elegant
young man developed a rapid friendship with my mother and
the result was that the gentleman from Ankara proposed
marriage to my gratified sister. He professed, so I gathered,
undying love for her and waived all notion of a large dowry.
In fact he went further. He declared with great passion and
feeling that he required no dowry at all, that my sister was
sufficient dowry in herself. This attitude delighted me but my
mother was shocked by such callowness on my part and said
that her daughter could not be allowed to go penniless to such a
proper, such an upright young man. She was quite firm on this

point and I gloomily had to prepare myself to spend much money. I had no great affection for the prospective bridegroom, but Muazzez and my mother insisted that he was very good looking and a model of propriety. My sister was determined to marry him and flooded the house with tears if one so much as criticised him.

A trousseau was bought and we clad her in bridal white with trailing flowers and my grandmother parted with her long-treasured jewels and my sister was married with great ceremony to the dapper young intruder from Ankara.

Muazzez shone brightly that day and a big reception was given, for which I was expected to pay, and the thought of this did nothing to improve my general gloominess for the alliance. The loving looks frequently exchanged between the newly wed pair began to fill me with boredom; playful, frolicsome ladies coyly suggested that it would be my turn next and I fled from them. I was able to return to normal however after the party was over and the bridal pair had departed for Ankara, where they still live to this day in great state and elegance as befits their nobility. And either the years have mellowed me or Ali has lost some of his unreal suavity, for nowadays, on the rare occasions when we meet, we find much in common. Muazzez has retained her wearable beauty, but her figure has prodigiously thickened and sophistication has overlaid the earlier charm of her girlhood years.

With the excitement of the wedding over, the house seemed strangely quiet and after a time my mother started to complain that she disliked the house and its prominent position on the station road.

I found another house on the south side of the city, on the crest of a hill, and I transferred my family there. For a long time my mother had been uneasy in the other house, for the funerals of the crashed Air Force victims wound their way past —sometimes as many as two in a week—and always she had lived with the fear that one day I also would be carried past her windows.

And in summer the dust was choking. Even with the windows tightly sealed, the dust would seep in, getting into food, between the sheets on the beds and leaving its fine white mark everywhere. But up on the hill there was no dust and no sound of the Funeral March and I hoped that in time my mother would lose this morbid dread she had of my crashing.

On the hill too, it was cooler and in the evenings one could sit on the old wooden, vine-clad balcony and look down to Eskişehir lying below, still hazy with the dust clouds, the heat and the flies.

CHAPTER XXV

FEMININE AFFAIRS

Up on the hill, alongside of our house, lived the Regimental Paymaster, who soon became very friendly with my mother. They both loved anything to do with food and spent a great deal of their time exchanging recipes, or sending succulent dishes to each other, all of which my grandmother viewed with the gravest suspicions.

He was a strange, odd person living an eccentric lonely life in his big house on the hill with only his batman to look after him. He did all his cooking himself. He devoted hours to this. Sometimes I would drop in on a winter's evening to find a couple of stray guests lounging in the salon—officers perhaps merely passing through Eskişehir and wanting a bed for the night, and since he was noted for keeping open house they naturally and automatically made for his home. More often than not he would himself be in the kitchen, a large apron enveloping him and his short-sighted eyes peering anxiously into whatever savoury dishes he was concocting by way of surprise for his guests. Sometimes he would let me stay in the kitchen but at other times he would send me away from him, telling me that to-night's dish was a secret, that I must not see what he was doing, since I might tell my mother and he did not want her stealing his recipes before he was ready to part with them.

I would take the stairs to the salon to stretch unmolested on a divan until a shout from below would tell me that the meal was ready.

There was a very ornate, rococo dining-room opening off the salon and sometimes he would have dinner served here when he wanted to show off, but dinner in the tasteless dining-room was a sombre affair. And he would not let us forget our politeness, chiding us severely if a drop of wine was spilled over his elaborate table-cloth, losing his familiar identity as our contemporary, becoming the Paymaster, a senior officer.

We liked it best when he allowed us to eat in the unrefined

atmosphere of the kitchen. Perhaps there would be half a dozen of us or so, and we would squat ungracefully over the huge open fire whilst he roasted slowly a whole lamb, cutting strips for us as they cooked. His batman would place glasses and raki on the bare wooden table and oil-lamps would glow kindly for there was no electricity in the kitchen. The lamb finished, he would produce stuffed tomatoes or some such delicacy. There would occasionally be freshly grilled fish—he furiously exhorting us to eat it immediately and not to wait for each other for grilled foods should be eaten directly they are cooked.

We would stuff ourselves to repletion, glad for once of the lack of women to curtail our gossip and our purely masculine jokes. When we could eat no more, we would stagger up to the salon, throwing ourselves inelegantly on divans and loosening our belts. Our host would turn on the lights in the domed ceiling and draw the curtains against the night. He would feed more logs to the already bright fire in the china stove, and presently the batman would appear with Turkish coffee to take the taste of grease from our mouths and a choice of cigarettes for the smokers. One of us would start up an old Turkish song and soon everyone would join in, well content with the world in that coarse atmosphere of unashamed belchings and loosened trousers. Disreputable and unglamorous we might be to-night, but the girls of Eskişehir would not know that to-morrow when they met us strutting through the city's streets.

Sinop, Samsun, Çarşamba—three cities on the Black Sea coast—and each of them had bought a plane to be presented to the Air Force.

My unit was given the plane which had been subscribed to by the good citizens of Sinop, and I the task of flying it there.

Samsun and Çarşamba had no aerodrome so the other two planes accompanied me from their different regiments to Sinop, where representatives from Samsun and Çarşamba would welcome them and name their respective planes.

We were to fly over all three cities and give an aerial display then return to spend the night in Sinop.

Everything went according to plan. We all three flew low over Samsun and Çarşamba, looping and rolling and spinning and diving, and when we got back to Sinop the aerodrome was crowded with well-wishers—peasants eager to see the planes close up, schoolchildren to shyly present gifts to us and pompous Municipal officers. The Governor arrived in his striped morning suit and a tall, shining black hat and we were quite put to shame by such elegance.

The Mayor was late for the ceremonial welcome, and the Governor showed signs of irritation. We all stood about waiting, we three pilots in Sinop and yet not in Sinop if you can follow my meaning. For until the Mayor made us welcome we could not strictly be regarded as being there at all.

Presently a knowledgeable man in the crowd shouted that the tardy Mayor was sighted and we all looked in the direction in which he pointed and we saw a very old donkey carrying a very small man coming down the hill. The Governor made noises in his throat.

'That is the Mayor!' he said bitterly for he had been educated in Europe and knew what was what.

Many of the happy people surged to meet the donkey and its precious cargo. The donkey suddenly began to trot briskly and reached the aerodrome at a terrific speed. The Mayor alighted from its back stiffly and welcomed us so affably and with so much enthusiasm that there was no longer doubt in anybody's mind as to whether we were in Sinop or not in Sinop.

When I returned to Eskişehir I discovered that Muazzez was temporarily installed in the house, her husband being in Rome on duty. The house had become like a private hospital with my mother in bed with one of her innumerable headaches and my sister complaining of pains in the most unlikely spots.

My grandmother and my batman ran the ménage—one as autocratic as the other and both of them driving the hired servant into constant outbreaks of semi-hysteria. Once, long ago, a far-away Hacer had had to put up with similar treatment.

One morning a doctor was called to the house and I was telephoned at the aerodrome, the doctor testily telling me that both my patients were to go to the hospital. Muazzez he said needed an immediate operation. My mother though was, in his opinion, a very obstinate woman indeed. She refused to listen to any suggestion of hospitals. He ended by saying that furthermore all her teeth had to be removed.

When I arrived home there was bedlam in the house with my sister having the most terrible premonitions of her death and begging my grandmother to look after her baby for her. My mother was sitting up in her bed crying and declaring that never, never would she go into a hospital and neither would her teeth be removed. This was the direst blow for her, that her strong, white, even teeth should be removed. We managed to calm her and told her that they would probably never have to come out anyway. Muazzez was our most immediate problem and we had her rushed to a hospital, where she was operated upon with astounding success, to recover with remarkable speed. She returned to my home for convalescence, cried constantly for her husband and her child and wrote reams of letters daily to all her friends, recounting with the most horrific details her operation. Dislike sprang up between us.

It was she who eventually persuaded my mother to have her teeth removed and when in the course of time my mother received her new ones, my grandmother examined them with great suspicion then handed them back, saying piously that thank God *she* did not have to wear them. This caused my mother to cry and declare she would rather be dead than put such monstrous things in her mouth. Maliciously my grandmother encouraged this attitude. One evening however I lost my temper to such an extent that my mother nervously promised to do whatever she had to do with the confounded teeth if only I would quieten down before the neighbours came in to investigate possible murder.

Not very long after this I was walking home one sunny afternoon from the aerodrome when I saw two fighter planes taking off from the field. They were flying very close to each other and I stood and watched them for a few moments, mentally criticising them. They started to attack each other in mock battle and they flew under and over each other and they flew just that much too close. I walked on towards the town, remembering the crazy things we had done too when we had first become pilots. When I reached the centre of the city I became aware that the sound of the engines up above me had ceased and I turned my face skywards and hundreds of pieces of plane were hurtling down. I remembered their dangerous, too-close flying and thought that I should have known that this would happen.

I hurried on towards home for I had suddenly become sure that my mother had witnessed or heard of the accident and I desperately wanted to reassure her that I was all right.

The streets had become crowded with people, with the wives and the children and the mothers of airmen. Their faces were white and frightened-looking, all of them wondering if it was their turn to become widows, orphans or the mothers of the dead.

An ambulance tore by, clanging with feverish urgency, and I had a fleeting thought that if the one pilot who had jumped by parachute was not already dead he most certainly would be by the time that jolting ambulance had got him to hospital over these uneven roads.

The pale, trembling wives and mothers rushed on me like an army of mad things, begging me to tell them the names of the pilots who had crashed and I replied that I did not know. But they held tightly to me, crying into my face that I did know, that I must know who was on duty. Still I said I did not know and they wailed that I would not tell them, beating my arms with their soft, impotent fists, begging the one question over and over again:

'Please!' they said, 'please, Lieutenant, tell us the names. Please, please, please. . . .'

I tore myself out of their grasp and their tormented cries pierced my ears all down the crowded street. Suddenly I saw my mother running on bare feet and for an incredible, unbelievable moment I was a child again and our house was burning and I saw her running thus down the desolate garden on her bare feet.

She was only partially dressed, having run out in the middle of changing, and my batman was running after her with a cloak in his hand. I was numbed with shock and felt coldness creep all over my body. When she saw me she stood still and the batman caught up with her and threw the protective cloak over her bare, white shoulders. I cannot forget her eyes, those wandering eyes that told their own story, only we were still too blind to read their message correctly, even though fear stirred somewhere, warning. . . .

We none of us knew then the madness that would one day leap out at us, when all the bottled thoughts and memories of a quarter of a century would darken the over-tired brain, dim the bright, mournful eyes.

'Take that uniform off!' she said to me, her voice so low and hoarse that involuntarily I backed away from her. 'You will send me to my death!' she said. 'You will make me lose my mind!'

Her voice died away in a great, strangled sob and she half collapsed into my batman's arms. He picked her up as if she were a baby and carried her home through the oblivious streets and I walked beside him. My mind was numb and cold and drained of all thought and I could only see before me, imprinted forever on the summer air, the gentle madness that had looked out of her eyes.

CHAPTER XXVI

THE WISE WOMAN OF ESKIŞEHIR

I SUPPOSE THE memory of that day never quite left me. Sometimes I would wake up in the middle of the night, bathed in sweat, tormenting myself with the reminder of my mother's eyes that tragic afternoon. She steadily declined—at least physically. She lost weight to such an extent that a doctor started giving her injections to fatten her. He said she was anæmic and recommended red wine so we bought her a bottle a day and thrust it upon her. He recommended plenty of red meat so we forced that on her too, but still she did not appear to improve. I took to watching for signs of mental illness and almost gave myself a nervous breakdown in consequence. Was it my uneasy imagination or did she seem ever so slightly neglectful of herself—not caring any more about her appearance, once her main concern? Did I sometimes only feel that one eye drooped just the littlest bit seemingly half shut, whilst the other ranged with every show of normality? Oh, I watched for a thousand signs and all the time the fear inside me refused to be stilled.

For days at a time she would be her old self, then, without warning, irritability would break out stormily; moroseness and dissatisfaction accumulated, and she would fretfully, like a child, complain of headaches.

I took her to a well-known nerve specialist, who questioned her, set little traps for her and examined her physical health—then said there was nothing wrong with her whatever. We came away from his consulting-rooms, I conscious of relief that was yet only half relief. Uneasiness persisted in the face of medical opinion. I could not trust them but I could not trust my own intuition either. I took her to another specialist with similar results—except that this one ordered a course of injections for her, perhaps so that I should not feel cheated in the face of the large fee asked. I did not know what to do. She *seemed* to be better and so pathetically eager to please me, so like a child wanting my approbation that my heart was wrung with pity.

I remember that during the winter of 1937, on a Saturday when I was doing a spell as Duty Officer, my batman telephoned to me in a terrible state and asked that I should return home immediately. He said that my mother was ill again and urged me to make haste. He sounded so agitated that I at once asked for permission to leave the aerodrome and was even given my senior officer's car to deliver me to my home with all speed.

When I arrived home, there was my mother sitting up in bed and with a swelling on her neck about the size of an orange. It was a ghastly, horrible thing, a great excrescence of flesh weighting down her neck and face. She was trembling with terror and I asked my grandmother if anything had been done about it.

'Oh, no,' she said, looking surprised. 'It came very suddenly a few hours ago, getting bigger and bigger until we thought it would burst and then we sent for you!'

'Great God!' I cried, exasperated, 'could you not have immediately sent for a doctor and me afterwards?'

My batman was sent for the doctor and I sat down to wait, unable to hurt my mother by leaving her room, yet at the same time totally unable to look at the large ugly swelling. Within a very short time a doctor arrived, an elegant, bearded fellow, his whole attitude very finished and complete. He examined the neck, prescribed medicine and directed that my mother should be brought to the hospital on the following Monday.

After he had gone I asked my mother if she was in any pain but she said no, it did not hurt at all, it just felt very heavy and she could not bear to look in a mirror. There seemed little that I could do so I left her to return to the aerodrome, sternly instructing my careless grandmother to be sure to call a doctor again if anything else seemed likely to go wrong and to telephone me afterwards. She meekly agreed that she would but I felt that her meekness was deceptive.

For the rest of that night I was consumed with worry and the vagueness of this continued illness that haunted the house. As soon as I was free on the following morning I rushed home on feet that had to be chided into hurrying, for the message the brain was sending to them was to go slowly—lest other, greater troubles be found at home awaiting me.

When I rang the electric bell which made a star of pattern on the air with its shrill sound, my batman opened the door, a large grin on his moon-like face. I looked at him enquiringly and he directed my gaze to the garden doors which opened off the back of the hall in a direct line with the street door. There an amazing sight met my eyes. The mother I had left in bed only the previous evening was calmly watering flowers, her face turned towards the house and the swelling, to all appearances, entirely gone.

I walked quickly out to her and she smiled at me. I caught her two hands in relief and the water-hose fell spurting to the ground and the smell of the wet earth came up refreshingly.

'Am I dreaming?' I asked. 'Or did you not telephone me yesterday? Did I not come home and find your neck three times its normal size? Did I not get a doctor for you?'

'You are not dreaming,' she said happily, her eyes childlike and wide yet concealing their secrets.

'Well, then!' I said, 'what is this? I cannot believe that the medicine cured you so quickly!'

'Oh—the medicine,' she said as though she had forgotten all about it. 'No, that did not cure me. In fact I am afraid that we threw all the medicine away. It was not necessary after all.'

'But——' I protested, utterly at a loss, perhaps even thinking a little bit impatiently: these women and their feminine secrets.

'Come,' she said. 'Let us tell you all about it, my son. You will see—doctors are not always necessary.'

I turned to the grinning batman behind me and asked what the devil it all meant and then I heard a most curious, almost unbelievable story—except that it happened, thereby giving credence to it. But for the fact that there were three witnesses, besides my mother, I should have thought I had been the victim of a hoax.

Now there was in Eskişehir at that time a reputed Wise Woman—an Albanian, old and wrinkled like a crab-apple and at least one hundred years old. My mother, having been born in Albania of Albanian parents, had a very soft spot for this old woman and, because she lived in appalling poverty, now and then sent food and other things to her by my batman. Incidentally they both fondly thought that this was being done behind my back, but in point of fact there was not much that happened in the house without my knowledge—even though I did not always make use of that knowledge.

It appears that after I had gone back to the aerodrome the previous evening and the batman had returned with the medicine prescribed by the doctor, a little conference had taken place around my mother's sick bed. My grandmother automatically distrusted all doctors—especially after they had ordered the removal of my mother's teeth, nearly causing her to bleed speedily to her death. She had eyed and smelled the medicine with great suspicion. The servant had made sympathetic noises in her throat to intimate her profoundest suspicions too; she had then gloomily said that medicine would never cure *that* swelling. This dire prophesy had alarmed my already alarmed mother, who was suddenly all for rushing to the nearest hospital to have the offending, painless lump removed by a surgical operation.

At this the servant snorted and said that that would be useless too, and the conference was temporarily in a state of deadlock. But the servant, resuming authority as the undisputed leader in this affair, slyly reopened negotiations by remarking that in such a case as this the Wise Woman ought to be called in. Seeing no noticeable reaction to this, she followed up by saying that the Wise Woman had already performed a remarkable number of cures in the district and pointed out some of them to my mother, who was in no position to argue with her as many of the cases were already quite well known to her.

The result was that my batman was despatched to the mud house of the Wise Woman to ask her assistance.

She came to my home with him, in a great state of fear for she half expected that I would return from the aerodrome and ruin everything. I might even have her arrested, she confessed to my grandmother.

My grandmother pooh-poohed this idea uneasily, then briskly said a prayer that I would not suddenly take it into my head to come back and bade my batman double lock all the doors so that in the event of my return I should have to ring the bell, thereby giving them warning. She even thought of a place to conceal the Wise Woman should this happen. When the doors had been locked and they felt safe from all outside interference they set about the serious business of what was to be done with the offending growth on my mother's neck.

The Wise Woman looked at it with one eye half closed, then heavily pronounced that undoubtedly someone had put the evil eye on my mother. Everyone readily agreed that this indeed might be so and the servant said with triumph:
'There's doctors for you!' or words to that effect.

'Lie back on your pillows,' commanded the Wise Woman, having the situation well in hand now that she had so satisfactorily gained the entire confidence of her 'patient'. She added that my mother would be quite better by the next morning.

She then turned to my batman, that poor, long-suffering soul at the mercy of three determined women, and commanded him to go to the graveyard and bring her back the bone of a dead person.

This terrible, unexpected request almost shook his determined loyalty to my mother, for the thought of scrabbling about in a dark cemetery with all the blinding white tombstones to watch him, made him shiver with fear. His fear of what I might have to say when I heard about it was infinitely more manageable.

Despite his terror he still had sufficient spirit left to argue with the Wise Woman and told her that he could not be expected to find the bones of any dead people since they were all safely in their coffins and he absolutely refused to prise open any coffins.

The Wise Woman remained completely unmoved by this state of affairs and said that she wanted a bone from a dead person and that was all there was to it. She told him with obvious knowledge that all he had to do was to go to the old part of the graveyard where none were buried any more and there, just beneath the soft earth, he would be able to find plenty of bones for her. She assured him that she knew there were bones there and, alarmed that, if he refused, she might turn him into a toad or a frog or something even worse, he set off on his gruesome errand.

His eyes revealed the remembered horror when he told me of the darkness of the night, the tall cypress-trees guarding the lonely dead, the sinister sound of the wind in the poplars, the screeching of the owls and their terrible swooping about his head, and he all the time scrabbling furiously in the earth until at last he found a bleached, dry human bone. It was so ghastly-looking, so frightful to the touch; then his vivid imagination looked for ghosts to lay their clammy fingers on him and he perspired until all his clothes were soaking and he had ran, terror-stricken, from the cemetery.

Re-entering Eskişehir he had tried to control his shivering and had become conscious of the odd-shaped, gruesome object in his hands. He had thrust it swiftly into a pocket where it unpleasantly jabbed his thigh and had sidled past a policeman, anxious only to get home before anything more unpleasant happened to him.

When he arrived home, still in an abject state, instead of receiving thanks that he had gone at all on such an errand, he had been severely chided by my grandmother for being so long away. Her whole attitude suggested that had *she* gone she would have brought back an entire skeleton in that length of time.

The Wise Woman took the bone from him and went out to the kitchen to cleanse it. She then demanded an egg which she broke into a bowl, another bowl which she filled with cold water, and then handed the batman a lump of lead which she instructed him to heat for her. When she had finished her preparations she went back to my mother's room, the batman following her, for having done so much for the cause he could not bear now to be excluded from the rest of the ritual. For quite a long time nothing was done. The Wise Woman sat reading from the Koran and all the others remained uncomfortable and silent in the face of such holiness. Then the Wise Woman stood up and massaged the swelling with the cleansed human bone and asked that the heated lead should be handed to her. She placed a large towel over my mother's head and stood the bowl of cold water over this, balancing it precariously with one hand; but by this time everybody was too openmouthed in amazement to care very much whether the water upset or not. The lead was put into the water and made a sizzling sound, then the egg was poured in and the Wise Woman said with appalling anti-climax:

'Everything is over. I shall remain here all night so let us have something to eat now.'

The batman was disappointed that nothing more spectacular had occurred and sat down to his meal in a very disgruntled frame of mind, for he rightly felt that after so much effort on his part, something really dramatic should have happened.

After she had eaten, my mother was told to sleep and forget everything and, amazingly, she was able to do this.

When she had woken up on the following morning her first thought was to feel for the offending lump but to her amazement it had entirely disappeared.

She had rushed to a mirror only to find her neck back to normal once more; then she had started to cry with joy and immediately called all the household to witness her marvellous recovery.

I listened to their combined story with growing horror and indignation, furious that my mother had allowed herself to be persuaded to employ the wiles of an old half-crazy woman.

I gave tongue to my feelings but when I had finished, my grandmother said perfectly reasonably:

'But what is there to be cross about? The swelling has gone and your mother is better.'

This I could not dispute.

My batman brought the bowl to me so that I could see the aftermath of the wonderful cure for myself and when I looked into the bowl I saw the queer, twisted shape of the lead and the egg floating on top, looking indeed oddly like a giant eye.

'And what about the bone?' I asked, feeling that they were quite capable of having kept that too.

The batman looked sheepish and hung his head.

'It's back in the graveyard again,' he said. 'I was told that it had to be put back there before the dawn came, otherwise something awful would have happened to me.'

CHAPTER XXVII

KUTAHYA AND İZMIR

AT THE LATTER end of 1937 I was ordered to Kutahya on duty and I travelled there one bitterly cold morning in search of a house to which my family could be transferred, for they had made it quite clear that they had no intention of remaining alone in Eskişehir. At the station of Kutahya I hired a Tartar phaeton to take me into the town. The bleakness and loneliness of the place were depressing and I remembered the much-maligned Eskişehir with positive affection.

The scenery was flat and uninteresting, the few houses we passed were old and so dreary-looking with the eternal kafes on the windows. When we got near to what looked partially like civilisation I called to the driver to stop. I had no desire to go any farther.

I turned in at the door of a café to get warmed but the music blaring from a loud speaker, the thick blue fog of smoke, the terrible noise from innumerable tric-trac sets caused me to hastily back out again, deciding it would undoubtedly be better to die in the cold.

I saw a chemist's shop and I entered, ostensibly to purchase aspirin, but I soon fell into conversation with the owner of the shop, who was bored with the rough life around him and eager to exchange pleasantries with a newcomer.

I said that I was looking for a house and he said he did not think I would be successful in this respect. He introduced me to a fat, short man who said that he knew everything there was to be known in Kutahya and everyone and he readily offered to accompany me in my search for somewhere to live.

I asked if he thought it possible for me to find a brick or cement house and he threw back his leonine head and roared with laughter.

'There are only two brick houses in the whole of Kutahya,' he said, 'and both of them are occupied—one by an Artillery Major and the other by a Russian Captain.'

'What the hell is a Russian Captain doing here?' I asked.

But he did not know and I thought it extremely odd indeed. Although why it was odd I did not know—perhaps because he was a Russian. That day we discovered five empty houses but none of them was suitable. In particular, two of them were in the older, lower part of the town in streets so narrow that it was possible to shake hands from your windows with the occupants of the opposite windows.

The ancient houses were so tall that one could not but wonder if the sun ever shone in these dreary streets, or if it was only a remote brightness out of sight in the far sky. All the windows were tightly latticed with kafes so perhaps in the long run it did not matter whether the sun reached these streets or not, for the rooms of these houses could never have felt its warm touch or the cooler chill of the wind.

We entered one of the houses and the ceilings looked as if colonies of bed-bugs lived there—in the dark, broken wooden beams—and no light filtered through the close kafes. I was suddenly depressed and longed to get out into the cold harsh air again, into the light. I could not imagine my mother living in a house such as this.

In the end the only place I was able to get which seemed to be in any way suitable was the house that had once been the chapel of the Melewi Dervishes, before Atatürk had abolished them. It had apparently lain empty for some time for people had a reluctance to make it into a home.

It was a big, roomy place though with many windows and was arranged very compactly on two floors. Unfortunately the tomb of a Melewi leader lay in the garden and I could not think I should feel entirely comfortable with him in such proximity. Since the front and the back of the house appeared to be alike, nobody ever knew for certain which was which so we all took to using the door which came handiest to our approach.

From one side of the house we faced other houses but on the opposite side we looked right across to an old Melewi cemetery which was at the bottom of a high, bare mountain. At the apex lay another grave and to look out to such continual greyness and unrelieved bleakness seemed to be like looking at the edge of the world.

Surprisingly my mother liked the strange house, loving the largeness of the rooms and the tall, bright windows, but my grandmother complained that badness lay over it and could not be persuaded to like the house the short time she lived there.

We had bought a dog whilst we were in Eskişehir, a small ball of white fluff whom we had called Fidèle with I wonder what unconscious memories stirring of the dogs who had roamed the gardens of Sariyer so long ago. This dog was now full grown and more my mother's dog than anyone else's, and when he entered the house with us that day in Kutahya he ran sniffing everywhere then came back to lie at my feet, whining a little.

He could not be coaxed to mount the stairs voluntarily and I had to carry him up, he all the time shivering as though some terrible thing was about to leap out to him from the shadows.

From the very beginning my grandmother was difficult about the place. She chose a bedroom overlooking the other houses and steadfastly refused to remain alone, even during the daytime, and almost succeeded in frightening us all. She kept looking over her shoulders at odd moments and would sometimes pause in the middle of a conversation to ask what was that peculiar noise and from whence it came. I am reasonably certain that she never saw or heard anything she would not have seen or heard in any other house, but because she knew that the Melewi Dervishes had once been here she never failed to associate evil things with their name. We could not fathom why.

My mother's health sadly deteriorated here. She grew more and more morbid and absent-minded and complained all the time of headaches. Eventually I managed to obtain a transfer to İzmir on the strength of the doctor ordering a change of air for her.

Mehmet, who was at the time stationed also in İzmir, arranged to find a house for us and I sent my family on ahead of me whilst I remained for a few days longer in Kutahya to clear things up.

Mehmet and I had not met for over two years and when we saw each other in İzmir we embraced each other warmly and commented on the apparent ruddy health of the other. He told me that my mother and grandmother had already settled down very well in the house he had discovered in Karşiyaka, a pretty house, he said it was, on the other side of the harbour.

He and I sat in a Casino overlooking the harbour and we discussed my mother.

'She is very neurotic, of course,' said Mehmet with detachment, as if she were just a patient and not his mother.

I envied him his indifference and then I remembered that he had not lived at home for a very long time. I thought too how little we all knew about each other, how—springing from the same root—we had nevertheless divided until now we knew less than nothing about each other's dreams. Mehmet's decisive eyes looked as if he were not interested in dreaming. He was only interested in the physical ailments of humanity and the best way to cure them, anxious to make well the pain, not studying too deeply the psychological pattern the mind made.

He asked me what it was I was thinking about so seriously, and I said it was nothing, unwilling to share with him the intimacy of thought. I suggested that we should go home.

The new house stood squarely in a garden full of palm-trees and roses and a large sloping lawn at the back gave on to a patch where lemon-trees grew stockily and tangerines; and what was it about that house that reminded me of another house that had stood squarely in its gardens, that had been burned so long ago?

There was a terrace which overlooked the harbour and I hoped that this peaceful spot would give my mother back her health.

There was a balcony too at the front of the house and my grandmother never tired of sitting here to watch the passers-by, but my mother sat at the back and watched the boats that sailed to far places. And she would talk of Istanbul and the Bosphor and I knew that her heart would remain in her beloved city forever. Far into the nights they would sit together talking with the moon riding high in the clear skies, throwing its reflection to the water, lavishly gilding a path in the sea, softening the outlines of the houses that by day could look so harsh. My mother appeared to be contented. She had her sons with her once again, she complained less and less of headaches, but she talked about Istanbul with nostalgia as if she would never return to it again.

I wish I had the words to paint the strange enchantment of İzmir—the little crooked streets with their air of secrecy and squalor; the haphazard shops in the sideways; the open carriages and the noisy trams and the hooting of the boats that over-rode all other sounds; the Casinos fronting the harbour with the never-ending strains of music issuing from them; the hot sunlight and the blue sky and the golden sands; the tree-lined roads and the wistaria and bougainvilia that hangs everywhere like a scented purple curtain.

Many times Mehmet and I rode in the open carriages, drowsing under the evening warmth, the steady clip-clop of the horses' hooves beating their rhythmic tattoo. The tall green mountains rose steeply behind the city, the half-tropical vegetation grew rankly and luxuriantly amongst the old, sun-warmed stones.

On hot nights we would sometimes visit the swimming-pool, which was filled with sea-water, and we would walk back home together in the moonlight, the houses we passed standing in sleep in their tranquil gardens. The smell of tangerine- and orange-trees would hang heavy on the air, the lime-trees giving off their own soporific essence. Most of the houses had vines growing and fig-trees and exotic palms and near the harbour were tree-lined new boulevards and always, no matter what the hour, the twanging of a guitar or the strains of a Turkish tango from the casinos to break the stillness sweetly.

There was a fishing village just beyond Karşiyaka and occasionally I dined there alone in a little café where the fish were cooked upon request. The owner of the café showed me the sea-pool where swam the fish and invited me to take my choice and I would spend many a pleasant hour there, choosing and eating and drinking raki until my belt had to be igno-miniously loosened.

Farther on lies Güzelyali, where the houses march up the green hills facing the sea. There is a cool, hillside café here with terraces and tropical vegetation in the gardens and good food to make the journey worth the while. And everywhere in İzmir in crazy profusion are the flower-beds, with their hot splashes of colour to hurt the eyes and beat upon the senses, and İzmir still looks foreign—a cosmopolitan city with only the Mosques and the slender minarets to remind one that one is still in Turkey.

CHAPTER XXVIII

THE BEGINNING OF THE END

LIFE IN İZMIR was a great deal easier than anywhere else I had ever been.

Duties at the aerodrome were not onerous and the summer passed pleasantly with my mother seeming to grow stronger and better with each day. She spent most of her time in the garden, eternally planning new borders, new arrangements of flower-beds, finding an outlet for energy in the design of growing, living things. Sometimes we found her embroidering—something she had not done for many years. She would sit out on the terrace, a scarf protecting her head from the heat of the sun and a pile of shining embroidery silks on a small table beside her. Seeing her thus the years fell away from all of us and we were back again in a gracious house where my father had walked, and where the rafters had rung with the shouted laughter of my Uncle Ahmet.

My sister arrived on a visit to us from Ankara with a baby and an Arab nurse, and looking at the dark face of the nurse the illusion of childhood was complete: it might have been Inci again or Feride.

Muazzez appeared peeved when told that she and her unnecessary entourage crowded the little house. She flew from my sarcasm to the spoilings of my grandmother and complained that I was becoming embittered.

She remained with us for a month, her husband joining us for the last week of the visit, and every day my mother appeared better and we heard her joyous laughter for the first time for many months.

Mehmet and I, noticing this, told each other that she was getting better, that she would never slip back into depression again.

On the 10th of October Kemal Atatürk died and great was the sense of bereavement when we heard the news. Turkey wept and wailed for her lost leader, the whole nation plunged into mourning. I got permission to go to Istanbul, travelling in civilian clothing. I realised my error afterwards, when I was caught in the press of frenzied people whilst uniformed officers strutted freely where they might. I joined the never-ending crowds entering the Dolmabahçe Saray, where Atatürk lay in state and the police tried vainly to keep order. Old women and young women wept for their hero who would never come again. Bare-headed men shuffled silently into the vast hall of the Sultans where the Father of Turkey slept his last long sleep.

They had draped him with the Turkish flag and four officers stood on guard about him, their swords held upwards in their clasped hands. The weeping, desolate people he had liberated filed past him, paying tribute, and I remembered many things about him. I remembered my first sight of him close-to, on the tenth anniversary of his Republic, almost five years ago. I remembered how the lean, fanatic's face could light with a smile so dazzling that even his enemies forgave him much and how, more frequently, the pressed-in lips smiled when the eyes remained dark and sombre, challenging.

The day they took him to Ankara I managed with incredible difficulties, with much unchivalrous jostling, to get a place in one of the boats leaving Galata Bridge. We followed the battleship that was taking him to his capital, the city he had wrested and built out of Anatolia, but we only followed as far as the islands in the sea of Marmora. There we waved farewell to him for we could go no farther. We watched over the rails as the bleak battleship rode the unquiet sea and Atatürk— perhaps one day to become less than a memory—continued his voyage alone. We who had been privileged to know him even a little would look for a long time and in vain for the figure that would not come, the tall stern leader with the hard eyes that could so suddenly soften, the welcoming hand on the shoulder and the amused, harsh voice that said:

'Well, Lieutenant, still running the Air Force?'

The lack of ceremony surrounding him upon formal occasions had not perhaps been in keeping with his impatient, autocratic temperament, yet sometimes he had affected simplicity. We had never known when he would drop into the Officers' Club, what he would next suggest. As I looked back to the battleship I remembered the person he had been and I felt the tears rise to my eyes, as if a friend had gone.

December 1938 and winter touching İzmir kindly with the lightest of fingers, and specialists once again were called to my mother. Injections gave her some temporary relief and quietness, but my grandmother's straight shoulders sagged permanently now under the great weight of my mother's illness.

The early spring of 1939—my nerves reduced to tatters after the long months of tension at home—then Mehmet bringing home a small, fair girl with babyish blue eyes, telling us he was engaged. Bedia her name was and she looked frail as a doll and one could not help wondering what sort of doctor's wife she would make. But they were so much in love, she seventeen, he twenty-seven, that one could not remain indifferent. My mother received the news calmly but my grandmother, dear martinet, loudly demanded to be told where the girl had come from and who were her parents. I think Mehmet must already have warned Bedia for she showed no surprise, no trace of indignation at the questions, only smiling her gentle angelic smile, moving closer to the dark Mehmet, who gave the information my grandmother required.

For a space my mother came out of her dream world and dinner-parties were arranged and she bought new clothes to attend other parties. Muazzez wrote peremptorily from Ankara, growing more and more like my grandmother in her younger days, and demanded that the happy couple visit her in order that she might have an excuse for giving parties too.

And that incredible, undying beauty came back to drape my mother so that one was always caught by the exquisite surprise of it and the years dropped away from her like magic and she became a young girl again, to match Bedia's innocent youth.

One evening she asked me when I would marry too, and before I had time to make any answer my grandmother said with a coarse laugh that half the mothers of İzmir wanted the same question answered. I could not but laugh at her sublime, conceited exaggeration and my mother repeated her question.

I kissed her hand and replied:

'When I love.'

She answered:

'That you will never do. You have no heart; I should know that.'

Then she started to cry, long tremors running through her body and impatience swept cruelly upwards in me so that I left the tearful house and spent the evening in a bar, deserting the dinner-party where I was to have been host. When I returned my mother was in bed again, Mehmet pushing injections into her.

Mehmet was ordered to Istanbul in May and my mother's favourite doctor also left İzmir to take up residence in Ankara. She brooded alone, worrying more than ever about her health, about Mehmet and Muazzez in far-off Ankara, about Bedia, feeling now that she would not make a suitable wife for my brother. She began to eat alone, sometimes not eating at all, then she grew careful again and would eat only if I were at home. So I curtailed my visits to friends' houses, or to the casinos, and ate at home each evening, trying not to chafe too much under this new restraint. She bound me with chains of love, even taking to waiting up for me at night, watching from the terrace to see me walking up the street. Even if I did not arrive home until three in the morning, still she waited in a corner of the terrace, never saying anything, never letting her presence be known, yet I could feel her mournful eyes watching me out of the darkness. I took to coming home earlier so that she should get some sleep. Her gaunt look grew more pronounced and my grandmother complained that she kept her awake at night. They shared a room now since my mother did not care for the İzmir servant we had engaged, and grew very grand and regal at the thought of having her in her bedroom.

One night during dinner she looked really ill. Her hair was unkempt and uncombed and one eye seemed to grow smaller and smaller as I watched her. I asked her why she sat at the table like this and she looked startled for a moment, as though I had rudely interrupted some far-away, private thought, then she stammered that she was not well, that her head ached. Suddenly she lay her head down amongst the dishes, so wearily, so uncaringly that my heart was wrung with pity and my grandmother rang for the maid and she was put to bed, coaxed and petted out of her clothes like a child.

Later when my grandmother and I sat in the salon drinking

Turkish coffee, I said I thought the time had come when my mother needed constant, experienced nursing and put forward the suggestion that she would be better off in a private institution I had heard of.

I remember that my grandmother looked at me very oddly, then she said:

'Your mother is not bad enough to separate her from her family and everything she has always known. That would be great cruelty, my son. She is only neurotic and the doctors all say that her headaches are migraine——'

'I suppose they must be right,' I said uneasily, unwilling to set myself up as an authority, in the face of medical opinion, on nervous disorders.

'If one day she has to be sent away,' continued my grandmother, following her own train of thought, 'I pray God that I may not be here to see.'

She looked away from me but I could see old bitter memories struggling in her face and I knew that though she and my mother had never liked each other, one always resenting the other, still they could not live apart for long. They had been together for too many years now, had shared all the important things that had ever happened to them.

We sat silent for a long time and then I rang for more coffee and my grandmother came out of her reverie.

'If only there was something more I could do,' I said and my grandmother put out her hand and touched my knee lightly.

'You have done everything that was left in your nature to do——'

The odd words startled me and revived the times I had had of impatience, the harsh words I had uttered. My grandmother watched my struggle and said sadly:

'It is too late now to torment yourself. You grew away from us a long time ago, shutting us out and perhaps the fault was our own. I have seen how you have tried with your mother, how you have forced yourself to do as she wanted but it was all false, my child. She knows that too, but you could not give more than you had to give so there is no need to reproach yourself. You have done more for her than many sons who loved her might have done.'

'You make me feel ashamed,' I said to her, hating my unnaturalness, remembering too the restraints that Mehmet had never had. 'I *can't* come closer!' I shouted in desperation, 'I can't give her all my thoughts!'

My grandmother's wise old face looked understandingly at me. She nodded her head.

'Hüsnü should not have died,' she said, pressing my hand tightly. 'She should not have been left alone so young in life.'

She shook her head sorrowfully, her eyes bright with tears but none were falling and I took her old, worn hand and kissed it.

I felt her looking down at my bent head and then she said irrelevantly:

'How like Ahmet you are!'

CHAPTER XXIX

DISINTEGRATING FAMILY

MEHMET RETURNED TO İzmir in August 1939 for his wedding and Muazzez and Ali arrived from Ankara, adding grandeur to the little house.

I never saw Mehmet married, for the day before I was ordered to a manœuvre and had to leave all the bustle and the excitement behind me. The manœuvre lasted ten days and when I returned home I was unutterably shocked for my grandmother had left us for good, returning to Istanbul with Mehmet and Bedia. My batman was in hospital.

It had previously been arranged in the family that when my grandmother went to live with my brother and his wife my mother would go to Muazzez in Ankara. My grandmother would never have left us at all but for the fact that Mehmet was more often away at sea than he was at home. It was felt to be unwise to leave the youthful Bedia unchaperoned. Perhaps this chaperonage would be quite unnecessary in other countries but to leave Bedia at seventeen alone in Istanbul, where scandal false or true needs but the slightest flicker to grow into a roaring flame, was unthinkable. There were far too many traps for unwary young wives in Istanbul.

When the arrangement was originally suggested my mother professed herself pleased, telling me in confidence that she had perhaps lived too long with my grandmother and that living in Ankara would do her good.

It was therefore a surprise for me to return to İzmir and find her still there and that she was alone in the house made it seem far worse.

'Where is the servant?' I asked.

'I dismissed her. She was lazy,' returned my mother, who hitherto had always extolled her.

My mother herself was in a terrible state. I trembled when I thought of the heartless criminality that had left her alone in that echoing house. She was unwashed, uncombed and slatternly and, worst of all, she was unaware of this.

I cursed Mehmet for having done such a thing but could scarcely blame the flighty Muazzez, who was always much too concerned with her own affairs to have bothered very much when my mother refused to accompany her.

I enquired for my batman and was told that he had gone to hospital. She started to complain in a high, whining voice of the maid she had dismissed. And all the time her hands were twisting, twisting, busily rending a lacy handkerchief. She looked as if she had not eaten for days and the house was a shambles. Most of my grandmother's furniture had gone to Istanbul and the few pieces that remained were pulled out from the walls. Beds were unmade and the kitchen littered with the remains of meals, obviously several days old.

I took her into the stuffy, airless salon and flung wide the windows. Here was shambles too. It was heartbreaking to see my mother like this, in this dirty, uncared-for house.

'Why did you not go with Muazzez?' I asked her gently and she stared at me for a moment or two and then she replied:

'And who would look after you if I had gone?'

I bit back the searing retort that burned on my lips and she said fretfully:

'I told your grandmother not to look back when she left the house. I said that if she did it would bring us bad luck. But she ignored me and she stood at the corner, looking back for a long, long time and I had to shout to her to go, go, go!'

My mother's voice was high with hysteria and I stirred uneasily, seeing the scene again through her eyes. The old woman leaning on her stick at the corner, looking back to a place where she had been happy, and my mother on the terrace shouting at her, attracting attention perhaps, my batman trying to pull her back to the silent house.

She watched me unwinkingly, trying to find out my reaction to what she was telling me. I said nothing. She had been silent for so long alone that talking was necessary to her now.

'Your grandmother did not want to go. She said that I wanted to be rid of her. That is why she turned back when I had told her not to, so that she could leave her curse on this house and everyone in it. I know'—she nodded to me. 'She hopes I will die!'

'Oh, Mother!' I said, wondering when this feud would cease between them.

Still I could see the departing figure of my grandmother and I wondered if we had done the right thing, we younger ones who had thought only to separate them, to keep them from fighting as they had done all through the years. I thought of my mother, remaining here for me, and could not see her in the alien atmosphere of my sister's house in Ankara. I did not know what I could do with her now, when only I was left with her. I had tried to be good but had failed somewhere, perhaps many years agö. I felt helpless sitting there, watching her. The others had shelved their responsibilities and had gone away, leaving us alone, the one thing I had always dreaded.

When my batman returned after a few days the house was normal again, and I was glad to leave her in his hands each morning when I went to the aerodrome, knowing no harm could come to her.

At the end of August I was sent to Kayseri, to bring back a new plane for my Unit, but on September 3rd I received a telegram from the Commanding Officer ordering me to return immediately.

War had again come to Europe and Poland had been invaded and all the lights of the world were going out again, one by one. When I arrived at Eskişehir for re-fuelling, I saw that all the planes were out of their hangars in the fields. Tents were out and lorries and I wondered if Turkey would come in and, more important, on whose side.

I was told in Eskişehir that all leave had been cancelled, that all officers had now to remain in the aerodromes day and night. I took off for İzmir, wondering about my mother. Who would look after her now?

At İzmir excited friends crowded about me but I could not listen to them. I sought out the Commanding Officer and begged him to relax the new rule for me, just for one night, as I was anxious about my mother. He knew of her illness and gave me permission to go home immediately, saying that if I should be wanted he would send a car for me.

When I got home my mother appeared quite calm, greeted me affectionately and said that she had heard over the radio that War had been declared. She also had heard from neighbours that I should no longer be able to come home at night. I was relieved by her normality.

During September everything went all right, for my batman

was excellent with my mother and I spoke to her each day by telephone. A new servant was engaged and at first she spoke highly of her, then the old dissatisfaction began to creep back to her voice and she no longer seemed pleased with her.

In October my batman was demobilised, having finished his military service. A new one came to take his place and my mother hated him, telling me he was too stupid to do anything or understand half what she said. I sent another one and another one and then another but they would not stay and, in any case, she disliked all of them on sight. Then she threw the servant out and she was now alone in the house with the dog.

I was half frantic with anxiety and would circle in my plane over the garden each day, to see if she was all right. I wrote to Mehmet, explaining the situation and suggesting that my mother go to his house in Istanbul, where at least she would not be alone.

I managed to get home one day and discussed this with her.

'Your grandmother is there,' she said. 'And perhaps we have missed each other more than we know and anyway, I shall be back again in Istanbul.'

Mehmet replied promptly, saying that Bedia would be glad to have my mother with her and to send her immediately.

Again I obtained leave, helped my mother to pack her things and took her to Istanbul.

Bedia welcomed her kindly and showed us the large, airy room she had prepared for her. My grandmother only looked thoughtful as though wondering how this *ménage à trois* would work out.

Alone I returned to İzmir and went to the empty house and wondered what to do with the furniture that was left. The dog, Fidèle, refused to eat his meals, all the time crying quietly to himself, watching me anxiously as though he was begging me to tell him what was the matter.

Now and then he would pad softly to the door, sniffing the carpets, then would come dispiritedly back to me, flopping down beside my chair.

My batman brought dinner and the silent room seemed filled with ghosts. Fidèle had followed me to the table but he would not eat. He lay down, resting his nose on his paws, only moving to cock an ear if he heard a sound. He waited all the time for my mother to walk into the room, but she would not come here again.

The house was given over to silence and the remembrance of all the unquiet things that had happened beneath its narrow roof.

CHAPTER XXX

GOOD-BYE, ŞEVKIYE

My MOTHER PROVED troublesome in Istanbul.

She soon left Bedia's house and took a room for herself in a tall old house in Sişli, saying she preferred to be alone. Sometimes she would visit my grandmother and she and Bedia soon noticed her rapid deterioration, the carelessness of her dress. She told people that her children did not want her. She started to go without food, giving most of her money to poor people whom she met in the streets. She would talk to all the beggars of Istanbul, inviting them to her room in Sişli, where she would give them quantities of food to take away. She could not bear to see people in tattered clothes and started to give them her own. At other times she would walk miles in the course of a day, returning home weary and hungry but without money left to buy food for herself. She used to go to the old places where she had lived before, frequently taking taxis, haughtily telling drivers to wait for her and then when she could not pay them would direct them back to Bedia's house. She bought quantities of sweets to distribute to the slum children and once she was discovered sitting in the rank, over-grown garden of our ruined house—the house my father had bought for her before he went to the War. I could not get leave to go to Istanbul and could only write frantic letters, imploring her to return to Bedia and my grandmother, where she would be well looked after.

These letters she completely ignored.

From the time she left İzmir she never communicated with me, even indirectly through my grandmother's scrappy letters. I grew despairing, wondering what would be the end of this bad business.

On February 2nd, 1940, I received a telegram from Bedia, asking me to go to Istanbul immediately as my mother was seriously ill. I went to the Commanding Officer and showed him the telegram. He took one look at my face and gave me permission to leave the aerodrome. I left Bedia's address with him and hastily booked a seat by train to Bandirma. From Bandirma I took the boat for Galata, impatient of the slow-seeming journey, my heart continuously in my mouth. When I finally arrived at Mehmet's house, Bedia's tear-stained, swollen face did nothing to reassure me that all might after all be well.

'Is my mother dead?' I asked her, clutching her arm and my grandmother came through the narrow hall and drew me into the salon. She seated herself and bade me do the same but this I was totally incapable of doing.

'Tell me,' I said to her quiet face. 'Is she dead?'

'No,' she said. 'Better by far that she were.'

I walked up and down the room, seeing the familiar furniture that still could remind me of childhood and hunger, even though I had nothing to fear on that score nowadays. All the houses we had lived in, even when prosperity had come back to us, were linked with those early insecure years, because the heavy old furniture was always there to remind one. There was never any escape from memories.

'Come, sit down,' said my grandmother gently; 'there is nothing to be gained by walking up and down the room or by hysteria.'

I sat down on a brocaded chair, once beautiful but now fraying at the edges through long usage.

'Where is my mother?' I asked. 'What has happened to her?'

And I think I knew the answer before anyone replied. It was Bedia who told me, Bedia who started to cry and irritated me with her persistent tears, yet who had the courage to say what was difficult for my grandmother.

'She has lost her mind,' said Bedia with a dignity in her voice and I was glad that she was here, new to the family, able to speak of hurting, hidden things as we others would not have done. So new to the family that our horror could not touch her too much.

My grandmother stood up very erect, her face without colour and her stern eyes filled with compassion. She put a hand on Bedia's young shoulder and said:

'There! my child. There is no need to cry!'

And she went on patting the thin shoulder absently, her eyes looking to something we could not see, and I leaned against the window, my body light as water, and waited for them to tell me everything.

It was Bedia who was the story-teller.

'Mother came to visit us two nights ago,' she said, 'and she looked very ill. She said she was hungry and I gave her something to eat and then she asked if she might spend the night with us. She complained that her head ached and, of course, I said that I should be glad if she stayed with us, not only for one night but for always. For awhile she was all right then she began to get irritable and would not have the radio on, saying that it made her head worse, so I turned it off. When I had done that she remarked on how obedient I was and asked me if I did not find it difficult living with grandmother. I said no, I did not, and she grew quarrelsome and said that grandmother was a most difficult woman, that all mothers-in-law ruined their daughters-in-laws' lives and that that was the reason she would not live with me. She said she wanted me to be free of older people's influence and then turned to grandmother and said she ought to leave me and take a room by herself somewhere. "You are foolish to remain here," she said; "Bedia does not want you. When one is old one is useless," she continued, "children do not want one any more." '

Bedia paused uncertainly and I was aware of my grandmother's still, immobile face from the shadows of her winged chair, of her contemplative hands demurely folded on her lap. Bedia went on:

'Mother started to get angry because grandmother would not answer her. She seemed to direct all her talk to her; she was really only using me as an excuse. I could see that. Then she told me that she hated grandmother, that she had hated her for many years and was responsible for a house that was burned —a long time ago, I think,' added Bedia apologetically, not yet being familiar with family history, not knowing of the square white house that had burned to the night skies. 'Mehmet is in Bandirma, he went there by torpedo-boat a few days ago so he was not here for all this. Mother kept asking for him and kept forgetting that I had told her where he was. Then she burst out that she could not understand what I was doing in her son's house. "I know you are his wife," she said, but with an awful contempt in her voice, "but I do not like your painted mouth. Nobody in this family ever used paint on their mouths."

Then she told grandmother that she would cure her deafness for her and asked me to fetch her some olive oil. She said she would heat it and pour it into the bad ears. I did not want to do it but she insisted so I went to the kitchen and got what she asked for. When I came back she was looking at a knife that was still on the table and which she had not used when she was eating.' Here Bedia shuddered, in remembrance, her eyes going dark. 'And she said in an odd sort of voice that the knife had a lovely edge, that it was so clean and shining. And she looked at grandmother all the time she spoke but grandmother only watched her, not having heard anything she had said. I took the knife from mother and put it away and when I turned back to her she said, "But is it wrong of me to admire the way you keep your cutlery, Bedia? Did you think perhaps I was going to injure grandmother?" I said, no, I had not thought that and then she came over to me and I screamed and she looked surprised and asked why I did that and I did not know what to say. And all the time grandmother sat there, not saying a word, not interfering, making mother more and more angry and I was terrified of what was going to happen,' she added naïvely; 'grandmother is very obstinate, you know.'

I nodded, remembering that obstinacy from other years.

'Yes, I know,' I said to Bedia. 'Go on.'

'There isn't very much more to tell,' she said. 'After a while mother said that she would go to bed, that she could not bear the aching of her head and asked me if I had any aspirins. I had not, so she said it did not matter. When she had gone to her room, grandmother suggested that we should get a doctor for her. I asked why, and grandmother said that she knew her daughter-in-law very well, that she had given trouble for years and that in the mood she was in tonight she was capable of doing a lot of troublesome things. Anyway, I went to get a doctor and he came straight here with me, wondering what was wrong for really I had been unable to explain very much to him. When he went to her room she was still awake and asked me who he was. I told her that he was a doctor and that he would give her something for her headache. She seemed very suspicious of him but allowed him to examine her and leave some tablets, and then he came to the salon with me and began to ask grandmother all sorts of questions about mother. Finally

he said that it would be better if she were put into an institution for a few months where she could get good nursing and
good food. "She looks as if she has been starving herself," he
said. Then he left us but we had not realised mother had heard
everything that had been said. You see, the doctor had had to
shout to make grandmother understand him and she had
shouted back at him, without knowing that she was shouting.
It was terrible. Mother came back into the salon in her nightdress and said: "Do you think I am mad that you want to put
me away where I shall never see my children again?" Grandmother tried to pacify her, although mother was very quiet,
but upset too, and she sat down on the divan and looked at me
pitifully. "Bedia," she said, "do you think that I am mad?
Is it madness to want to help the poor, to love my children too
much, to fear for my eldest son's death? Is it madness to live
alone so that I shall not be a burden to the married happiness
of you and Mehmet or Muazzez and her husband?" And I
said no, I did not think so. She sounded so terribly sane and I
began to think we had done the wrong thing by calling a doctor
to her and by telling him so much afterwards. Mother sat
there and then she burst into tears and ran back to her room,
where she locked the door. I ran after her but she would not
let me in and I could hear her moving about all the time,
crying, and then grandmother came and banged on the door
and roared out to her to open it for us. But her voice seemed to
set mother crazy. She suddenly flung open the door—she was
already dressed—and she pushed us out of her way saying to
grandmother: "You are responsible for everything that has
ever happened to me," then she flew down the stairs and out
of the house. I ran after her immediately but I could not catch
her. She seemed to have the strength of ten people. We heard
afterwards that she had run almost to Şişli and had called a taxi
but when she was getting into the taxi she had fainted. She was
weak of course for she had not eaten anything for days—only
the small amount I had given her that evening. The taxi-
driver took her straight to Medical Jurisprudence; the police
came to tell us so this morning. They said she had screamed at
them in the police station and had fought to get away. They
had called a doctor and he had given her injections and then
sent her in an ambulance to Jurisprudence——'

Bedia stopped speaking and I looked at her, not yet eighteen, to have seen so much passion unleashed, to have witnessed the outbreak of the sores that had rankled for twenty-six years. And I thought that she had emerged from it all with the little touching look of youth gone from her face forever, her little fragile air vanished like snow before the wind.

'Where is she now?' I asked.

'I do not know,' replied Bedia wearily; 'the police will tell you. I would have gone myself to ask but I was waiting for you to come.'

My grandmother laid a hand on my shoulder and I thought of the listening, straining face that must have watched my mother, the closed ears that had heard nothing, even though she must have been aware of danger. I thought of the indomitable courage that had held her in her chair in the face of the bright, sure blade of the knife, when one unguarded movement might have incited my overwrought mother to use it on her. My heart turned over and I felt my skin begin to creep. Of the pain and the heartbreak and the jealousy of the long years, of the teeming, crowded brain of my mother, I would not let myself think. Not just yet, I said. Not yet. Time enough to think of that later on. If you think of these things now, you will hate Bedia and your grandmother for not having understood. Think of something else.

I went to Medical Jurisprudence and the doctor who had admitted my mother granted me an interview.

He was an old, white-haired man with kind eyes, and when I asked him if I could see my mother he said gently:

'She is not here any more. You are a young man and an airman and you have witnessed many tragic things; it would not be right to subject yourself to such torture.'

I pleaded with him but he was firm.

'She is not here,' he repeated. 'We have sent her to Bakirköy. She will be well looked after there.'

I remembered the red, windowless ambulance that had just driven off as I had arrived at Jurisprudence and suddenly I knew it had held my mother. They had boxed her up in that airless place, to make sure that the already unstable brain would crack. I felt the sweat break out coldly on my forehead. Was there no humanity anywhere? Was it necessary to treat her like a possessed, witless creature who had no feelings, who knew nothing? I knew as surely as if she had been speaking to me that she was perfectly aware of what was going on, that she had known why they put her in the windowless ambulance. How her own heart had always been wrung with pity whenever she had caught sight of these ambulances in the Istanbul streets.

'Poor things,' she had said. 'They are unwanted by their families. They are being taken to Bakirköy, where they will not be allowed to give anybody any trouble.'

I could not rest until I had tried once again to see her, to comfort her if she could still be comforted.

I left Medical Jurisprudence and got a train for Bakirköy, fretting at the long wait at in-between stations, cross because I had not taken a taxi for the whole journey.

I managed to get a phaeton at the station and was driven to the Mental Home, a grim building enclosed in lovely gardens and high, unscaleable walls all about it.

I walked in through the gates, after a porter had sharply enquired my business. He looked at me suspiciously and but for the fact that I was in uniform I do not think he would have admitted me at all.

A man came towards me, a perfectly normal-looking man, and I asked him where I could find a duty doctor. He grinned at me and made vague gestures with his hands and I looked at his luminous eyes and passed on. I could not control a little shiver of apprehension.

I went up some steps and inside in a hall I saw a door marked: 'Private. Secretary.' I went in and stated my business.

'When did she arrive?' the Secretary asked fussily, thumbing through a sort of ledger.

'To-day,' I said, risking the shot in the dark, and he looked in a file on his desk and said, yes, she had been admitted that morning. He directed me to an opposite building for further details. He spread his large, white hands indicating that he was only the Secretary, he could not know everything.

I went out into the hall again and found that it was now full of patients, with their sleeves rolled up, all waiting for injections. I passed through their tidy ranks, feeling horror if I had to touch them, perhaps half afraid of them. They looked at me incuriously and I passed through their lines quickly, my head bent, embarrassment uppermost in my alienability to them.

In the other building I found a doctor who informed me that on no account would I be permitted to see my mother.

'Come back in six weeks time,' he said thoughtlessly. 'Perhaps you can see her then.'

Beaten by his obduracy I asked if she could be moved into a private room and he shrugged, intimating that the treatment afforded her there would be no better.

'She will feel more private there,' I said. 'She will not be all the time aware of the other patients around her.'

Coldly his eyes raked me.

'Lieutenant,' he said with terrible hardness, terrible lack of understanding, 'she is not in a condition to be yet aware of anything.'

I hated his cold, precise voice but I insisted nevertheless that she should be moved to a private room. He arranged for this whilst I was there, accepting the cheque I handed him with a doubtful air, as though suspecting that it might not after all be valid. As he was writing out a receipt for me he said:

'It is preferable to pay with money, Lieutenant. I wonder would you be good enough to remember that the next time you come?'

I did not reply and he stood up, indicating that he was a busy man, that the interview was at an end. As he said good-bye his white hand lay limply in mine, his eyes seared through me so that I realised here was a man with a mission, that given half a chance he would put me under observation too.

I left Bakirköy, having accomplished very little. All the way back in the train I speculated wildly as to what they would do with her. Would there be a window in her room, to give her all the fresh air and sunlight that she loved? Would there be a view over the gardens or would they keep her strapped down on her bed, helpless in the face of their sane ministrations? The tears were never far from my eyes and I did not return to Mehmet's house. There was nothing more to say and I did not want to meet the questions in my grandmother's eyes, the compassion in Bedia's.

I returned to İzmir and threw my energies into work and waited for news. Mehmet wrote several times but I did not bother to reply. What was there to say? I hated their continual harping on the subject of my mother. Could they not leave her alone now?

I was glad to be living in the aerodrome, where companionship now assumed a precious quality.

In March 1940 I was given permission to go to Istanbul and took passage in a boat from Galata Bridge; when I disembarked, I went straight to Bakirköy, by-passing Mehmet and his family. I was eager to learn about my mother for myself with no secondhand information to influence the mind.

By great good luck it was a visiting day when I arrived at the Mental Home and the lovely gardens were crowded with visitors and patients, and sometimes I had great difficulty in distinguishing one from the other.

I stated my errand to a crisp-looking, hard-faced nurse and as she walked away from me I hoped she did not have the handling of my impatient, impetuous mother, otherwise her chances of recovery were nil.

I waited in the gardens, feeling unequal to sitting tidily in the bare waiting-hall. My heart almost choked me and my stomach kept turning over and over in the most unmanageable way. Suddenly I felt unequal to this and wished I had waited until Mehmet had been free to accompany me. I felt foolish and full of insecurity as I hesitated on the springy, dry grass and I looked about me at the patients and the visitors, and thought that one should have nerves of steel and the imagination of a brick wall to come here.

There was a tall old man making an impassioned speech to a dim, elderly lady who might have been his wife. He talked at her without ceasing, scarcely seeming to pause for breath, his bony fingers wagging before her passive face. Occasionally he would thump his chest with a massive, destructive gesture and let out a roar like an angry lion. A doctor halted by me, his distinguishing marks in all this mass of doubtful humanity being a white coat and a stethoscope dangling from his pocket. 'The old man is not really so bad as he looks,' he said amusedly to my disbelieving face. 'We hope to have him completely well again in another twelve months.'

A young girl held court with her father and mother, who watched her with fond, anxious faces.

'So of course I could not marry him,' she was saying in a light, scornful voice, 'I could only refuse him——'

She looked all around her, so pretty and young and witless with her chestnut hair and large eyes. She caught sight of me and smiled entrancingly, pointing me out to her parents.

'Look,' she said. 'That is my husband. Do you not think he is very good looking?'

I pulled the doctor by the arm, hurrying away across the lawns. I asked him about my mother.

'Has she any chance of recovery?' I asked and he paused for a moment and I paused too, turning to face him. 'Tell me,' I said. 'I should like to know.'

He replied, not looking at me:

'She has very little chance. She became worse suddenly, you know, and we have to keep her quiet with injections——'

I saw her in my mind's eye, knowing the place she was in, wanting to get away to freedom, becoming violent because they had thwarted her, kept quiet with the injections that would be ruthlessly, relentlessly shot into her. We must have quietness here, I could hear them all saying. This patient is not quite mad enough yet. She needs disciplining.

The doctor was watching me now, reading perhaps many things from my face. He said gently:

'She will die soon. You would not wish her here for perhaps many years, would you?'

I thought of my grandmother and the words she had spoken that morning in Istanbul, when Bedia had told me the awful truth.

'Is she dead?' I had asked and she had answered sternly:

'Better if she were.'

But I could not face the thought of her death like this. She still represented all the things I had looked for in life, even though I had never found them in her. I started telling the doctor all the things I had thought to be forgotten, things from childhood that suddenly for this brief, illuminating second stood out in high relief. I told him of my father's going away, of the fire, of poverty, of the years in an orphanage in Kadiköy, of my mother's working in the Sewing Depôt at Gülhane Park, of the old, old hatred that persisted and magnified with the years between my mother and my grandmother. I spoke of the love that had tried to chain me, of the restraints imposed, and all the time the doctor listened, nodding now and then as if he were beginning to understand her better. Presently he left me and I stood alone on the sunlit grass, trembling, glad to have spoken of these things to another person.

I waited for my mother.

Presently I saw her coming, with two nurses, one on each side of her, supporting her. Her high, querulous voice reached me across the space that separated us and she tried, in vain, to rid herself of the encompassing arms of the sturdy nurses. My heart bled for her and I thought it would have been better not to have come here, not to have seen her so defenceless.

She stopped in front of me and I said, 'Mother,' and I saw a wary, trapped look come into her eyes.

She looked at me as if she did not recognise me. I said: 'Don't you know me?'

Then she said:

'Oh, it is you? My eagle, my airman son——'

But there was no emotion in her voice, nothing save haughtiness, the voice she would have used to a stranger. She pointed to a man and said:

'He is our cook. Not a very good one, I am afraid, but we could not get anyone else.'

I looked at the man she pointed to, a visitor, and she saw my look and added:

'He is really far too distinguished to be a cook, but there you are——'

Her voice trailed off and she turned away from me, ignoring me and began to tremble with such frightful violence that the nurses had to lead her to a seat.

I followed them and when she was sitting down I took one cold hand in mine and kissed it but she did not pay any attention to the gesture. All the time she persisted in treating me like a stranger. After that first flicker of recognition in her eyes she had withdrawn from me. She felt me watching her and turned her head to me, saying:

'Once I had a son too who was an airman like you. He broke my heart.'

The calmness of her light voice was terrible.

'Oh, mother!' I said, trying not to weep for her and for myself too. 'Don't you know me?' I asked.

It was cruel to go on knocking at memory like that but I could not help myself. She did not answer me, only commenced to hum a little nameless tune, an odd thin sound, and the shivers still spasmodically shook her frail body. I gave her some Turkish Delight and she ate it and then asked, with incredible courtesy, if she could have some more as her friends were too poor to buy any for themselves. I handed her the box but her hands were too unsteady to hold it so that it fell to the grass, spilling its contents and the nurses stooped to pick up the pieces for her.

She turned away pettishly, refusing to speak to me any more, and all the time she trembled. Her body and legs and arms were wasted, only skin and bone remained of her. She persisted in keeping herself turned from me and presently one of the nurses said she would have to be taken back to her room. She was to be put to bed.

She went away with them docilely, never looking to me, never turning her head backwards from the door as she went through, not caring that I stood there looking after her, not knowing who I was.

I stood there for a long time, watching the dragging, bent, trembling figure of my mother and I thought I should not come here again. Silently I said my good-bye to her and then she vanished from my sight. I felt the tears running unchecked down my cheeks.

I wept for myself and for the young lover who had once imprinted herself on the memory, the day she bade my father good-bye in the gracious salon of a long-dead house. I wept for the beauty who had flashed jewels and hospitality, who had brought poetry into a house in a back street of Bayazit. I wept for the pale young girl who had drudged untold hours in an army depôt, sewing coarse linen for soldiers. I wept for the middle-aged woman of the fugitive, persistent beauty, who had worn a flower in her hair against my return from the aerodrome, who had once sparkled and shone like the noonday sun and who had withered to dust inside the body of this bent, trembling old woman who knew none. But I wept most of all for my mother.

A light touch on the arm made me turn to see a nurse with a face of great gentleness, of compassion. She said:

'We have put her to bed now. Would you like to see her room?'

'No,' I said; 'no, thank you. There is no need. I am sure she is very comfortable.'

She did not say anything to this and I asked:

'Is there a window in the room?'

Her eyes lit with that rare understanding that comes so seldom in the world.

'Yes,' she said. 'She likes us to keep it open for her. And we bring her to the garden quite often too. She loves gardens, you know.'

'Yes,' I said, and saw the gardens she had made in Istanbul, in Eskişehir, in Kutahya and İzmir and I wondered if loving hands still tended them.

'She had green fingers,' I said irrelevantly and the friendly nurse smiled.

'Well, good-bye, Lieutenant,' she said. 'Come again, won't you?'

'No,' I said. 'I shall not come again. It is better not.'

And suddenly the face of the friendly nurse closed up and grew hard, unable to understand. She said tartly:

'But you can help her so much, you know.'

I remembered that the doctor had said she would not live for long, that she would never get better and I wondered at the terrible, ruthless sanity of the sane, of the stupidity that asked me to come back and see my mother, to force awareness of myself upon her when she did not want to be reminded, when her son was dead for her because once he had broken her heart. Such pitiless cruelty I had thought was alien to the friendly nurse. But there was no way of explaining to that closed face that there was nothing more to be said between my mother and me, that both of us were gone from each other.

My mother had travelled farther than we who stood here in the sunlight. She had gone to that world of soft illusions where she was always a young girl, the world to which she had tried to escape when her home was burned, when she learned that her husband had died on a far-away road under a blinding sun. She had wanted to go there long ago but always we held her back, called to her to stay with us but now she no longer cared and could not have been persuaded to stay any more.

I turned away from the gardens. The same man still speechified impassionedly, the same young girl haughtily told her parents that she could never marry. All of them living in their illusory world where hurt could not touch them. Their voices followed me to the high, iron gates and the porter opened them for me to pass through. I went out to the quiet, country road.

On the 18th of May of that eventful European year of 1940, my mother died but for me she had been dead this many a day.

I received the telegram the morning they were burying her, when it was too late to go to Istanbul and too late for anything else to be done by me.

Alone of all her family, Mehmet saw her lowered into her grave outside the fortress walls of Istanbul. An Imam read the Koran for her and presently Mehmet was left alone with her for a little while, then he too had gone, leaving her with the sun and the kindly rain and the eternal nights still to come.

Later we erected a tombstone for her and a low stone wall about the narrow grave. We put rose-trees at her head and her feet and her name was carved into the shining marble of the stone: 'Şevkiye Orga,' we wrote, '1893–1940—Ruhuna Fatiha —pray for her', and the name looked lonely there amongst all the nameless dead about her.

Then we left her alone, a little outside the Istanbul she had loved.

FINIS

AFTERWORD

'Other people's lives are always interesting. The gossip of the village or the gossip of Europe – it does not make much difference'
John Betjeman, reviewing *Portrait of a Turkish Family*, 16th August 1950

'Irfan', in Turkish, means knowledge, enlightenment, culture. My father carried his name with head held high. He was a gentle and kind person, a man of wisdom and sensitivity, of psychology and perception, a man of honour. His recipe for life was his mother's opinion that 'it is very vulgar to boast', and his grandmother's warning that you should 'never let anyone know when you are desperate. Put your best clothes on and pride on your face and you can get anything in this world . . . otherwise you will get nothing but kicks'. 'A good soldier,' he says in *Portrait*, 'needs no imagination, no feelings of humanity'. Perhaps this, along with a lack of ambition discovered early on, explains why ultimately he had so little enthusiasm for soldiering, why, by this definition, he was a bad soldier. He was too much of a dreamer, a questioner, a lover of life's spirit. One is thankful he never had to be put to the test in the way his father had been at Gallipoli, or his uncle in the deserts of Mesopotamia and Syria.

My father, I remember, had an enormous regard for justice and fair play. His capacity for love was wonderful to experience, his family feeling was all consuming. He was the fortress of our existence. He ran his life (and ours) by simple black-and-white beliefs. To him dignity, truth, loyalty, faithfulness and self-discipline mattered more than anything else. He was a stern task-master, a man who had a temper and could, given cause, punish. But I knew, too, that he was possessed also of the most infinite, intimate tenderness. He was a good human being.

The *Portrait* is an autobiography of tears and good-byes. Dedicated to my mother, and first called *On the Shore of the Bosphorus*, it was originally much longer and dealt in detail with my father's time as a cadet and junior officer. He further planned a sequel based on his years in England. It was the agent, Curtis Brown, in a letter dated 30 August 1949, who suggested its present form, with a narrative confined to childhood and family life in Turkey across the transitional period between the last sultans and Atatürk. My father agreed; an advance of £75 was offered, and a contract was signed with Victor Gollancz on the 25th January 1950. Gollancz published the book on the 14th August, price sixteen shillings. It proved to be such a major critical success that a second printing had to be rushed through within a fortnight. No bookshop in London was without a copy, it dressed most windows. On my birthday of that year, Macmillan of New York issued it in America. 'One of the memorable books of 1950', hailed the *New York Herald Tribune*.

The story of the *Portrait* as it stands (the original was destroyed long ago) stops essentially with my grandmother's death and my father's impending departure for England in 1941. It is an evocative but incomplete history. For some reason it is silent over my father's liaison in Eskişehir with one of Atatürk's adopted daughters, a girl of strong will with whom marriage was apparently discussed. It casts no light on why the 1st March 1908 is given on some papers as his birthday. Contrary to his opening statement, he himself had frequent doubt as to exactly when he might have been born. It didn't trouble him—error, he would say, was something you learnt to live with in old Ottoman Turkey: if you had no papers, it was common practice among officials for an arbitrary date to be fixed for a child, arrived at by matching a mother's description of circumstances around its birth with public events at the time—but it did leave him wondering. He once even raised with me the possibility of 1909.

And it reveals nothing about how our family name originated when Atatürk made surnames compulsory in Turkey in 1935. Before then my father had always been known as 'Irfan, the son of Hüsnü and Şevkiye of Bayazit'. 'Orga' he would tell us around winter fires, came to him one day by opening a map and sticking a pin in it. That pin came to rest by a river between Kazan and Gorky, the Urga. Wanting a harder-sounding, less ethnically suggestive, more Turkishly associative identity, he changed the 'U' to an 'O'—'Orga'.

My father set foot in England at Liverpool on the 16th July 1942, following a two-and-a-half month sea voyage via the

Levantine coast of Syria and Palestine, the Suez Canal, South Africa and Lisbon. After a stay in Torquay, he took charge of young Turkish officers completing their training with the Royal Air Force. He flew Spitfires as a guest of the RAF and had an office at the Turkish Embassy in London. Home was a room at 29 Inverness Terrace ('Mr John's' as it was always known in our family).

He met my mother, Margaret Veroni[y]ca, sometime during the early autumn of that year. A highly-strung, nervy, lapsed Catholic who was to eventually smoke and drink and hate herself to death (in October 1974), she was then a slight young woman of haughty beauty, the daughter of a landed gentleman racehorse-owner and breeder of independent means, deceased. In the late 1920s and 30s she had been sent to the convent of Notre Dame de Sion in Bayswater, before going on to finishing school in Paris. Norman-Irish by descent and conscious of her aristocracy (her mother was a Wicklow D'Arcy), she worked for ENSA and at the time of meeting my father had only just got married: her civil wedding to one Leonard Gainsboro of the Royal Engineers had taken place at Westminster Register Office a matter of weeks earlier, on 8 July, her 23rd birthday. Previously she had lived in Dolphin Square; then she had a room at 'Mr John's'. Later she and my father went to Raynes Park, Wimbledon, my father commuting daily to Waterloo.

For some time, it seems, my father's risqué affair was kept secret. Not surprisingly: quite apart from the inescapable fact that she had a husband, he must have been only too aware that for an officer to live with, let alone marry, a foreigner was to break Turkish law. At any rate, he was still in service at the time of my birth in 1944, and on his return to Turkey in 1945 he remained so, being posted to Diyarbakir. He always told me, however, that he felt this posting to have been a first sign of official awareness and reaction: Diyabakir on the Tigris was in the east of Turkey, a hot, inhospitable place of sand and drought and scorpions—not somewhere to send a successful career officer just back after a politically responsible posting in wartime London.

Whether my father resigned or was dismissed from the Air Force is debatable. He always maintained the former; the Turkish authorities couldn't quite decide. He himself used to say that he was offered a deal: either renounce his child and wife and keep his commission, or else get out. From things said, I believe he left some time early in 1947. In concern for my mother he had stopped flying by then. And his term of fifteen years service contracted for originally by *his* mother had by this time been fully honoured.

We followed my father to Turkey, making the journey by train through Athens, Salonika and Adrianople (modern Edirne). We lived at 40 Savaş Sokak in the Şişli district of Istanbul. My mother, it appears, was well liked by Mehmet and by our Greek neighbours, but was mistrusted by Bedia who believed her to be a loose woman unfit for her brother-in-law. As I grew up, I could never quite understand this. It always seemed to me an unfair slur.

By the end of 1947 my father, now a traffic officer for British European Airways working in Ankara, found himself in an impossible situation. Friends warned him of an impending arrest. He contemplated escape through Iraq and Syria, using the help of Kurds and Armenians he had befriended while in Diyarbakir. The idea proved impractical. Somehow he managed to secure a passport, in the name of *Mehmet* Irfan Orga with his occupation given as 'employee'. On 19 December the British Embassy issued him with a 'short visit' one-month visa. He left Istanbul on the 22nd.

I thought of my mother [he was to write later] lying outside the fortress walls, of my father and my grandfather. Yes, I remember you and you and you. Dead images clothed in flesh and blood who have walked across the pages of this narrative for your brief moment; your terrible silence mocks the puny, noisy wisdom of the living. You keep your own counsel . . .

When I think of you who are gone, long-dead dreams rise up again to catch me by the throat this last evening . . . All the graceful life you represented comes back in full measure to haunt this jaundiced eye, to torture this foolish heart for the things that might have been had Time stood still.

The long line of the Bosphor I see too in the mind's eye that discerns everything so clearly this night and Kuleli lying under the quiet sky and far away there is a square white house that will for me burn eternally to a disinterested heaven . . .

'Good-bye,' we shout. 'Good-bye . . .'

He landed at Northolt the following day. On the 25th, Christmas Day, at ten-past-four in the afternoon, my mother sent a telegram from Beyoğlu: 'Arriving Saturday Meet Air Offices Victoria Love Margaret'. On the 27th, a high moon on the rise, we were re-united.

My parents' wedding rings carry an engraved date in the Turkish style, '22/7/943'. It was a date spasmodically acknowledged by them as marking their wedding, notably in 1968, the occasion, they said, of their Silver Anniversary. Clearly it held some special meaning for them. An enshrinement perhaps of a pact? Certainly, we now know, it was *not* the year of their marriage. For the first twenty-five years of my life I had no reason to question this. But then one night at Tunbridge Wells station shortly before my father's death my mother surprised me. She spoke of a previous husband. I failed then to take in the startling implications of this revelation. Only now, in researching this Afterword, has the truth fully come to me: in 1943 they were in fact quite unmarried. And were to remain so through my birth (in 1944), and for another three years. There was good reason for this delay: documents at Somerset House show that my mother's divorce (with my father cited as co-respondent) was only made absolute on the 7th January 1948. Two days later, at Paddington Register Office, they were married. (*Now* I realise why Bedia felt as she did . . .)

In that blizzard winter of 1947/48 my father faced the possibility of deportment, separation, trial and imprisonment. Friends, made in London during the war, came to his aid. In February a letter arrived from the Aliens Department of the Home Office in High Holborn, granting him permission to stay in Britain and to take up employment.

Home for three-and-a-half years was a small fourth floor front room with one window rented for £3.10s a week at 35 Inverness Terrace, a boarding house owned by a wiry old Greek ship owner, Ferentinos, and his large, generously kind, wife. Bayswater and Queensway then, as now, was very much a cosmopolitan community, a haunt for emigrés and refugees, for prostitutes and fugitives. A place perfumed by the smells of the East, dominated by Bertorelli's, crowded out by small shopkeepers and pavement cafés, crowned by the glory that was Whiteleys. Here my father wrote the *Portrait*, took me to

Kensington Gardens, and, with great patience, gave me my first lessons in reading and writing. Here, too, he began to learn that although he was still seen to be the head of the family (to whom his brother and sister would refer in the event of important decisions), it was going to be my mother who would be the bread-winner from now on. Psychologically, he could never quite accustom himself to this idea. It questioned his manhood. It had a lot to do with the depression of his later years.

How wise my father had been to flee Turkey in 1947 came home to him twenty months later. On Monday 12 September 1949 in the Third Law Court of First Instance in Ankara he was prosecuted *in absentia* by the Turkish Treasury in the name of the Ministry of National Defence. Identifying him as Irfan *Urga* of Ankara, the plaintiff's case centered around a Complaint Petition that had been registered on the 13th October 1947, accusing my father of living with a foreign woman. The judge found in favour of the plaintiff, and my father was fined 45,904 liras 42 kuruş (in today's money over £60,000).

For more than ten years my father from England was to contest this finding—in the event unsuccessfully, despite many long letters of pleading and despite appeals from my mother to the Turkish President, Celâl Bayar, and to the Prime Minister, Adnan Menderes, and despite, after the *coup d'état* of 1960, my father making contact again with such close old friends from the Harbiye days as Irfan Tansel, by then Commander-in-Chief of the Turkish Air Force. My father never returned to Turkey.

I was brought up very much within a Turkish environment. We survived by being a close-knit, self-contained, insular trio. Each of us worked for and supported the other. Strangers were not welcome. I was instructed to keep Turkish visitors at bay, away from my father for fear of what they might try to do (only once, in 1957, was this relaxed when two old students of his, both now high-ranking officers, managed to convince him, through me, of their otherwise good intentions). We kept our own identity, our foreignness, our pride. No one knew anything about us or our situation. If fictions sometimes had to be created to support the fabric of our existence, then they were (for a long time I was told, and believed, that I had been born in Istanbul, an exotic fancy without a grain of truth).

At home we spoke a mixture of Turkish and English, me with

a stammer so bad that at times my only means of communication was through a sing-song patter. I was never to go to school because it was felt that I would be corrupted and anglicised and would have to wear a Christian cap: my mother, further, favoured a private rather than state education (typically somewhere like Ampleforth), for which, clearly, there was no money (at best she was then earning five or six pounds a week, while my father could not even find employment as a hospital orderly). When I was six years old, it was decided that my father should take me in hand.

Remarkably, he was to give me a solid education for the next ten years. He encouraged me to study for myself, and within our solitude we made astonishing progress. Lessons were strict and daily, from 9 in the morning until 3 in the afternoon, followed by an hour or so of exercise and play in the park up the road (comfortingly watched over by my father some distance away). Regular homework was expected each evening, and exams, devised by both my parents, would take place at the end of each term. I was given long 'private school' summer holidays. Annual pilgrimages to Foyles ensured I learnt from the latest books. With my father I covered reading, writing (later typing), arithmetic, algebra, geometrical drawing (plus a little Euclid), geography, Turkish language, Turkish history, and, towards the end, music and piano (which he taught himself in order to help me). With my mother I studied English and French. BBC school programmes and museum visits fostered other insights. This made me enormously self-sufficient from a very early and formative stage. I learnt a lot, I was allowed to develop at my own pace, and I was encouraged to read as much as I wanted: by the age of thirteen I knew no Shakespeare or Dickens but my command of Homer and Herodotus, of mythology and Arthur Ransome, of the Napoleonic Wars was prodigious. What it failed to do, inevitably, was to give me any kind of competition or contact with my own generation. I mixed with few children apart from those I would meet in the park during the week (we never went there at weekends because my mother thought it 'common'). Still, I am grateful for those amazing days.

The Turkishness of my upbringing was underlined in many ways. We ate mainly Turkish food, supplemented by the odd sausage but almost never by Christian pork. The radio alternated between the BBC Home Service and the shortwave crackle of Ankara or Voice of America. Turkish news and music (of both the traditional and casino variety) were always part of our evening listening. Turkish papers like *Cumhuriyet, Vatan* and *Hürriyet* were posted weekly by Mehmet. For years he and Ali, writing in old Ottoman Turkish (Arabic) script, would send letters to my father, keeping him abreast of events.

Then there was marriage, the arranged marriage. Unexpectedly, for a man of his liberated behaviour, my father quite warmed to the idea: throughout my childhood it was always tacitly understood that I was intended for my pretty cousin, Oya (Mehmet's and Bedia's daughter). Later he compromised his ideas. Even so, in favour of my awakening love for a Slovak beauty from Bratislava and my later stirrings for a Polish girl of entrancingly vivacious sparkle, contact with anyone English was dissuaded. My father could never rid himself of an irrational fear that, were I one day to marry someone English, he would be banished from my house and left to starve. My mother, who in her arrogant, dismissive, cutting manner, felt the English to be somehow inferior specimens of the human race, only helped fuel this insecurity.

My father believed himself to be cursed, to be dogged by ill-luck. Whenever things began to look up, especially financially, disaster would always strike. My mother, inevitably, unwittingly, seems to have been at the centre of these calamaties: they happened *because* of her. Within two months of their marriage she was diagnosed as having pulmonary tuberculosis, in those days a serious, even fatal, condition. She had to go to hospital where my father would visit her, and where I, dutifully, would wait outside. Contact between myself and her was kept to an absolute minimum and I was only ever allowed to drink out of a cup put aside especially for me—a habit I was to remain conditioned by for the next quarter of a century. By June 1951 she was better, though her consultant at the Paddington and Kensington Chest Clinic considered that she should still be kept 'under periodic supervision for the next three to five years'.

Later, at the end of 1958, she went down with such a complete nervous breakdown that she was to be incapacitated for a year, unable to walk. Flat on her back in bed, in considerable discomfort with her spine out of alignment and agonising pain in her legs, heavily sedated, moody and vicious in temper during her more lucid moments, puffy yet haggard, she attributed her recovery to a mixture of self-therapy (she painted bottles and glass with abstract designs) and visits to a faith-healer off Baker Street—through whose laying-on of hands she found herself in the care of a physician of ancient Egypt called Hemput who would bathe her body in waves of blue light and glowing heat.

Physically, my father survived these shocks. Emotionally, they took their toll. He began to age visibly, his hair thinned and whitened. He resorted to taking nerve tonics.

On the morning of Wednesday 4 July 1951 we left by train from Euston, heading for Ireland. Though my father's stay in Ireland was limited officially to six months, his intention in going there was to make it our home. The idea especially appealed to my mother, a woman as full of southern Irish spirit as she was of family pride and history (strange how no mementoes of her childhood or parents, no photographs, have survived: she used to say she destroyed everything when her father died. Or was it simply that all her possessions had been abandoned in her first marital home?).

Packed in large, ribbed, trunks all our belongings, all my father's uniforms, books and silk Sparta carpets, came with us, nothing was left in England. I never questioned the existence of those rich carpets, they were always around me. Looking back, pondering the nature of my father's exit from Turkey, I wonder now how they ever got here? Had they perhaps been left in storage in England during the war? Had they been secreted out at some time? Where are they today?

In Ireland we took up residence in Blackrock along the coast between Dun Laoghaire and Dublin—at 82 George's Avenue, a quite splendid (if modest) double-fronted detached house dating from some time before Victoria. It was occupied then by a widow called Mooney whose husband had been in the horse-racing world and was once connected with the *Irish Independent*. She let us have some rooms at a rent of £12 a month.

The Blackrock days were at first full of hope. Most evenings we used to walk out to sea across the sand flats, my father would write, we would take the sun in at Howth and Killiney. We would go for lunches and teas in wealthy houses owned by people I didn't know. Then, with cold nights on the wing, all this began to change. We waited for offers, we got rejection slips. That Celtic summer we had thought the world ours. That autumn we knew it wasn't. It had all been a fantasy. Fire was the *idée fixe* of my father's life. The *Portrait* tells us that. When I was born he gave me the name 'Ateş'—Turkish for 'fire'. One night at George's Avenue the flames came again for him. I set the house ablaze. My father managed to put it out, but not before burning his leg with a kettle of boiling water provided by one of the Mooney daughters, an absent-minded girl. My father, in great pain, was taken to hospital in Dun Laoghaire. He stayed there for some time, apprehensive of the nuns, visited every day by me and my mother. He left under a cloud: there was no money to pay the bill.

We had embarked for Ireland by First Class. By Third Class, four months later, we were now to leave, penniless and possessionless save for a Turkish dictionary and a ceremonial sword. Everything else we left behind. My parents promised to return for them one day. They never did. Darkly, the boat-train brought us back to England. Blackly, the underground returned us to Inverness Terrace.

Ireland behind, the euphoria over, the *Portrait* as spent as a supernova, life in London in the early 50s was grim, grey and smokey. It was a time of rationing, of under-the-counter deals, of thick choking yellow smogs, of bomb-sites, jagged scars of the Blitz, lit by gas lamps. In winter we were so cold that my father would seal the window cracks with paper and flour paste; so hungry he would go down to Portobello Road market to rustle what he could from the barrow boys. Warm clothes were not easy to come by: wrapping ourselves with newspaper, especially our feet, helped, but not much. Food parcels from Mehmet and Ali gave us essentials like rice and beans, *sucuk* (a Turkish sausage) and olive oil, but little else. Perhaps sometimes there was the luxury of silk stockings for my mother, well hidden from the Customs. Toys certainly never.

Mrs Ferentinos, our kind former landlady, would give us a pound or two. When that failed, we would sell the odd book for a few pence. Then there was Davis the pawnbrokers by Bayswater station: it was here, in a final act of desperation, that my father one day parted with his gold Longines.

He no longer had the courage to go into his bank for fear of refusal. 'Dik yürü', he always used to say to me. 'Walk straight'. He didn't. We had become a part of London's faceless tenement poverty. Life was about fights and arguments, about stale left-overs and gnawing mice, about being kept awake by the people next door and trains rumbling through the night deep in the ground, about cabbage and a balloon for Christmas. It was never to be so bad again.

After a few years in a tiny room at the back of 21 Inverness Terrace, we moved to 7 Pembridge Square, an elegant large Nineteenth Century town-house, where in time we acquired several furnished rooms across the top floor. We liked Pembridge Square. During the week, my father and I would take to long walks around Holland Park and Notting Hill, a nice backwater then. On Sunday afternoons we would go to Paddington Station to savour the wiff of trains from Fishguard and Cheltenham, to watch the *Cornish Riviera Express* shuddering into Platform 8. In June we would go as far as the Mall to watch the Queen ride side-saddle at the head of her troops, and to Hyde Park to be deafened by salutes from the Royal Horse Artillery.

Pembridge Square saw a change in our fortunes. Up to the spring of 1957 my mother had had a good job working for a German printing machine company in Westminster Bridge Road, spoilt only by her being loved and courted there by a handsome Pole—an episode which made for a stressful atmosphere at home, however much she would protest her innocence. Then at the end of June of that year she joined the publishing house of Secker & Warburg in Bloomsbury, initially as a secretary, latterly as an editor. She was paid a salary of £14.10s a week. We felt ourselves rich, the more so since at the same time I was earning some money by keeping the post-book for a travel agency in the Courtyard off Queensway.

For the first and only time during my father's life in England, we went away on holiday, on one of those big trains of promise down to Totnes in Devon, to a farm called Blue Post. It was a good fortnight, us three striding out under open skies, taking in the sea at Paignton, waiting at Avonwick for trains that never seemed to come despite all the smoke in the valley, for once at one with each other and rurality.

We went to vibrant autumn parties at Fred and Pamela Warburg's book-lined Regent's Park flat in St Edmund's Terrace. Here my father found himself suddenly taken up, admired by a literary set who may have wondered at his less than fluent English, but said nothing, thinking it quaint and attractive instead.

All but two of my father's books were published in the 1950s. Many more, short stories as well, were sketched or completed, but they either remained in manuscript or were destroyed. When the *Portrait* appeared, a number of critics expressed surprise at its command of English. Harold Nicolson in particular, in *The Observer* (13 August 1950), closed his long and generous review with a note of surprise that someone who had not known one word of English in 1941 'should now be able to handle the intricacies of our language as easily as if it were his native tongue'. A fortnight later Barbara Worsley-Gough, writing in *The Spectator*, likened my father as a story-teller to 'something of a masculine, Muslim George Eliot'.

In their different ways these critics questioned and exposed the truth more acutely than they might have imagined. In the late 40s my father's spoken command of English was fractured; by the late 60s it was fluent but still quite limited in vocabulary and strong in accent. His understanding of the *written* word, on the other hand, was rich: he read widely and avidly, from Dostoevsky and Pasternak to Galsworthy, from Churchill to Freya Stark. When *Atatürk* was published by Michael Joseph in 1962 he insisted (though much against her will) that my mother should be seen to be his co-author. Just so. He, after all, better than anyone, knew that it was in fact *she* who was the stylistic and linguistic force, the mentality sometimes, the persona often, behind all his work.

In writing his books, my father's method, so far as I can remember, was to prepare first a sketch in old Turkish Arabic, which he would then translate and expand into new Turkish Latin script, followed by a basic draft in English. This he would hand over to my mother who would absorb, interpret and discuss before fashioning a literary metamorphosis suitable for publication. Later I would join in, too, reading each chapter, preparing indexes, and, on one occasion (*The Caravan Moves On*), taking care of the eventually printed end-paper maps.

His two most significant books of the 50s were *Phoenix Ascendant: the Rise of Modern Turkey* (Robert Hale), dedicated to the memory of my grandparents, and *The Caravan Moves On* (Secker & Warburg), an account about the little-known Yürük nomads of Karadağ in the High Taurus. Both appeared in 1958. The *Caravan* aroused interest. *The Geographical Magazine* thought it to have 'ethnological importance'. Freya Stark, a seasoned Anatolian traveller, enjoyed it. Kinross in *The Daily Telegraph* spoke of its illumination. *The Times Literary Supplement*, not always kind in reviewing my father's books, found space to praise. To his surprise (but pleasure) my father found himself hailed variously as a poet, a traveller of the best sort, a master story-teller, a companionable fellow, a writer of brilliance.

My father's two most effortless books of the 1950's, both published by André Deutsch, were to do with cookery, one of my father's genuine pleasures in life: *Cooking with Yoğurt* (1956), a thoroughly unusual book in its time about 'one of nature's blessings to mankind', and *Turkish Cooking* (1958). Both enjoyed financial return and were still in print twenty years later. The astonishingly primitive way given by my father for making yoğurt, complete with a 'nest' of cotton twill and feathers in the fireplace of our room, was a ritual I witnessed every evening at Pembridge Square. Prompted by a need to build up my mother's strength after her tuberculosis, the result had a deliciousness and texture quite unlike anything that was then available. Nothing today can still compare with it.

Two educational books for children also appeared: *The Young Traveller in Turkey*, dedicated to me (Phoenix House 1957, and later in Holland), and *The Land and People of Turkey* (A & C Black 1958). This last, sold outright for £75, was published under a pseudonym, Ali Riza—a useful invention that happened not only to be the identity of Muazzez's husband but also the name of Atatürk's Albanian father. A *nome de plume* was wanted, the publishers said, so as to avoid clashing with the *Young Traveller*. They were also worried about saturating the market with too many books under the Orga name (apart from my mother's breakdown, 1958 was a good year for us). My father didn't mind. He needed the money and was glad to have a chance to write something for his young nephews back in Istanbul, Kaya (Mehmet's son) and Erdal Aretikin (Ali's).

In the late fifties and early sixties a new way of life began to take us over. We started to look for houses to rent. At weekends we would go to St Albans, to Pinner and Chesham, to Northwood Hills and Amersham. Metropolitan countryside became our regular hunting ground. Occasionally we would venture south: a Pullman tea on the old *Brighton Belle* is a happy memory. Then we put an advertisement in *The Times* and got one reply. We pondered, we visited, we fell in love.

Spike Island, owned by the van Thals (Bertie had been in publishing, Phyllis edited *Vanity Fair*), was a long, low, late 18th century weather-boarded East Sussex cottage. In one-and-a-half acres of isolated wilderness, of wooded, nightingaled, seclusion, it nestled by a rampant ancient hedge down a sloping, rutted, grassy farm lane just up from Wadhurst station. No more than an hour or so from Charing Cross (on the Tunbridge Wells spur), it was like nothing we had ever seen before. It was romantic and rustic, a haven within heaven. It was not ideal, we kept telling ourselves (just two front rooms, bathroom and kitchen—which meant I would have no bedroom of my own), but was anything better likely to come up? After all, we'd only had one response to our optimistic advertisement and we wanted to get away from London. We rented it for a song (5 guineas a week). Later, in March 1968, my mother bought it for £5,500.

In 1962 my father published two contrasting books: *Cooking the Middle-East Way* (sold outright to Paul Hamlyn for £200), and *Atatürk* (against which Michael Joseph advanced us £500). *Atatürk* (which anticipated Kinross's study by two years) was a re-working of the second part of *Phoenix Ascendant*. The Turkish Embassy didn't like it. 'The portrait of Atatürk . . . is a source of astonishment and indignation to Turkish people everywhere,' wrote the press attaché to the *Evening Standard* (20 January). 'I take the strongest exception to the words used to describe Atatürk's character . . .' (The *Standard* had suggested that the book made 'no secret of the black side of Atatürk's nature': their reviewer's most vitriolic adjectives had in fact very little to do with what my parents wrote.)

Coincident with this criticism from the embassy was a letter received from the Turkish Consulate in Portland Gate requesting my father to attend for an interview to answer some (unspecified) questions. He never did, he never heard further, he never renewed his papers of citizenship.

As for books, these, too, were to be no more. He compiled a voluminous tome of recipes using rice but no one wanted it. He contemplated a book on Mahomet but it was never more than an idea. With me he researched and wrote some chapters for a definitive biography of Hayrettin Barbarossa, Süleyman's admiral; had it been completed, it might have been his most definitive work. Omar Sharif wanted to film *Atatürk*, with himself, an ideal cut of a man, in the title rôle. He paid us a large option fee. But this, too, came to nothing.

Spike Island gave my father peace of mind. It was the next best thing to his boyhood dream of ending his days fishing by the Golden Horn. But it also perhaps gave him too much time to think. He saw almost nobody, visitors were few. He felt he had no status or authority or class. Materially he was totally dependent on my mother. His life in England, he would confide to me in a mixture of temper and tears, had long been celibate. My mother's flirtations angered him, her affair with an RAF wing-commander tortured him. By then, in her mid-forties, coolly attractive, flighty, extravagant, she was senior editor at W.H. Allen, travelling daily to Cannon Street, with a life-style coloured by literary luncheons, cocktail parties, and—from what she would tell me—by more than the odd illicit rendezvous. Rows, moods, hours, days of silence . . . My mother no longer used to walk out on us (as she had done so often in London). But she knew exactly how to punish my father. Our house may have resounded to our fun, but it trembled with our tension, too.

My father's regime at Spike Island revolved around his daily gardening and cooking, his chickens, cats and one dog, learning to live with country footpath laws, and watching television (including, with all the animated fervour and knowledge of an England supporter, the 1966 World Cup). Following the bitter winter of 1963, when we were snowed in for a week, we formed a literary agency, International Authors. We ran this from home. My father did the typing and filing, my mother did the advising, and I went after the contracts and commissions. I also dreamt up ideas for books and made them a reality. We had a small but respectable stable of clients. None of us I think ever thought that we really had an agent's mentality, but it was a way of creating an occupation.

Music was increasingly important to my father. Having once in Pembridge Square heatedly opposed my musical aspirations, only giving way on condition that I prove myself within two years, he did everything in the 60s (once I had fulfilled my side of the bargain) to encourage me, to buy music and books, and (in my late teens, early twenties) to support my first steps into journalism and criticism.

Our concert-going in the 50s had been sparodic but not unknown. In the 60s we'd walk across Kensington Gardens to the Royal College of Music to hear all their brightest and best students play every Wednesday evening at 5.30. The Goethe Institute was another favourite of ours, where we could get concerts, a reception and food, and a chance to chat informally with artists—all for nothing.

Going to Spike Island did not inhibit my father's desire to keep up our concert life. There was a refined 150th anniversary Liszt recital given by the handsome young Hungarian Tamás Vásáry, with five dazzling encores including the Sixth Hungarian Rhapsody (whose oriental rhetoric my father found appealing). And we enjoyed war-horse piano concertos given class by Rubinstein and Giulini. We discovered the Proms, we experienced the 20th century no less than the past: Bernstein and the New York Philharmonic, Solti, Boulez, Copland, Ozawa, Penderecki, Xenakis, Horenstein, Ormandy, Oistrakh, Barbirolli, Boult, Ashkenazy fresh from his Moscow triumph in the Tchaikovsky Competition, modern music at the ICA . . . For long after my father's death it seemed inconceivable to go to a concert without him. He taught me how to enjoy music and how to show my pleasure. He could never understand, he resented, the mentality, the attitude, the apparent lack of response and applause he witnessed among so many professional music critics. Why, he would ask? I had no answer. I still don't.

My father lived at Spike Island for a little more than nine years. In that time he saw my mother become successful but remote. He saw me off on my own future. He saw himself with nothing to live for. I know of no-one who cried out for death to come more than he.

In the first morning hour of 29th November 1970, he died. He was 62. Brought home for one last night, his coffin shrouded with a red Turkish flag crossed by his sword, that same sword we had brought back from Ireland, he was, at his wish, cremated. A simple service. Some music—the Intermezzo from *Cavelleria Rusticana*, Chopin's *Funeral March*. Flames.

His ashes we cast to the winds around the place he had come to love so much. A few I kept aside. I buried them with my mother.

© Ateş Orga
Guildford,
16th August 1988